Perspectives in Reading No. 18

reading in the middle school

Gerald G. Duffy
Compiling Editor
Michigan State University

Harry W. Sartain, Reviewing Editor, University of Pittsburgh

ira International Reading Association
Newark, Delaware 19711

INTERNATIONAL READING ASSOCIATION

Library of Congress Cataloging in Publication Data
Main entry under title:
Reading in the middle school.

    (Perspectives in reading ; 18)
    Includes bibliographies.
    1. Reading (Secondary education) -- Addresses, essays,
lectures. I. Duffy, Gerald G., ed. II. International
Reading Association. III. Title. IV. Series.
LB1050.P4 no. 18 [LB1632] 428'.4'0712 74-23428
ISBN 0-87207-118-9

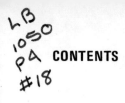

CONTENTS

FOREWORD

In May of 1973 in Denver, Colorado, the International Reading Association held its Eighteenth Perspectives in Reading Conference, focusing on Reading in the Middle School. The purpose of such conferences is to offer those who attend an organized body of knowledge about a topic of current importance in the field. The publication of *Reading in the Middle School* brings the views of the speakers to a wider audience and a record to those who attended the conference.

The speakers in this case were reading specialists from Canada and the United States. The subject was a relatively new outgrowth from concern for the education of the preadolescent, who has for many decades now attended, during grades seven, eight, and nine, either an eight-year elementary school and a four-year high school or a junior high school.

Much has been written in the past decade about the middle school organization as contrasted with that of the junior high school. Sometimes when new organizations are evolved, reading gets lost. Either it continues to be what it was in a previous structure or it is crowded out by the major purpose for reorganization. Old attitudes toward responsibility for the improvement of reading through opportunities for reading and instruction are often inheritances which hobble change.

The present book edited by compiler Gerald Duffy and reviewer Harry Sartain delineates positive effects of the new organization upon the learner, the content teacher, and the reading teacher.

The middle school is not the last form of organization which will appear on the educational horizon to herald a long-delayed millennium for the preadolescent, but the conditions it creates and their possibilities for beneficial changes in procedures and attitudes are worthy of careful study. Nothing of this magnitude ever happens without leaving its mark on our thoughts and attitudes, and eventually our behaviors.

Constance M. McCullough, *President*
International Reading Association
1974-1975

The International Reading Association attempts, through its publications, to provide a forum for a wide spectrum of opinion on reading. This policy permits divergent viewpoints without assuming the endorsement of the Association.

INTRODUCTION

Much has been written about the middle school since that time in the early 1960s when most of us began to realize that this new school organization was somehow different from the junior high school. Most of this writing, however, has focused on the structure, the goal, and the uniqueness of the emerging middle school concept with little being said regarding the role of reading. Indeed, a casual perusal of much of the middle school literature leaves one wondering whether reading even has a place in the middle school!

This book is designed to remove any doubt. To the question of whether reading has a place in the middle school curriculum, the answer is a resounding "yes." Part One directs itself to the unique characteristics of middle schools and middle school pupils; Part Two focuses on the organizational problems of middle school programs; Part Three describes reading content and instructional strategies; and Part Four predicts the future of middle school reading.

In writing the various chapters of the book, each contributor adhered to a single guideline — the contents of the book should be practical and field-oriented. The goal was to provide a usable book for the practicing teacher in the middle school, whether he be a reading teacher or a content area teacher. While the contents are based on both research and experience, the goal was to create a pragmatic handbook rather than a scholarly treatise.

The authors hope that you will find this book readable, realistic, and, most of all, practical in meeting reading problems in the middle school.

GGD

PART ONE

A Frame of Reference

CHAPTER ONE

CURRENT THEMES
AND PROBLEMS
IN MIDDLE SCHOOL READING

Gerald G. Duffy
Michigan State University

This book attempts to answer four basic questions about reading in the middle school:

1. How are the middle school and the middle school student different and how do these differences affect the reading program?
2. If one wishes to implement a reading program in a middle school, what are the components of organization and administration with which one must be concerned?
3. Once the program is organized, what should be taught and what strategies are most useful in achieving these instructional goals?
4. What does the future hold for reading programs at the middle school level?

As one seeks answers for the questions related to the four major parts of the book, certain prevalent themes and problems about middle school reading become evident. To provide a frame of reference for the reader, they are summarized here.

THE MIDDLE SCHOOL AND ITS STUDENTS

A prevalent theme throughout the book is that middle school theory sometimes exceeds practice. The middle school is supposed to be a unique educational structure designed to meet the special needs of the preadolescent. In practice, however, the middle school is often simply an administrative expediency for dealing with building problems or shifts in the school population.

The middle school age group is undergoing dramatic physical, mental, and emotional changes and the students are, in a word, volatile. The result is an unstable student population representing a mind-boggling breadth of abilities and attitudes in which any given student may change dramatically on almost a daily basis. In theory, the middle school program reflects this uniqueness of its clients and provides the security of a home base, while simultaneously offering a variety of experiences. The program efficiently utilizes instructional personnel in team organizations to effectively meet individual needs; and the middle school provides extensive exploratory programs which are based on strong guidance responsibilities shared by all instructional personnel.

It is important to acknowledge, however, that in practice some middle schools are simply junior high schools with changed names. These schools are typified by rigid departmentalization, a heavily emphasized academic curriculum based on traditional offerings, and teachers who view students as miniature replicas of high school students. Such schools may impede, rather than enhance, the development of the preadolescents they serve.

A school's reading program reflects the philosophy of the school. Where the middle school concept is taken seriously, the reading program differs significantly from that found in a traditional junior high school. Rather than being exclusively remedial in nature, the program attempts to meet the needs of all students. Rather than being confined to the efforts of a single specialist, it pervades all offerings of the school; and rather than rigidly homogenizing all students, it flexibly meets individual needs.

To be effective, the emerging middle school must not become a high school for younger children. The various forces which caused the goals of the junior high school to fail must be avoided in the middle school movement, particularly in the area of reading. The typical middle school child requires a highly flexible reading program which capitalizes on variations in his ability, interest, and attitude. This goal will not be realized, however, if the school simply gives the old junior high school a modern name.

ORGANIZING THE READING PROGRAM

The organization of middle school reading programs depends primarily upon the effectiveness of the reading coordinator. The role of this person constitutes a major theme in middle school reading.

In contrast to the reading specialist found in the traditional junior high school, the middle school reading coordinator is a new breed. He no longer confines himself to a tiny cubbyhole in the basement and his clientele is no longer restricted to severely disabled readers. Instead, he is an agent for change whose strategies for working with teachers are as important as his strategies for working with children. As such, he spends a significant part of his time working in content area classrooms. Here, he demonstrates instructional strategies and helps teachers implement these strategies. He is a leader who has a vision of what the middle school reading program should look like and who has the knowledge, wisdom, and tenacity to implement his vision. He is an activist who, by one means or another, creates a reading program which involves all the instructional staff. And, despite his fervor, he is tactful and cautious, realizing that the old saying about "every teacher a teacher of reading" unfortunately is a myth which, when quoted pugnaciously to a group of typical middle school content teachers, will create more antipathy than sympathy. Finally, the reading coordinator is patient, realizing that any change takes time.

The reading coordinator, then, is concerned with improved reading instruction throughout the middle school. To accomplish this, he organizes the middle school reading program out of his special knowledge and implements it by using all his accumulated guile to create change. In the process, he must make judgments about everything from tests to instructional materials; he must involve students, faculty, and the community; and he must simultaneously keep his principal happy and supportive.

The task is gargantuan. However, if we are to break the old junior high school mold and make reading an integral part of the middle school program, no less an effort will suffice.

TEACHING MIDDLE SCHOOL READING

This book reflects two major thrusts regarding the teaching of middle school reading: *who* teaches reading and *how* it is taught.

Who teaches reading in the modern middle school? The answer is "everybody." All staff members in the middle school share the responsibility. This means that every teacher is responsible for teaching his content; every teacher is responsible for insuring that each student achieves at his potential.

Does this mean that the middle school content area teacher must teach first grade reading skills to the severely disabled reader in his class? The answer to this question is "definitely not." Such a task requires a specialist, and an untrained content teacher may do more harm than good if he attempts to remediate a severe reading disability. By the same token, however, the presence of severely disabled readers in his class does not absolve the content teacher of all responsibility. To the contrary, he must be flexible enough to differentiate his instruction to accommodate such students, providing means other than reading for them to meet the objectives of the course. He also must take responsibility for obtaining the special reading instruction that the child needs.

Further, reading involves both pronouncing words and thinking about what the words say. While a content teacher can justifiably excuse himself for not teaching basic word recognition skills, he cannot deny a responsibility for teaching his students to think. Consequently, every teacher in the middle school must know the thinking skills that are required in his content and must possess the instructional competence to develop these skills with his students, whether it is in a listening situation or in a reading situation. Thinking *is* comprehension, and whether a student comprehends depends largely upon whether he understands the interpretative demands of the rhetoric he faces in a given content area. Teaching the child to understand specialized content material is an integral part of being a content area teacher and the responsibility cannot be dodged.

Regarding *how* reading and thinking should be taught in the middle school, this book focuses on the concept of individualization. This is, of course, consistent with the central philosophy of the middle school which, in theory at least, professes to emphasize individualized instruction.

Individualization is an extremely broad concept. It encompasses the problems of grouping, differentiation, selection of materials, management, and many other facets of instruction. It usually fails to be implemented effectively, despite all that is written about it, because teachers tend to take the rather naive view that there must be an easy way to individualize instruction.

Nothing could be further from the truth. Individualized instruction requires highly refined skills of organization and instruction, to say nothing of diligence. To work, individualized instruction must spring from a strong conceptual base, be supported by a flexible and efficient management system, and be actualized by a teacher who believes in actively teaching what needs to be taught. It cannot be achieved by sitting back and waiting for something to happen incidentally or by buying a commercial program which is promoted as the cure-all for everything that ails the middle school reader.

Finally, individualization demands teachers who care. They must care because individualization requires commitment and diligence. If a teacher's level of caring does not go beyond viewing his task as a nine-to-four job, little individualization will occur.

THE FUTURE

There are many problems involved in effectively implementing the middle school concept for today's preadolescents, but the final section of this book predicts even more problems for the middle school of the future. While today's middle school students are volatile, those of the future are likely to be more volatile. While today's middle school must be flexible to meet the unique needs of its students, the school of the future will need to be more flexible. While the reading teacher of today's middle school must be a person of diverse skills, the reading teacher of the future will need a still greater diversity of skills. Clearly, the major trend for the future of middle schools and their reading programs is toward ever greater flexibility to meet the unique needs of the preadolescent age group.

CONCLUSION

The middle school has immense potential for both today's students and those of the future. The goals and philosophy, if implemented as espoused by its advocates, will result in excitingly appropriate instruction generally and in significantly improved reading instruction particularly.

It is important to note, however, that it is currently a matter of conjecture whether the middle school and its reading programs will achieve this potential.

The danger is very real that the "in-between" school is changing in name only. Whether its potential is reached depends upon those of us who staff the middle school. If we accept the challenge and implement a true middle school, the future is bright; if we are content with the junior high school model, our reward will be mediocrity. The choice is ours.

CHAPTER TWO

THE MIDDLE SCHOOL: A HISTORICAL FRAME OF REFERENCE

Thomas H. Peeler
Dade County, Florida, Schools

Middle school reading problems cannot be fully understood without also considering the growth and development of the in-between school itself. This movement, which began nearly seventy years ago, provides a perspective within which specific curricular problems, such as reading, can be viewed in sharper focus. Consequently, this chapter provides a historical frame of reference regarding the growth of the middle school and suggests some implications for current programs.

THE JUNIOR HIGH SCHOOL MOVEMENT

The first middle school, the junior high school, came into existence at the turn of the century. This reorganization movement in secondary schools developed through the combined efforts of several noted educational leaders.

Early Leaders

In the forefront of this movement was Charles W. Eliot, former president of Harvard. He was interested in lowering the college entrance age of students. Eliot suggested that there would be an economy of time by placing high school subjects in the upper elementary grades (7 and 8), thereby allowing high school students to graduate at a lower age.

Just before the turn of the century, Nicholas Murray Butler, president of Columbia University, became an energetic worker for the idea of a reorganized secondary school. He pointed out the difference in functions between the elementary and secondary schools and the importance of adolescence in educational adjustments made for the upper grades (11).

During the latter part of the 19th century and early years of the 20th century, writers in the field of educational psychology focused their attention on student needs. Noted psychologist G. Stanley Hall advocated educational re-organization to meet the needs of the adolescent youth.

The efforts of these writers, as well as various social and economic factors such as increased population, demands for vocational education, pupil dropouts, and the need for new buildings, led to the growth of the junior high school. The first ones opened in 1909 in Columbus, Ohio, and Berkeley, California. The popularity of the junior high movement was apparent from the increase of junior high schools from 387 in 1922 to 2,372 in 1938 (*11*).

Goals

The goals of the junior high schools are to:

1. provide vocational career preparation;
2. provide for the needs of early adolescence;
3. provide for a smooth transition from the elementary to the secondary school;
4. help youth understand the nature of the society in which they live;
5. provide an opportunity for youth to discover and understand their interests, capabilities, and aptitudes;
6. provide an educational environment which would reduce the number of dropouts; and
7. assist pupils to make the fullest adjustment possible for self-realization and service to the society in which they live.

Evolution of the Junior High School

As might be expected, the curriculum changes for implementing the above goals evolved slowly. Prior to 1930, grades seven and eight were characterized by elementary subjects such as reading, spelling, penmanship, grammar, arithmetic, geography, and American history. Grade nine was very similar to the senior high school program and subjects such as English, algebra, foreign language, and general sciences were taught.

In the 1930s, subjects in all grades were combined under English, social studies, general math, and science. The development of courses such as home economics, industrial arts, and fine arts found their way into the curriculum. It was also at this time that teachers in the junior high became more highly specialized. Departmentalization became the standard mode of organizing teachers for instructional purposes.

As time passed, many curriculum innovations were made in attempting to modify the strict departmentalized mode of organization. Perhaps the best known effort was the introduction of the core curriculum. This concept had several purposes and definitions. Basically, the core program, combined with block scheduling, attempted to correlate subjects such as social studies and English around central themes. Teachers either became proficient in both subjects or combined their talents for instructional purposes.

Attempts to modify the predominant mode of organization were never highly successful, although core programs, block scheduling, and interdisciplinary team teaching have been utilized in junior high for the past three decades.

Criticism of the Junior High School

During the late '40s and early '50s, a mounting series of criticisms were aimed at the junior high school by educators who advocated different organizational and curricular patterns for the intermediate school years. Some of the criticisms, as enumerated by Kindred (*11*) were as follows:

1. The junior high school tended, by and large, to pattern itself after the senior high, despite the excellent theory behind it. This was evident in the extension of departmentalization downward to include grade seven, in the extracurricular fanfare associated with interscholastic athletics and marching bands, in elaborate graduation exercises, in social events, and in class scheduling. In fact, it became a high school for junior pupils.

2. Pressures on the junior high school to place more emphasis upon academic subjects, such as mathematics, science, and foreign languages, meant less time and energy for fine arts, industrial arts, dramatics, and homemaking projects which are equally important in a general education program.

3. Study assignments and homework loads increased considerably because of the thrust downward of senior high subjects; the amounts given probably were detrimental to the physical and mental health of junior high students.

4. Junior high school programs, in many instances, were badly out of line with the needs of the preadolescent and early adolescent youngster.

Many educators, sociologists, and psychologists began questioning the junior high school as an effective organization structure. Their concerns were centered mostly on ninth grade students. The studies conducted by educators and social scientists indicated that the ninth grader of the 1950s had greater maturity, social sophistication, and more rapid maturation than students of twenty years earlier. Their recommendations were for the ninth grade student to be included in the senior rather than the junior high school.

The Junior High School in Perspective

In reviewing the junior high school movement, there appears to be a weakness which is now common to many educational practices — namely, that of translating theory into practice. The goals and objectives of the junior high school were sound but the implementation of these goals and objectives fell far short of expectation.

An example of this theory-practice deficiency can be found in a survey conducted by Howell (*10*) in 1947. One hundred junior high school administrators were asked to react to the original aims of the junior high. The respondents selected the following aims as being as valid as ever, although there was little evidence that the aims were being achieved:

1. a suitable environment for children 12-16 years of age;
2. exploration of interests, abilities, and aptitude of those ages;
3. adaptation of training and education to individual interests and needs;
4. guidance to help the individual find himself;
5. provision for individual differences in the various subjects;
6. special care for retarded students;
7. participation of pupils in school government activities;
8. physical diagnosis and remedial work for individuals;
9. recognition of the nature of the child at adolescence; and
10. guidance exploration and provisions for individual differences.

The junior high was originally intended to be a bridging institution between elementary and senior high school. Instead, it became a school more like the high school and was better geared to the adolescent than to the preadolescent. Departmentalization gets much of the blame. Leonard (12), for instance, states that departmentalization is out of harmony with what we know about human growth and development. Junior high youth do not possess the adjustment characteristics needed for quickly changing from the guidance of a single teacher to that of five, or for shifting from a unified emphasis to a specialized interest. Briggs (4) further indicates that any bad effects of sudden departmentalization of the beginning of the ninth grade are likely to be worse when introduced at the seventh grade or earlier.

The failings of the junior high school also are blamed on teacher training. Burnett (5) contends junior high school teachers must understand adolescents and be able to work with them, have a knowledge of the techniques of guidance and homeroom leadership, and possess a balanced background of general education with the ability to teach in several subjects. Teacher training programs to develop these needs among junior high school teachers have been sparse. Hansen (8) contends that teacher education institutions place more emphasis on the training of elementary and high school teachers than they place on the training of junior high or middle school teachers. Moss (15) indicates that after sixty years only a handful of states have recognized the junior high as worthy of separate teacher certification, while Conant (6) states that neither the elementary school teacher nor the senior high school teacher is well enough prepared to give instruction in grades seven and eight. Finally, Hoats (9) found that forty-six states accepted the secondary certification for grades seven through nine while only twenty-one accepted the elementary certificate. Bossing and Cramer (3) summarize the teacher training situation by stating that the junior high school has served too long as a small imitation of the upper division of the secondary school.

It is apparent from the above review of literature that the junior high school movement failed to accomplish several of its outlined functions. The major criticisms revolve around three central themes. First, the curricular and organizational patterns became mere replicas of the senior high rather than new patterns different from the elementary and secondary schools. Second, teacher training institutions and state certification bureaus did not generally promote programs which train teachers for working with junior high students. Third, the body of knowledge concerning the study of the physical, intellectual, emotional, and social development of the junior high student has been largely neglected in school programs.

THE MIDDLE SCHOOL MOVEMENT

The junior high school critics had their impact on the educational scene. The decade of the sixties evidenced a rapid movement toward reorganizing the conventional 6-3-3 pattern of operation and substituting a middle school pattern. Although there are no clearly defined guidelines for what constitutes a middle school organization, most advocates recommend placing the ninth graders in the senior high school for reasons cited above. Such patterns as the 4-4-4, 5-3-4, and 6-2-4 have emerged while the traditional 6-3-3 programs are less in evidence.

The apparent rapid growth of this movement can be found in surveys which indicate 500 middle schools in 1965-1966 (7), to more than 1,000 in 1967-1968 (2), to at least 1,300 in 1969-1970 (13).

Characteristics of the Middle School

As a result of numerous studies and surveys concerning the rationale for the middle school, Alexander (1) indicates that certain features characterize this new organizational pattern.

1. A home base and teacher for every student to provide for continuing guidance and assistance to help him make the decisions he faces almost daily regarding special needs and learning opportunities.
2. A program of learning opportunities offering balanced attention to the three major goals of:
   a. personal development of the between-ager,
   b. skills of continued learning, and
   c. effective use of appropriate organized knowledge.
3. An instructional system focused on individual progress, with many curriculum options and with individualized instruction in appropriate areas.
4. The use of interdisciplinary team arrangements for cooperative planning, instructing, and evaluating.
5. A wide range of exploratory activities for the socializing, interest-developing, and leisure-enriching purposes of the bridge school.

Despite the apparent clarity of the above characteristics, some of the first studies to emerge on the middle school movement are somewhat disappointing because of poorly defined purposes. This is because the middle school came into being as an administrative device before goals were specified. There is a parallel here between the early history of the middle school and the history of the junior high school. Both came into existence as administrative organization structures with goals and objectives being developed after the fact. Most school reorganizations take place because of enrollment pressures, building needs, or budgetary problems — in other words, for reasons that are more administrative than educational. This has been true of the junior high school and is equally true of the middle school.

This phenomenon is reflected in Alexander's study (*1*) of the middle school. When principals of the schools surveyed were asked to indicate reasons for the establishment of the middle school, the most frequently reported reason was the elimination of crowded conditions in schools. Other reasons somewhat unrelated to the educational program, were "to utilize a new school building" and "to aid in desegregation." Integration has been the greatest single reason for creation of the middle school in large cities such as New York.

Current Status of the Middle School

In attempting to summarize a few of the salient points in Alexander's study, it appears that many of the frequently cited weaknesses of the junior high are being carried over to the middle school:

1. It appears that there is not a great reduction in interschool athletics.
2. Departmentalization as it functions in junior high has not been significantly changed in the middle school.
3. Generally stated aims, such as "to remedy the weaknesses of the junior high school" and "to provide a program specifically designed for the age group," are not generally reflected in either the curriculum or the organization of the schools surveyed; instead, both the program of studies and the departmentalization pattern of the junior high school is predominant even as low as grade five.

Mellinger (*13*), states that the prevailing curricular pattern in Illinois middle schools also leaves much to be desired. His statewide analysis indicates that 1) exploratory programs are skimpy and unimaginative, 2) study halls are legion, 3) the Carnegie Time Unit is very much alive, and 4) few middle schools limit their athletic activities to the intramural type.

Studies such as those cited are alarming. Consequently, it might be appropriate for middle school educators to view the next several years as the "period of transfusion" if the middle school movement is to avoid becoming another junior high school.

Encouraging Signs

In the past two or three years, encouraging moves at several universities, state departments of education, and local school districts indicate a renewed interest on the part of educators to eliminate the weaknesses cited.

One of the frequently mentioned deficiencies of both the junior high and middle school has been the lack of formal training programs for teachers of intermediate age students. However, several universities around the nation are now offering preparation programs for middle school teachers. The University of Florida has recently instituted such a program, and the University of Georgia has developed a competency-based field experience program for the preparation and certification of middle school teachers. State accreditation standards in Florida are being rewritten to accommodate the change created by middle school training programs, and several other state departments of education are in the process of changing secondary certification standards (*14*).

Another hopeful sign in the middle school's attempt to put theory into practice is the move to more individualized programs. Recent curricular changes utilizing learning packages and programs such as the Individualzied Mathematics System are finding their way into the middle school programs. The most encouraging changes, however, are occurring in the language arts area. Reading programs are being continued in grades seven and eight with students having an opportunity to choose from a wide variety of reading material. A wide choice of books of a high-interest, low-readability nature are now being provided for students who are reading below grade level.

Innovative instructional plans are gaining support in many middle schools. In grades five and six, the traditional elementary self-contained organization is often modified to allow for instruction in art, music, physical education, industrial arts, and home economics by specialists in the field. Also, team teaching and cooperative planning allow classroom teachers either to exchange students for certain academic subjects or to combine talents in the planning stages of instruction. The core program which achieved moderate success in the junior high, is now being proposed for the middle school with the addition of a strong emphasis on guidance. Moss (*15*) describes the following guidelines for a core program:

1. It is centered around expressed interests of children aged 10-14.
2. Certain social needs of our democratic society are fulfilled through study of a few well-defined problem areas.
3. While embracing the broad areas of English and social studies, core utilizes these content subjects as background materials necessary to develop understandings about the problem being studied.
4. One teacher is responsible for a group of twenty-five middle school children assigned to a two-hour class.
5. Core students are heterogeneously grouped.

While the early middle school seemed frequently to be a junior high school with a different name, the more recent trends in both teacher-training and middle school instructional programs provide hope that the failures of the junior high school will not be repeated.

SUMMARY

The middle school movement is still too young to permit one to generalize firmly regarding organizational and curricular trends. One thing, however, is certain – the middle school is now a major organizational pattern on the American scene. The number of school systems having middle schools has been growing and is continuing to grow.

However, the history of the "in-between" school provides us with some perspective on the emerging middle school movement. Much like the junior high, the middle school come into existence for reasons which have little relationship to the stated goals and objectives. While the past few years have seen the initial development of programs and curricula which address themselves to these goals and objectives, considerable additional effort must be expended to insure that the middle schools do not become modified senior high schools, as did the junior highs.

Middle school teachers concerned with reading, through their actions in the respective schools, can influence the degree to which the middle school achieves its goals. It is fervently hoped that these teachers, as well as other middle school personnel, will support and implement the curriculum innovations which will make the middle school a real bridging institution between the elementary and the high school.

References

1. Alexander, William M. "How Fares the Middle School?" *National Elementary Principal*, 51 (November 1971), 10-11, 163-186.

2. Alexander, William M., et al. *The Emergent Middle School* (2nd ed.). New York: Holt, Rinehart and Winston, 1969, 164.

3. Bossing, Nelson L., and Roscoe V. Cramer. *The Junior High School.* Boston: Houghton Mifflin, 1965.

4. Briggs, Thomas H. *The Junior High School.* Boston: Houghton Mifflin, 1920, 110.

5. Burnett, Lewis W. "Core Programs in Washington State Junior High Schools," *School Review,* 59 (February 1951), 97-100.

6. Conant, James B. "Some Problems of the Junior High School," *Bulletin of the National Association of Secondary School Principals,* April 1960, 314.

7. Cuff, William A. "Middle Schools on the March," *Bulletin of the National Association of Secondary School Principals,* 51 (February 1967).

8. Hansen, John H., and Arthur C. Hearn. *The Middle School Program.* Chicago: Rand McNally, 1971, 55.

9. Hoats, W.R. "Junior High School Teacher Certification," *Bulletin of National Association of Secondary Principals,* 47 (October 1963), 47.

10. Howell, Clarence E. "Junior High, How Valid Are Its Original Aims?" *Clearing House,* 23 (October 1948), 75-88.

11. Kindred, Leslie W. *The Intermediate School.* Englewood Cliffs, New Jersey: Prentice-Hall, 1968, 21, 29-30.

12. Leonard, Paul J. "Frontiers in Junior High School Education," *Bulletin of the National Association of Secondary Principals,* 24 (February 1940), 112-119.

13. Mellinger, Morris, and John Rackauskas. *Quest for Identity: National Survey of the Middle School, 1969-70.* Chicago: Chicago State College, 1970, 3.

14. "Middle School Status in Ten States," *National Elementary Principal,* 51 (November 1971), 70-72.

CHAPTER THREE

THE MIDDLE SCHOOL STUDENT AND THE READING PROGRAM

H. Thompson Fillmer
University of Florida

The history of public school education reveals numerous efforts to improve the quality of education at both the primary and secondary levels of education. Until recently, there has been a dearth of research, programs, and innovations in the grades enrolling approximately one-third of the school population — the middle grades. Now, a new type of school organization is emerging that provides an administrative unit to accommodate this third of the school population who are neither children nor adolescents but are in a transitional stage somewhere between the two extremes, children whom Eichhorn (5) classifies as *transescents*.

In theory, the emerging middle school is designed to meet the unique educational needs of this group of in-between pupils. As is pointed out in the previous chapter, however, there is a danger that the middle school will become just another junior high school, thereby failing to achieve its unique function. This is no less a danger in the area of middle school reading programs. If reading instruction is to be effective in the middle school, teachers must consider both the characteristics of the transescent and the uniqueness of the middle school as foundations to build a reading program which will effectively meet the needs of the students.

CHARACTERISTICS OF THE TRANSESCENT

Great disparity in physical development exists among pupils in the middle grades. A growth lag occurs prior to the onset of pubescence, followed by a tremendous spurt. This burst of growth is accompanied by the development of the reproductive system and the appearance of secondary sex characteristics.

Accompanying the radical physiological changes are many characteristics which are related to changes in mental processes, attitudes, relationships with others, and self-concepts which might be classified as psychosocial characteristics.

Intellectual Characteristics

Intellectual processes also, show lags and spurts during the period of transescence. Some pupils still rely heavily on concrete experiences for concept development, while others have entered the period that Piaget classifies as the formal operations stage in which they are able to reason abstractly without the use of concrete props. Pupils who have arrived at the stage of formal operations naturally have different interests and differ in degree of creativity and imagination from those yet in the concrete stage of cognitive development. The wide range of intellectual development has implications for the teacher of reading with regard to the extent of concreteness, number of concepts, and type of comprehension to be studied by different pupils in the class.

Attitude Formation

The rapidity of physical development, the onset of sex characteristics, and the awkwardness in performing motor activities with their new body configurations are responsible for the changes in attitudes and the emotional turmoil of transescents. Pupils respond to the disconcerting sexual urge with guilt and uncertainty. They try to fill their sex role appropriately. Although interested in members of the opposite sex, they are clumsy in mixed social situations. As pupils strive to gain emotional independence from parents and other adults, the need for peer approval assumes gigantic proportions. This new role causes the pupils to reexamine their values and self-concepts and frequently motivates them to seek a model or "hero" with whom to identify.

At the risk of oversimplification, it might be stated that the transescent's major preoccupation is his search for identity. Erikson describes this search as follows (*11*):

> The central problem of the period is the establishment of a sense of identity. The identity the adolescent seeks to clarify is who he is, what his role in society is to be. Is he a child or is he an adult? Does he have it in him to be some day a husband and father? What is he to be as a worker and an earner of money? Can he feel self-confident in spite of the fact that his race or religion or national background makes him a person some people look down on? Overall, will he be a success or a failure? By reason of these questions, adolescents are sometimes morbidly preoccupied with how they appear in the eyes of others as compared with their own conception of themselves, and with how they can make the roles and skills learned earlier jibe with what is currently in style.

Summary

The middle school pupil is a volatile creature. He is encountering radical physiological changes, his intellectual growth is erratic and may at any given time be quite different from the intellectual behavior of a given peer, and he is striving to develop basic attitudes about himself as a person. The combination of these characteristics is unique and requires a unique school program.

UNIQUENESS OF THE MIDDLE SCHOOL PROGRAM

Because the transescent has special needs, the general school program must also be special. It must serve as an axis around which the pupil's search for self-identity can revolve.

Cognitive Domain

To nurture the transescent's rapid intellectual growth, the middle school program should provide a full range of activities concerned with the cognitive domain.

The cognitive domain includes activities which require the pupil to recall facts or information, communicate knowledge, apply information in specific situations, identify the interrelationships between ideas in a communication, put together elements to form a whole, and make judgments about the values of materials and methods for a particular purpose (2).

The majority of curriculum activities are presently found in this domain. It has been suggested that the majority of reading activities deal with cognitive objectives at the lower end of the hierarchy, such as literal comprehension, to the detriment of the objectives at the higher end, such as analysis, synthesis, and evaluation.

Affective Domain

A more neglected phase of classroom activities lies in the area of the affective domain. Activities for attaining affective objectives provide pupils with opportunities to become aware of the existence of various phenonema; receive or take notice of particular stimuli; respond or attend to stimuli; develop or change interests, values, and attitudes; organize one's value system; and respond consistently to the environment on the basis of this internalized value system (9).

Because the middle school years are characterized by turbulent emotions engendered by a pupil's search for identity, the examination and analysis of interests, values, and attitudes should occupy a significant portion of the middle school program.

Psychomotor Domain

The transescent's physical growth spurts and lags necessitate a comprehensive and diverse physical education program. As a growth spurt occurs, there is often a temporary lack of psychomotor coordination. At the same time, pupils are interested in becoming proficient in a wide variety of games and sports. An appropriate psychomotor program for the middle school would include activities designed both to practice fundamental physical skills and to reinforce the understandings of cognitive and affective skills.

Psychomotor activities appropriate for the middle school grades are: role playing, dramatic play, creative dance, sensory activities, games, stunts, tumbling, and calisthenics. Many psychomotor skills, such as control precision, response orientation, and reaction time, may be directly related to reading skills and might well be correlated with the reading program.

Summary

The effective middle school program must be structured to accommodate the unique characteristics of its clients. The cognitive activities must reflect the broad range of abilities of the pupils, the affective activities must be designed to help pupils develop the values they are so diligently striving for, and the psychomotor activities must be consistent with the physical growth spurt typical of this age level. Failure to provide appropriate activities to meet the unique needs of the middle school child minimizes the chance that the middle school will achieve its function.

COMPONENTS OF A MIDDLE SCHOOL READING PROGRAM

The reading program, as well as other curricular areas, should be in harmony with the unique characteristics of the preadolescent pupil and the philosophy of the emerging middle school. Traditional reading instruction, conducted in a remedial setting or in a single group in which all the pupils are considered to be the same, is not likely to meet the unique needs of the middle school child. The reading program, regardless of how it is organized and administered, must be designed to accommodate the unique client being served.

Since many middle school reading programs are directed by avant garde, stylish young ladies, the characteristics of an effective middle school reading program may be organized into the acronym MOD MISS:

M Motivation
O Objectives
D Diagnosis

M Materials
I Individualization
S Systems
S Saturation

Motivation

The United States is second only to the U.S.S.R. in published materials available. The amount of literature available, however, does not seem to reflect the amount of reading performed. Surveys by the National Opinion Research Center indicate that citizens of the United States read fewer books than citizens of Great Britain, France, Germany, Holland, Switzerland, and the Scandinavian Countries (7). Approximately 10 percent of our population reads approximately 80 percent of the books. Less than half of the adult population of the United States has never read a book all the way through. One-third of the college graduates participating in the survey had not read a book completely in the past year. Perhaps even more disappointing is the fact that less than one out of five adults could name a book that they would like to read.

Despite these discouraging statistics regarding the reading practices of our citizens, there is evidence that persons will read if motivated to do so. Such motivation does not occur naturally but must be planned for in the middle school setting.

For instance, a laboratory approach, as opposed to a reading lesson approach to reading instruction, provides many motivational advantages for meeting the diversified needs of the middle school pupil. Such an approach is characterized by a wide variety of reading goals. Some pupils participate in enrichment activities, such as word power development; others participate in remedial activities.

Some middle school teachers find that the reading hardware frequently found in laboratories adds a novelty effect to reading instruction and, therefore, serves as a motivator. Hardware is rather costly, however, and is a dispensable part of the reading program. The reading teacher must list priorities carefully and then equip the laboratory within budget restrictions.

The laboratory approach motivates because each pupil can establish his own purposes for working in the laboratory. Since all pupils will be assigned to the laboratory for a certain number of hours each week, the stigma that is sometimes attached to a remedial clinic is avoided. Every pupil plans an individual program with the help of the teacher. Each time he comes to the lab, he knows exactly what to do and keeps daily achievement records. Periodically, he and the teacher review his accomplishments and readjust his program appropriately.

In addition to the self-direction and responsibility developed in such an individualized program, there is some evidence that boys learn to read more effectively when allowed to work independently in self-instructional materials (10). Since boys in the middle and lower achievement ranges tend to be inferior to girls in reading performance, practices favoring boys' learning could noticeably affect the mean reading achievement of an entire school system.

The laboratory approach increases the motivation of middle school pupils for reading because it provides the atmosphere and flexibility needed by children of this age level. It is geared to the unique characteristics of the transescent. A more detailed description of a laboratory approach in action can be found in Chapter 9 of this book.

Objectives

A middle school reading program should have general objectives based on the needs of the pupil population. Some pupils need a review of the word recognition and comprehension skills taught in the primary grades. All pupils need to develop more complex skills in locating information, using library resources, improving reading rate and flexibility, and expanding comprehension skills.

Heilman (8) suggests that certain principles and objectives may be deserving of special emphasis in the middle school grades.

1. Individual evaluation should take place to determine the capacity of students and the present level of achievement in facets of reading including:

a. sight word vocabulary
b. word attack skills
c. level of silent reading
d. meaning vocabulary and concepts
e. ability to profit from listening situations including oral directions
f. oral reading skills
g. facility in finding information, use of reference materials
h. work habits and attitudes
i. rate at which curricular materials can be read*

2. Following diagnosis, the teacher should devise a flexible reading program to take care of individual differences and needs revealed in the initial diagnosis.

3. Reading instruction must be deliberate and systematic. Inestimable damage to children can result from the philosophy that "children learn to read in the primary grades and read to learn at the intermediate level." They must do both at each level.

4. In addition to specific reading instruction per se, instruction must also be incorporated with the teaching of all subject matter. Children must be *taught to read* science, mathematics, health, and social science materials.

5. The child should be helped to expand his stock of concepts. This is essential in all content areas.

6. Practice should be provided in various types of functional reading — in newspapers, magazines, and books — to supplement basic texts in subject areas.

7. Guidance should be given in reading for recreation, pleasure, and personal growth.

8. The child's reading interest should be broadened to build a foundation for life-long reading.

9. Appreciation should be developed for good literature, poetry and drama.

10. A wide selection of materials should be available in all fields — science, literature, biography, current events, and social studies.

11. A program should be devised for guiding the intellectually gifted children.

12. Children should be helped to increase the rate at which they can comprehend printed word symbols in combination. This skill is important at this instructional level since curriculum materials in the various content areas make increasing demands on readers.

*Editor's Note. Teachers might add to this diagnosis a number of points related to attitude and appreciation. The middle school pupil who does not like to read will have problems almost as serious as those of the pupil who cannot read. – HWS

13. Steps should be taken to improve the critical reading skills:
    a. coping with figurative or picturesque language
    b. drawing inferences
    c. classifying ideas and selecting those that are germane to the reader's purpose
    d. evaluating ideas and arriving at the author's purpose or intent
    e. detecting bias and differentiating between fact and opinion
14. The following reading-study skills should be developed and extended:
    a. using books effectively — making maximum use of the index, table of contents, and appendix
    b. acquiring facility in the use of dictionaries
    c. using reference books effectively
    d. understanding graphs, maps, charts, and tables
    e. using library resources, card catalogues, and periodical indexes
    f. note-taking and outlining materials for a given purpose
15. Diagnosis should be continuous and ongoing throughout each instructional year. An initial diagnosis serves only for initial procedures.

Many collections of behavioral objectives for reading are available in the literature. Yet, objectives in the affective domain frequently are omitted from lists of objectives, especially when behavioral terms are used. The following affective behaviors are listed under the general objective of "Reading for Enjoyment" in the reading assessment program published by the Division of Elementary and Secondary Education, Florida Department of Education.

1. The learner will explain what he liked or disliked about the stories or books he selected and read.

2. The learner will volunteer to read a favorite poem or selection to the class.

3. The learner will indicate that he enjoys reading activities in class.

4. The learner will recommend to others the reading selections he has particularly enjoyed.

5. The learner will indicate that he enjoys and reads many different types of reading materials.

6. The learner will indicate that he often reads in leisure time independently of school requirements.

7. The learner will indicate that he is acquainted with a wide variety of children's literature.

If appropriate objectives for each pupil are clearly spelled out in behavioral terms and if these objectives accurately reflect the specific needs of the pupil, the teacher is well on his way to accomplishing the desired learnings.

Diagnosis

A critical part of any reading program is the diagnostic program. It is virtually impossible for a teacher to provide appropriate reading activities for a pupil without ascertaining his achievements in detail. This is particularly true in the middle school where there is such a wide range of capabilities.

In interpreting test results, the reader must be aware of some limitations of formal and informal tests: 1) test items represent a minute sample of the behaviors being assessed; 2) test items may not measure the behaviors they purport to measure; and 3) test performance may be affected by many unrelated variables. Despite these limitations, the use of tests to make generalizations about pupil behavior is an efficient and generally accepted practice.

There are many reading tests and other assessment instruments currently available to teachers. Instead of presenting great lists of assessment materials, this paper will explore areas in which assessments should be made. The first area is the pupil's instructional reading level — that level at which the pupil is able to pronounce correctly 95-98 percent of the words in a selection and score 75 percent on an informal comprehension test. Reading material at this level provides new words to challenge the pupil, yet presents material which does not become frustrating.

Several standardized oral reading tests are available for assessing the instructional reading level. A teacher can obtain approximately the same results by selecting a 100 word passage from each book in a graded reading series and preparing five comprehension questions from each paragraph. The passage from which the pupil pronounces correctly 95-98 percent of the words, and answers at least four of the questions, represents his instructional reading level.

After assessing the pupil's instructional reading level, the teacher should then estimate his expected reading level. Since the reading process is correlated with mental ability, an acceptable way to gauge expected reading level is to consider the pupil's mental ability. Obviously, if the pupil is a poor reader, it is useless to base one's judgments on an IQ obtained from an intelligence test that requires reading skill.

Perhaps the most accurate formula for gauging the expectancy age (XA) of a middle school pupil is the Horn formula (6) which is stated: $XA = \frac{2MA + CA}{3}$. To illustrate, Tom is twelve years old and has a mental age of ten. Using the formula, his XA will be ten plus twelve divided by three, which gives him an expected reading age of 10.7. We can expect, then, that Tom will read at approximately the level of a child who is 10.7 years of age and has average intelligence.

Martha is in Tom's class and is also twelve years old. She has a mental age of 14. Her XA is 13.3. Although Tom and Martha are the same age and in the same class, there is more than two years difference in their expected reading age. If Tom reads one year below his age level, he is reading well. If Martha is reading at age level, she is reading below her ability level. All teachers, but middle school teachers especially, must learn to evaluate a pupil's reading level in terms of reading expectancy rather than in terms of chronological age or grade level.

A third required diagnostic assessment is a sight-word test. Even at middle school level, many pupils are not able to recognize instantly the most used sight words. Both standardized and informal lists of "instant words" classified by grade level are available to teachers, and can be used to assess the pupil's repertoire of sight words. If the pupil is below expectancy in this area, he should be taught these words immediately to help him attain the repertoire of sight words that is essential for reading proficiency.

The fourth step in the diagnostic pattern is the assessment of the pupil's word attack skills. This is necessary only for those who are not fairly fluent readers. Beginning with the pupil's knowledge of letter names and sounds, this assessment should include blends, digraphs, diphthongs, prefixes, roots, suffixes, inflection, compound words, and syllabication skills. There is an abundance of informal and standardized instruments available for teachers who desire to assess the word attack abilities of their pupils.

Since reading involves a combination of word attack and comprehension skills, the fifth step necessary in an adequate diagnostic program is the assessment of the pupil's comprehension skills. Pronouncing words correctly without getting meaning from the context in which the words appear is not reading.

Although informal questioning techniques can be used to estimate a pupil's ability to comprehend written material, comprehension must be broken down more specifically if corrective instruction is to be effective. Some of the specific comprehension tasks include the following:

finding main ideas in paragraphs
recognizing and organizing facts and ideas
detecting the writer's mood and purpose
evaluating what is read
predicting outcomes
perceiving relationships or comparisons
suspending judgment
drawing inferences and conclusions
interpreting figurative and picturesque language
detecting bias and slanting
filtering facts
differentiating between fact and opinion
weighing facts as to their importance
analyzing opinions

By assessing each pupil's skills in the five areas stated, the teacher will be better able to help the pupil establish goals for his reading program, guide him into appropriate materials, establish a sequence of activities, and work with other teachers in planning appropriate activities. The wide range in cognitive ability among middle school pupils makes diagnosis an essential element in middle school reading programs. For further insight into this crucial component, see Chapter 6 of this book.

Materials

It is a truism that one learns to read by reading. An indispensable component of middle school reading is a wide variety of reading materials to match the wide variety of middle school pupils. Several general categories of materials are listed here with a more specific listing appearing in Chapter 8.

The school library is the most readily available source of reading materials. Books of various reading levels, interests, and topics will meet the needs of any pupil in the class. School librarians, if given sufficient notice, might prepare a mobile library to serve temporarily as a classroom library. Such a library could be planned to meet specific topics and reading levels requested by the teacher.

The most widely used books in reading programs are those in basal reading series. They are sequentially organized and contain extensive practice exercise and assessment instruments. Basal readers may be used as the central focus of the reading program or as a supplement to it.

High interest — low readability series are useful books for the many readers whose ages exceed their reading ability. These books usually are fast-moving, action-packed adventures; they cater to the interests of older pupils but offer primary grade readability.

Adapted classics include such works as *The Count of Monte Cristo* and *Huckleberry Finn*, rewritten in simplified passages. These books are intended for pupils who otherwise would not be able to read the original classic.

Several commercially prepared reading programs, classified as classroom laboratories, are available to reading teachers. These programs usually include a pretest to determine where the pupil should begin the program, reading selections which are color coded according to difficulty and followed by comprehension questions, exercises designed to increase reading speed and to build vocabulary, and answer sheets for exercises to enable pupils to score their own work and keep progress records.

Excellent sources for meaningful reading exercises are the newspapers and magazines prepared specifically for this purpose. A teacher's edition, which accompanies the pupil issue, suggests appropriate activities and supplementary readings.

Graded series of exercise booklets designed to provide practice on specific skills are available, especially for word attack and comprehension skills.

Some authorities may condemn publications such as comic books and believe them to be responsible for adversely affecting the attitudes, personality, and behavior of children who read them. Others may assert that healthy children are not moved to antisocial behavior through reading. Nevertheless, comic books do exist and most children read them; teachers should, therefore, encourage the proper use of comic books. The Walt Disney animal characters such as Bugs Bunny and Mickey Mouse are popular comics among middle school pupils. The high adventure story with fantastic characters such as Hercules, Superman, and Batman are also highly favored. Mature middle school pupils, if they read comic books, may prefer the realistic stories in *True* and *Classic*. The beginning middle school years are the most popular for comic books; interest falls rapidly as pupils move toward adolescence.

Programed materials texts are designed to teach specific reading skills by presenting them in a logical sequence, dividing the learnings into small steps, requiring an active response from the learner, providing feedback regarding the correctness of the response, and allowing the learner to proceed at his own pace. The programs generally include teacher's guides, workbooks, tests, filmstrips, overlays, and storybooks. Such materials should be useful in helping teachers to individualize instruction to achieve certain objectives.

Perhaps the most recent development in reading instruction is the availability of approaches that appeal simultaneously to the senses of sight, hearing, and touch. The teacher or individual pupil may project a lesson on the screen by use of a filmstrip while listening to the words from a record or tape. The pupil then responds orally or writes in a workbook. This type of multiple-sensory appeal is necessary in the reading instruction of certain types of disabled children and may be useful in providing individualization of reading instruction.

A wide variety of material is available for use with the middle school reader. Some multisensory materials may be expensive; other (such as comic books) may be very inexpensive. The middle school teacher must allocate financial resources wisely in order to accumulate reading materials which accommodate the wide range of interests and abilities found among middle school students.

Individualization

Extensive differences exist on all grade levels among the middle school population. Alexander and associates (*1*) demonstrate existing differences in level of maturity among children in the same middle school classrooms:

1. Some fifth grade girls already are biologically and physiologically fifteen-year-olds — usual for girls at the ninth grade level.
2. Some fifth grade boys still are biologically and physiologically only seven-year-olds — usual for boys at the second grade level.
3. Some eighth grade boys are biologically and physiologically seventeen-year-olds, and some eighth grade girls, nineteen-year-olds — usual for seniors in high school or freshmen in college.
4. Some eighth grade boys are only ten-years-old biologically and physiologically, while some eighth grade girls are only twelve-years-old physically and in terms of physiological dynamics usual for fifth graders.

Differences in intellectual ability, personality, and attitude are as striking as those in biological and physiological development and they combine to underscore the commonly stated, yet frequently ignored, truism that reading instruction must be individualized.

Some middle school pupils at the late childhood stage of maturity may need reteaching of the sound-symbol relationships, structural analysis, and development of other skills designed to help pupils unlock the written code. Others in the same classroom may be adolescents ready to use reading as a vehicle for comparing and contrasting abstract ideas. Undoubtedly, most pupils will be at a stage of reading proficiency somewhere between the two extremes presented.

Effective middle school teachers recognize these differences and teach primary, middle school, and high school level reading lessons in the same classroom. These teachers possess the ability to evaluate the reading skills of each pupil in the class and to follow through with assignments tailored to fit the needs of each individual. Such teachers encourage independence, provide feedback, insure success, accept pupils, and provide reinforcement as means for achieving individualization.

One of the primary goals of individualization is to encourage the pupil to become an independent learner. By participating in the establishment of his own goals, selecting appropriate materials to accomplish these goals, and maintaining a chart of his own progress, the pupil learns that he is in control of his own ability to learn.

Providing feedback on the reading the child has done is another important aspect of individualization. Aristotle made the following statement:

> We learn an art or craft by doing the things that we shall have to do when we have learnt it: for instance, men become builders by building houses, harpers by playing on the harp. Similarly, we become just by doing just acts, temperate by doing temperate acts, brave by doing brave acts.

He might well have continued that "a man learns to read by reading." By finding the pupil's instructional reading level and matching it with material in which he is interested, the teacher sets the stage for individualizing reading instruction. The most important part of the program is to encourage the pupil to read and read and read and to provide him with appropriate feedback regarding his performance. Extensive reading with no feedback does not constitute an individualized reading program. An individualized reading program requires that the teacher listen periodically to the pupil read, provide guidance, and keep accurate records of the quantity and quality of the reading. The student should also be provided with a management system which allows him to check much of his own work.

Insured success is still another aspect of individualization. The pupil who has succeeded in past performances of a particular behavior is likely to succeed in his next performance of the same behavior. The pupil who has failed in past performances is likely to fail in future performances. A pupil's program, then, must be planned to fit his level of readiness precisely so that he will experience success rather than failure.

Individualization requires that teachers accept their students. The traditional school rejects the poor reader. Really, it is the inability to read that is rejected; but how can one separate rejection of one's ability from rejection one's self?

The successful teacher should convince the disabled reader that he is accepted by asking him to read only materials that he can readily learn to read. If he is not ready to read, he should participate in activities that he can perform successfully. The teacher can permit the poor reader to acquire information in science and social studies by methods other than reading. The teacher should establish the attitude that all members of the class are desirable and wanted regardless of academic ability.

Finally, individualization requires reinforcement through rewards for jobs well done. Rewards may be objects of value such as money, candy, toys, games, and clothing; or they may be privileges such as free time, permission to listen to records, go on a trip, or shoot baskets in the gym. A smile, a nod of the head, a pat on the back, or some verbal congratulation can become an effective reward.

Unfortunately, research studies indicate that most reinforcement in classrooms is negative. The teacher should make an effort to stress positive reinforcement and seek to reward desired behavior rather than punish undesirable behavior. When a response is rewarded, the pupil knows exactly what he should do. When an undesired response is punished, the pupil may still not know what he is supposed to do and he is left without enough information to guide him in changing his behavior.

Individualization is an aspect of public school education which has long been talked about but which is seldom implemented. Middle schools cannot afford to neglect this phase of the reading program because of the diverse student population served. The techniques cited here and those detailed in Chapter 13 should be implemented to achieve this crucial component of middle school reading programs.

Systems

Educators are learning from industry that management systems can improve program efficiency. Learning sequences can be established with projected dates for completion. Alternate tracks may be provided in case the original sequence does not meet the specified need. Such a management system can be adapted to any plan of classroom organization and will clarify the role of both teachers and pupils.

In describing a system for teaching reading, Duffy and Sherman (4) list the following necessary characteristics:

1. It must reflect what is known about reading and how we learn to read.
2. It must be easy to apply and must produce the desired achievement.
3. It must specify what is to be taught, how to teach it, and how to determine what learning has occurred.
4. It must enhance and encourage diagnosis and individualization of instruction.

5. It must be easily adaptable to both group and tutorial situations, as well as to the various reading materials and methodologies currently being used in classrooms.

6. It must be easy for both the professional and the paraprofessional to use.

Although several excellent reading systems are available commercially, some school districts employ teachers during the summers to develop different systems which best meet the needs of particular pupil populations. One program is the Cognitive Reading Skills Planning System (3). The first volume deals with comprehension skills and the second volume deals with decoding and structural skills. Successive volumes will deal with other competencies essential to effective reading. In developing this management system the following steps were taken:

1. Consideration was given to theoretical background, published assessment systems, Florida State Department of Education assessment objectives, teacher produced objectives, and state adopted textbook content.

2. A continuum of cognitive objectives was written in the areas of decoding skills, structural analysis, and comprehension skills.

3. Checkpoints along the continuum were identified as key points for assessment.

4. Skills prerequisite to each checkpoint were identified.

5. Pre- and post-assessment instruments were written for each checkpoint.

6. Assessment instruments were written for each prerequisite skill.

7. A record keeping system was developed to be used for regular instructional planning and permanent record keeping.

8. Instructions were written for the use of the system.

9. A system was devised for organizing objectives, assessment, and teacher materials into a file box for use in the classrooms.

10. Materials were prepared for printing.

11. Materials were piloted for a year and revised in accordance with data collected.

Whether reading is taught in a self-contained classroom, developmental laboratory, or in conjunction with content courses, such a management system provides a comprehensive record-keeping system that can follow each pupil through the entire middle school program and into high school.

Saturation

The generalization that every teacher is a teacher of reading is essentially true. Yet, it is unrealistic to believe that teachers who have not been trained in reading can perform skillfully the many functions of a reading teacher. A saturation program of assistance is therefore essential.

One solution to this problem is to have the reading specialist work with other content area teachers. A program on reading in the content areas could be emphasized with the reading teacher suggesting activities. In a Florida middle school, for instance, each content area teacher accompanied his homeroom pupils to the reading lab. There the teacher worked on his own reading improvement along with the students. This resulted in an aura of respectability both for the reading program and for the homeroom teachers.

Sharing of information is also helpful in this regard. If an efficient management system is maintained, each pupil's folder should show his strengths and weaknesses. These folders should be examined periodically by all content area teachers. Special projects for content area classes might be suggested in the folder along with a progress system that could be marked by the pupil or his teacher.

Reading must be the concern of the entire middle school program. Through saturation devices such as the above, as well as through the strategies suggested in Chapters 4 and 7, reading problems can be met effectively throughout the middle school.

SUMMARY

The middle school, if it is to achieve its unique role and function, must avoid the failing of the old junior high school. Rather than clinging to the concept of providing a high school for junior pupils, it must structure a curriculum which matches the needs of the pupils it serves.

This is particularly important in the area of reading. The reading program must be structured to accommodate the special cognitive, affective, and psychomotor characteristics of the middle school pupil. It must use motivational techniques and objectives appropriate for the middle school child. Diagnosis must be thorough, a wide range of materials must be employed, the extensive range of individual differences in the middle school must be accommodated through individualization, a system of efficient management must be employed, and all the teachers in the school must be saturated with the assistance needed to meet effectively the reading needs encountered in their classes. These are the components of an effective middle school reading program. When they are present, the middle school can achieve its goals in the area of reading.

References

1. Alexander, William M. et al. *The Emergent Middle School.* New York: Holt, Rinehart and Winston, 1969, 28.

2. Bloom, Benjamin S. (Ed.). *Taxonomy of Educational Objectives.* New York: David McKay, 1956.

3. *Cognitive Reading Skills Planning System.* Gainesville, Florida: Alachua County School Board, 1971.

4. Duffy, Gerald G., and George B. Sherman. *Systematic Reading Instruction.* New York: Harper and Row, 1972.

5. Eichhorn, Donald H. *The Middle School.* New York: Center for Applied Research in Education, 1966.

6. Fry, Edward B. *Reading Instruction for Classroom and Clinic.* New York: McGraw-Hill, 1972, 258-259.

7. Gallup, George H. *The Gallup Poll: Public Opinion, 1935-1971.* New York: Random House, 1972.

8. Heilman, Arthur W. *Principles and Practices of Teaching Reading.* Columbus, Ohio: Charles E. Merrill, 1972, 416-418.

9. Krathwohl, David R., Benjamin S. Bloom, and Bertram B. Masia. *Taxonomy of Educational Objectives.* New York: David McKay, 1964.

10. McNeil, John D. "Programed Instruction Versus Usual Classroom Procedures in Teaching Boys to Read," *American Educational Research Journal,* 1964, 113-120.

11. "Midcentury White House Conference on Childhood and Youth, the Course of Healthy Personality Development," in Jerome M. Seidman (Ed.), *The Adolescent: A Book of Readings.* New York: Holt, Rinehart and Winston, 1960, 230.

PART TWO

Organizing a Middle School Reading Program

CHAPTER FOUR

THE READING COORDINATOR:
KEY TO
AN EFFECTIVE PROGRAM

Lois A. Bader
Michigan State University

Organizing a middle school reading program is not a simple task. There is no single prescription for how a program should operate since the precise nature of its functioning will be dictated by the differing expectations of children, staff, and community as well as by the differing professional preparation of the staff. However, the key to improved middle school reading is the person who coordinates the program, the person who provides the leadership and flexibility necessary for optimum program development. To be successful, this person must possess a broad knowlege base and a set of very practical strategies for creating changes.

KNOWLEDGE BASE OF THE MIDDLE SCHOOL READING CONSULTANT

The Field of Reading, K-12

Reading ability of children attending the middle school will range from K to 12. The gifted reader may not comprehend with the breadth and depth of an older child with more experience, but he can comprehend, to a considerable extent, materials considered to be suitable for high school readers. Conversely, the very poor reader cannot be considered to be functioning cognitively as a younger child, but he does need skills that are typically acquired at a much younger age. The result is that the middle school reading program must provide instruction which ranges over the entire K-12 spectrum.

Most classroom teachers in the middle school have not been prepared to understand the K-12 reading skills hierarchy. Yet, in middle schools without consultants, classroom teachers have had to function as reading teachers. For instance, recent visitors to a middle school observed two teachers managing a reading class of approximately one hundred children, seated at tables in an area that also served as a cafeteria, working with boxed reading materials — one box to a table. This was the entire "developmental" reading program. One teacher asked the visitor, "Tell me, are basals out?" The remedial portion of this program consisted of help for no more than ten youngsters a period. The teacher had a master's degree in school administration and no reading courses. Certainly, such teachers lack the knowledge base which is crucial in organizing an effective reading program.

When a middle school does have a reading consultant, that person may be the only teacher in the school who can arrange for instruction on an appropriate level for all youngsters. It is essential that the consultant be well prepared in knowledge of skills, instructional techniques, and materials appropriate for middle school youngsters who scatter widely along the developmental reading sequence.

The Structure of the Disciplines

There is irony in the instructional situation that provides close guidance for helping children understand a sequence of simple events in a basal reading series but no guidance in reading content area material written with complicated organization patterns. When a youngster comprehends the organizational pattern, he has a gestalt into which he can fit related details; but reading instruction based on an understanding of the structure of the discipline is often neglected.

Many reading teachers provide instruction in a facet of comprehension they consider discrete, such as main idea. Youngsters may learn to identify the topic sentence in a well written essay or they may specify main ideas for three or four related paragraphs. Their criterion reading tests may attest that they can identify the main idea. When this skill does not transfer to other reading in the classroom, what has gone wrong?

It is a faulty assumption that main idea, or any other comprehension skill, is a simple, discrete skill. Main idea in literature becomes a statement of the theme, frequently an analogy. Main idea in science becomes a statement of a principle, and in social science, a statement of theory.

The point is that to help youngsters comprehend material in the content areas, the reading teacher needs to understand the structure of these disciplines. This is true, also, if the reading specialist is to work with content area teachers to help youngsters. Further assistance in developing comprehension within the various disciplines can be found in Chapters 14 through 17.

Needs of the Population to be Served

Before an attempt is made to establish priorities in a reading program, the consultant should acquire as much information as possible about the population to be served. How have students previously been instructed? What is their attitude toward leisure reading? What are the predominant sports, hobbies, and social interests of the children? These are only a few of the questions that might be raised about the students.

The professional preparation — both preservice and inservice — of the teacher also needs to be known. Attitudes are important since previous experiences with reading consultants may color the present feelings of the teachers.

Also, it is important to define the knowledge and expectancies of administrators concerning reading programs. In the view of some principals, reading is pronouncing words. To others, reading encompasses comprehension, study skills, critical thinking, and leisure reading. Some administrators have taken undergraduate and graduate courses in reading; others have attended conferences or workshops, and still others have no background. Obviously, if the latter situation exists, it will be necessary for the consultant to provide the administrator with information about desirable procedures.

Finally, community attitudes toward reading need to be ascertained. Parents have been known to ask that their children be withdrawn from reading instruction because they think that only slow children are given special reading help. Gathering and using information regarding community needs and attitudes will help insure a successful reading program.

Program Forms

In a recent survey, reading teachers were asked: "What is your reading program?" The answers frequently were, "Houghton Mifflin," "Ginn," or "Sullivan," indicating that a set of materials dictated the curriculum. While materials from publishers may be important, the total program must be derived from the needs of the school and must be more comprehensive than a set of materials.

A comprehensive middle school reading program should include: 1) developmental instruction as an integrated language arts approach (listening, speaking, reading, writing); 2) content area reading and study skills instruction; 3) corrective instruction; and 4) development of interests and tastes in leisure reading. Depending on the population, supplementary programs may be created for children with English as a second language or for gifted children.

Several points must be made: 1) there is no best program, 2) all programs are attempts to distribute resources equitably according to the needs of the students, and 3) the choice of a program is highly dependent on the professional preparation of the staff and the organization of the school. In developing a comprehensive program, part of the consultant's time will be spent working directly with children and part will be spent with staff. Exactly what the division will be depends upon resources and other previously stated factors.

Evaluation Sophistication

As business enterprises continue to pursue the educational dollar, reading consultants must develop their evaluation skills. Recently, a contract for a workbook-tape set of materials was so worded that youngsters whose reading growth was within the standard error of measurement for the reading test being used were considered to have improved, thereby paying the contracting company for growth that was not substantiated. In another contracted program, youngsters supposedly learned to "Summarize in Science" by attending to word order in the paragraphs so that they could complete the cloze sentence that was the summarizing statement. The criterion test required the same type of operation, thus giving "proof" of the achievement of the skill. When the pupils were asked to identify or compose a summarizing statement from a section of a science text, however, they were unable to do so.

Finally, in a contract reading center processing fifty students per hour through programed material, the teacher was observed working separately with three or four youngsters at a time for fifteen minutes throughout the hour. His methods were quite different from the contracted program. When questioned, he replied that these were children who were failing in the contracted program, so he had to use other methods. Certainly this was the proper procedure; however, the achievement of those youngsters was credited to the contracted program that failed.

Whether a school contracts part of its reading program, evaluation requires professionals with technical and pedagogical insights. What constitutes progress for a particular population? Does the test really require the application of the skills taught? Is the Hawthorne effect operating? While the consultant may not possess highly sophisticated evaluation skills, he should be sufficiently knowledgeable to seek assistance and to work with program evaluators.

Roles of the Program Administrator

"Work expands to fill the time" is a principle that the reading specialist may well print on a sign and tack above his desk. Under it he may add, "Know Thyself."

It often seems that reading consultants engage in activities which are comfortable rather than those that should be high on the priority list. How else does one explain the time spent by reading specialists compiling skill charts, reading lists, and bulletins for teachers' mail boxes, when students need individual help and new teachers need instructional demonstrations in their classrooms? Perhaps it is because the roles of the reading specialist are so many and varied that he literally has a job that cannot be done. He needs to establish priorities.

Note the following list of tasks associated with organizing and administering a reading program. Which are most necessary in your middle school?

- development of sequences of objectives
- material selection and evaluation
- individual diagnostic assessment
- inservice instruction
- remedial and developmental reading instruction
- content area instruction
- public relations
- program evaluation

When priorities have been selected with the help of colleagues, some of the less crucial tasks may be delegated to volunteers, aides, or staff members, after providing necessary assistance or structure. As the program evolves, role priorities will change, necessitating a flexible approach. For a more detailed discussion of the myriad roles of the middle school reading specialist, see Chapter 5.

Supervisory Styles

The program coordinator must have knowledge of various supervisory styles and be able to choose those appropriate to a given situation. For instance, a reading consultant might: 1) visit teachers with a predetermined list of reading-teaching behaviors sanctioned by authorities in order to observe and report results to the teacher; 2) visit (on invitation) to observe a particular facet of instruction of concern to the teacher; 3) visit for a combination of both purposes; or 4) forego supervision and, as a team member or colleague, work with the teacher to achieve instructional goals important to both and to evaluate, jointly the results.

All approaches have strengths and weaknesses. Perhaps all have their place and the application might be considered situational. The ability to function in more than one style will give flexibility. It is crucial that the consultant have enough knowledge to achieve this flexibility.

Social-Psychological Factors in Gaining Cooperation

The coordinator of a middle school reading program usually finds himself in the role of change agent. To function efficiently in this catalytic role, he should be aware of social-psychological principles in reducing resistance. These include the following:

1. change originating within the school that is based on group diagnostic efforts is more acceptable than change brought by outsiders;
2. change will be more acceptable when endorsed by formal and informal leaders within the school;
3. change that does not increase workloads or threaten security and status is more acceptable than change that does;
4. change that offers interesting, novel experiences in harmony with the values and goals of those within the school is welcome; and
5. change, open to evaluation and modification, is more acceptable than irrevocable commitment to an unknown course.

These principles, along with the conditions of trust, communication, and respect which are necessary to good human relations, are the foundation on which a dynamic reading program is built. If the reading program is to create effective change, the reading consultant must know and use these principles.

Also, he must know the K-12 spectrum of reading skills, the structure of the disciplines, the needs of the population served, various program forms, evaluation techniques, the priority of roles, various supervisory styles, and the social-psychological factors which influence change. Then he will be prepared to implement what he knows.

STRATEGIES FOR THE MIDDLE SCHOOL READING CONSULTANT

The above knowledge base provides a foundation. However, knowledge alone is not enough to create a middle school reading program. The reading specialist must also know how to use knowledge; he must have strategies for putting what he knows into action.

Goal Setting and Consensus

A reading program devised by the consultant alone may exist on paper or in the mind of its creator, but it is not likely to have meaning for the staff; indeed, staff members may be unaware of its existence. One way to gain consensus is to form a reading committee which involves the staff so that they feel the program is theirs.

A reading committee may be formed through invitation and/or through open membership. Existing curriculum committees may be utilized. Care should be taken to invite representatives from each content area, an administrator, and special services personnel. Membership should be open to all interested teachers. Consideration should be given to student and parent representation whenever possible with such groups contributing to curriculum decisions while instructional decisions are made by professionals.

The consultant might provide the committee with brief descriptions of desirable programs. He should ask the staff, the principal, students, and the community to submit questions about reading status. After reporting on status, he should then request the committee to consider suitable goals for the school and to reach consensus on priorities. Such a strategy pays high dividends in the long run.

Continuous Evaluation as a Dynamic Factor

One of the common techniques in goal setting is to present current achievement data on students to stimulate consideration of the strengths and weaknesses of the present program. Since the results of evaluation produce the reaction, "What can we do about this?" evaluation can serve as a catalyst to change. This especially is true when the staff participates in gathering the requested information.

Not all facets of the program need to be evaluated at once, since this would be time consuming. However, the following data should be examined ultimately:

1. Standardized Test Results
   a. Are there large numbers of very poor readers — beyond the expectancy of the normal curve?

b. Are the students with high verbal intelligence achieving their potential?

c. Is progress fairly steady through the grades?

d. Does item analysis indicate areas of general weakness?

e. What are the component skills related to these deficiencies?

f. What are the students' attitudes? Are they doing their best? Do they finish? Do they guess?

2. Informal Test Results

a. How are students achieving in reading capabilities not tested by the standardized tests?

b. What are the students' content area reading skills?

3. Development of Broader Interests

a. Are students given time to read?

b. Do they have access to materials?

c. Are the materials suitable to the interests of the children?

d. Are the children capable of reading the materials available?

4. Instructional Efficiency

a. Do teachers possess effective and efficient instructional strategies?

b. Do they have materials necessary to teach the skills they need to develop?

c. Do teachers have efficient record-keeping systems?

5. Other Investigations

a. Reports on very poor readers have revealed high absenteeism (if children are not in school, they can hardly be taught); low energy levels; and poor health, in addition to other factors inhibiting to achievement.

These are a few of the considerations required during the continuous evaluation of a reading program. The reading consultant should use these data as spurs for encouraging improvement of the program.

Credibility Route vs. Authoritarian Policies

When a reading consultant is new to a school, teachers might well question his recommendations, particularly when reading has not been part of the teachers' professional training or experience. Time should be taken to establish rapport. The specialist might begin by working with teachers in their instructional setting on request. To illustrate, a history teacher commented that when the new specialist worked with him to construct, administer, and interpret an informal reading test, the teacher realized that he had made many false assumptions about the capabilities of his students. When a question arose concerning the best use of the specialist's time — working only with students or working with both teachers and students — the history teacher vigorously supported the latter approach.

The reading problems of individual students can be used as a wedge to work with content area teachers. The consultant can interpret the nature of the problems for the teacher and offer to help plan instructional strategies to enable the student to achieve at his present level of functioning. Another initial service that might be offered to establish credibility is the retrieval of standardized test scores from students' files and profiling these for departmental teams.

When the reading coordinator has established credibility within the school, suggestions are more likely to be accepted. Misinterpretations are less likely to occur and statements such as the following tend to disappear: "I would like to make some changes in my reading instruction but 'they' will not permit·me to do so."

Inservice Strategies

Inservice education should be ongoing rather than a one-shot attempt to change instruction or attitude. A program that extends over a period of time and utilizes a variety of strategies would appear to have the best chance of making an impact.

One strategy is the minilesson. The reading specialist might distribute a list of several fifteen-to-twenty-minute presentations he would be willing to make to interested teachers. Topics might include: Reading in a Specific Content Area, Readability Formulas, Open-Book Informal Reading Inventories, Reading Skill Games, Language Arts Classroom Centers, Classroom Libraries, Constructing Reading Guides, and Vocabulary Development. Those interested could return the list, after checking off the session or sessions they wished to attend. Sessions should begin and end promptly and they should include demonstrations with children whenever possible.

Workshop sessions are also helpful. These could be held for such purposes as making record-keeping devices, instructional packets, reading games, and learning activity center materials. Teachers should elect what they want to make. Samples, instruction sheets, materials, and tools should be ready. The potential and limitations of each device need to be discussed. Reading games, for example, are safer to use when accompanied by a brief criterion test.

In-house dissemination of ideas is often favorably received by teachers. After visiting teachers to collect ideas, the specialist may invite the teachers to explain and demonstrate their techniques in sessions, request permission to videotape, have other teachers visit the class, or describe the ideas in a bulletin, being careful to give proper credit. All teachers should be featured. No derogatory comments should ever be made.

Another technique is to invite teachers to observe and participate in the reading center so that they might improve their diagnostic methods, test instructional techniques, or evaluate materials.

A course may be contracted for graduate credit from an institution of higher education. Some schools pay for part or all of the tuition. These sessions are most effective when:

1. content and instruction are focused on the needs and interests of the staff;

2. instructional sequences, classroom applications, and class discussions are used to insure understanding and use of new methods;

3. culminating activities include the creation or adoption of methods and materials to be used by the participants; and

4. administrators participate in the course.

Finally, classroom demonstrations offer a powerful strategy. To the comment, "That sounds good, but it won't work with my kids," classroom demonstrations offer a convincing reply. Probably the most effective inservice instruction occurs when a teacher can observe, then adapt methods within his instructional setting. While this strategy is not efficient in terms of numbers, the effects are reasonably certain.

Research as a Neutral Stimulant

If the seeking of new or adjusted methods takes an action research aspect, the reading program evolves dynamically. Rather than suddenly adopting an approach, the school tests an approach, asking, "Is this the best course for our situation?" or "How can this approach be adapted for our situation?" The consultant does not pass judgment but, instead, assists the staff members to continually evaluate and improve their program. Thus teachers are encouraged to become participants in making decisions through their own investigations.

Articulation

The reading program needs to be understood by school personnel, students, parents, the school board, and the larger community. The supervisor should prepare bulletins, arrange displays, make presentations, and invite visitors to provide knowledge about the reading program. Such information should encourage the students to take advantage of program offerings; provide the superintendent and school board with data on which to make decisions about the allocation of resources; give school personnel an overview of the program, as well as information on facets of the program with which they have no immediate contact; and provide information to parents so that they can extend or support the program.

Research findings, summaries of conference proceedings, abstracts of articles and similar materials should also be circulated judiciously to school personnel. Many items or lengthy selections may go unread; however, most administrators and staff members like to be kept informed. An English department chairman requested the reading consultant in his school, who was leaving for a convention, to "Tell me what's going on. I like to stay abreast of the 'in' terminology." Administrators, who cannot be expected to be current with all facets of the curriculum, appreciate help in keeping up-to-date with the literature. They want to be knowledgeable about desirable programs.

Intangibles that Make a Difference

There are numerous intangibles that affect a reading program. One is the power base. In schools, as in other organizations, personnel exist who control resources. In some cases, this power is delegated; in others, the power seems to have been assumed. Certainly it is to the advantage of the consultant to identify these power bases and make every attempt to establish a harmonious relationship. Hostilities — open or covert — drain energies and detract from the program. An alignment with a particular "camp" should also be avoided.

When problems arise in such areas as rescheduling or information retrieval and the specialist is told that "nothing can be done this year," he might offer his assistance. Sometimes a pleasant relationship can develop when a task is shared.

Having the appropriate administrator present at meetings where problems of resources or program coordination are being discussed is helpful, because he can provide relief either through policy support or allocation of materials and services.

When the problems are severe, a neutral outside consultant might be invited to discuss the program with concerned administrators and staff in order to make recommendations. This person might be a reading specialist from another district, from the county or state, or from a university. The specialist should be one who will be able to use the strengths of all school personnel in making recommendations, rather than one who will make hasty judgments.

Personality is another intangible. A mature reading consultant observed with dismay, as her young colleague alienated a series of teachers and administrators, "I never thought I would make such a statement, but that girl lacks personality!"

Essentially, the crucial components of personality seem to be tact, flexibility, and acceptance of another's viewpoint as opposed to whether the person is vivacious, quiet, or whatever. Other characteristics that do seem to distinguish successful coordinators are competence and a willingness to work. In addition, the specialist should be approachable and sympathetic to the demands on a teacher's time other than for reading. He should keep confidences and, finally, he should be available and quick to respond to requests for assistance.

A final intangible is autonomy. The specialist should have some input in decisions in scheduling his time, in selecting and scheduling the children for reading help, and in selecting the tests and materials he will use. Too often, a specialist who could help many youngsters by working in the classroom with teachers, will see only a small fraction of the children who need help; youngsters with emotional problems who read quite well are placed with severely retarded readers; and tests or instructional materials that are undesirable are purchased, leaving no funds for materials sorely needed. When administrators permit consultants to participate in decisions concerning their areas of expertise, these problems are less likely to occur.

With the freedom to make professional decisions, however, comes responsibility. Specialists have earned the title "coffee-drinkers" by misusing their time.

Administrators who have hired such people are understandably reluctant to give autonomy to subsequent personnel.

As a strategy for gaining and maintaining partial autonomy, the consultant should outline the services he expects to perform and discuss them with the principal. Later, at regular intervals, he should submit a summary of his activities. An administrator who wishes to support a flexible schedule needs such data to substantiate his recommendations while the consultant, too, finds such records helpful in making yearly reports.

In summary, the coordinator of an effective middle school reading program must utilize a variety of strategies to implement needed innovations. These strategies include methods of gaining consensus, continuous evaluation, establishing credibility, providing for effective inservice, utilization of research, techniques for articulation, and various intangibles. The wise utilization of such strategies leads toward effective middle school reading programs.

OTHER PROBLEMS IN ACHIEVING EFFECTIVE PROGRAM COORDINATION

While the knowledge base and the strategies of the reading coordinator comprise the foundation of an effective middle school reading program, other problems persist which often impede effective organization. These problems tend to be grouped into three areas: training of consultants, expectations of the middle school personnel, and resources available.

The Training of Consultants

The training of many reading consultants is not adequate for the jobs they hold. The result is that they are often self-taught. To meet their demanding job responsibilities, they invent their own solutions or adapt ideas they read or hear about. Still other consultants, lacking confidence, retreat to the limited role of working with no more than ten youngsters an hour, conferring with classroom teachers only on request, and sending out an occasional bulletin.

Colleges of education have been training specialists to diagnose and remediate youngsters singly or in small groups, but little attention has been given to the knowledge and skills required of a consultant who must organize and direct a comprehensive program. Recently, some city and district school systems have redefined the roles of their specialists and have contracted with universities for inservice courses in classroom consulting and program development. More effort is needed in this direction if middle school reading programs are to be effectively organized and administered.

Expectancies of the Population Served

University reading specialists are frequently requested to speak on such topics as "Every Teacher a Teacher of Reading." The request is usually prompted by an administrator who is concerned about his staff members who wish to send many of their students to the reading specialist. Such a concern is justified. More publicity needs to be given to the desirability of making more efficient use of the skills of the reading specialist. One might begin by raising these questions: How can we justify a situation where a youngster with a severe reading problem has only one happy and achieving hour a day — in a reading class? Can we assume all content area reading skills will be acquired by students without help? Can we ignore research that tells us that average youngsters can be helped to make more improvement in reading than below average readers?

Adequacy of Resources for the Consultant

When visiting many schools, one will find striking inequities in resources. In one school, large numbers of consumable materials and hardware are present; in the next, the consultant prepares plastic sleeves to extend the life of a few workbooks. Some programs employ many aides; others have none at all.

While some of the inequities reflect the financial base of the schools, others reflect attitudes toward the importance of reading instruction. Although a consultant can find ways of extending existing materials and making materials, his energies should be put to other uses.

Publicity may be helpful in changing attitudes. Another possibility is to encourage persons controlling the resources to visit successful reading programs in order to obtain an estimate of a reasonable expenditure of funds for an effective program.

CONCLUSION

The development and coordination of a middle school reading program is challenging and demanding. Schools which previously have had a limited emphasis on reading may change more slowly than others. However, the foundations for an effective program are clear. The school must hire a reading coordinator who possesses the necessary knowledge base and, once hired, this person must utilize the strategies described here, plus others he devises himself, to establish the various components of the program. The task is not easy, since winning staff understanding and cooperation does take time. However, by establishing priorities and by setting realistic goals, a middle school reading program containing the characteristics cited in Chapter 3 can be established.

CHAPTER FIVE

ROLES OF
THE READING TEACHER

H. Thompson Fillmer
University of Florida

The emergence of the middle school in the educational scene has been attributed to the fact that the middle school pupil population is a unique group with special needs that have not been adequately met in the past. The reading program which serves this group of pupils also has unique functions. DeBoer and Dallman (*1*) state some of the chief reading tasks of the middle school student:

> ... 1) to become skillful enough in reading so that through reading he can greatly extend and enrich his experiences and can thereby acquire much information and knowledge; 2) to continue in the development of speech and silent reading so that he will be able to read easy material on his level much more rapidly silently than orally and learn to read at appropriate rates for various purposes using materials of varying difficulty; 3) to learn to read so well orally that it is interesting to listen to him; 4) to acquire complete independence in the ability to identify new words; 5) to develop skill in the use of the dictionary; 6) to acquire so much ability in comprehending what he reads that he can understand fairly difficult materials; 7) to achieve power in reading with discrimination; and 8) to acquire interest and skill in reading in various fields of learning.

As was pointed out in Chapter 4, the reading coordinator in the middle school has a monumental job in achieving the above tasks. He must be a versatile person since the unique demands of the middle school require him to play a number of roles. These include his roles as a professional, a diagnostician, a counselor, a resource person, a manager, and a researcher.

THE READING TEACHER AS A PROFESSIONAL

The successful middle school reading program cannot be an extension of the program designed for elementary pupils. Neither can it be a "junior" high school program. Rather, it must be a specific program designed for the particular needs of its pupil population.

Stradley (9) explains the general role of the middle school teacher by stating that:

> The elementary and the high school teachers are not directly concerned with each other in program sequence and articulation. The middle school teachers are directly concerned with both levels. They find that while they must primarily base their teachings on the elementary curriculum, they must prepare the students for the high school curriculum. If this were not enough, they must, in addition, continue to provide learning experiences that will be in keeping with the singular purpose of the middle school. The teachers must be constantly aware that the middle school is a stage, and time of transition for the students, socially, physically, and academically. They are not striving to turn out a finished product.

The middle school teacher, according to Hansen and Hearn (5) is basically a hybrid whose preparation contains more subject matter content than that of his fellows in the lower grades, and more knowledge of and empathy for children than that of his fellows in the senior high school.

The middle school reading teacher should be no exception to this description. It is recommended that the teacher of middle school reading be a certified reading specialist who has completed a graduate degree in reading or its equivalent and who has had several years of successful teaching experience, preferably in the middle school grades.

Since many states are now more concerned with the competencies of a teacher than the number of courses she has taken, the following are suggested as tasks in which a professional teacher of middle school reading should be able to demonstrate competence:

1. Identify the reading skills generally taught at the various ages from early childhood through high school.

2. Determine the validity and reliability of selected formal and informal instruments used in assessing reading competencies.

3. Administer and interpret selected formal and informal instruments used in assessing reading competencies.

4. Evaluate the most common techniques, hardware, and materials used in reading instructions.

5. Prescribe appropriate reading activities for individual pupils based upon diagnostic information.

6. Select reading materials that coincide with the interests and reading levels of the pupils involved.

7. Plan with pupils a reading program that meets specific objectives arrived at cooperatively by teacher and pupil.

8. Plan a record-keeping system to keep track of pupil progress in reading.

9. Help content area teachers plan activities to teach reading in the content areas.

10. Evaluate the reading program continuously in the light of pupil performance and revise it as needed.

Specific techniques and materials for teaching the various reading skills to middle school pupils are treated in detail in subsequent chapters of this book.

THE READING TEACHER AS A DIAGNOSTICIAN

By the time pupils reach the middle school grades, the ability range is considerable. The two-thirds rule is a rule of thumb that is useful to teachers in estimating the ability range of a heterogeneous classroom. This rule holds that by multiplying by two-thirds the mean age of pupils in any classroom, one obtains a figure that represents the range of pupil ability in years. To find the age range in years of a sixth grade class in which the mean age is twelve, the following computation would be performed:

$$Range = 2/3 \times mean\ age = 2/3 \times 12 = 8$$

Therefore, in a typical classroom of twelve-year-olds, the range of ability will be eight years — from second grade ability to tenth grade ability. In such a situation, the reading teacher must assess or diagnose the abilities of each pupil before appropriate reading material can be assigned to pupils.

Harris (6) comments on the nature of diagnosis as follows:

Making a reading diagnosis means studying the nature of the individual's reading performance and of the factors, both in the present and in the past, which have contributed to the development of the difficulties he is showing. In the process of making a diagnosis, it is necessary to collect facts, and tests can contribute many of the facts needed. But the heart of diagnosis is not testing. It is, rather, the intelligent interpretation of the facts by a person who has both the theoretical knowledge and the practical experience to know what questions to ask; to select procedures, including tests, which can supply the needed facts; to interpret the meaning of the findings correctly; and to comprehend the interrelationships of these facts and meanings. The natural outcome of a diagnostic study is a plan for treatment which involves two parts: a plan for correcting or minimizing those handicapping conditions which are still interferring with learning; and a plan for remedial instruction that is most likely to be successful in the light of what has been found.

Some of the questions that must be answered in a diagnosis of reading skills are:

- What is the pupil's instructional reading level?
- What is the pupil's expected reading level?
- What are the pupil's strengths and weaknesses in word attack skills, comprehension, study skills, rate, and flexibility?

- What are the pupil's reading interests?
- What reading skills should receive priority for each pupil?
- What particular methods, materials, and activities seem to be most successful in teaching this particular pupil?

An important but frequently overlooked function of a diagnosis is the assessment of pupil strengths. Any effective reading program, remedial or developmental, must guarantee the pupil some success. Few middle school pupils will continue to expend time and effort on an activity at which they consistently fail, whether it be tennis or reading. The reading teacher should plan each reading activity to insure that every pupil can achieve success. In order to do this, the teacher must be aware of particular pupil strengths. In this respect Wilson (10) says:

> While a child's weaknesses naturally might be the concern of the teacher, diagnosis for strengths is equally important. Since instructional adjustment should start with areas of strengths, deliberate diagnosis to determine those strengths is necessary. However, as we observe diagnostic reports of children with reading problems, we seldom find mention of their strengths. *All children have strengths.* Each child should be made aware of them and the teacher should note them with as much accuracy as he notes weaknesses. In fact, given a choice, this author would favor diagnosis for strengths. What a child knows is important. What he does not know can be assumed from what he does know. Unfortunately, many case reports seem to indicate that the child has only weaknesses.

Once the pupil's strengths and weaknesses have been assessed, the middle school reading teacher must plan with each pupil those activities that will improve areas of weakness by utilizing areas of strength. Such a program will insure success and nurture a positive attitude toward self as reader.

THE READING TEACHER AS COUNSELOR

All teachers are in a counseling role with pupils because of the very nature of the teacher-pupil relationship, the school function, and the activities therein. The reading teacher especially is in a counseling situation because of the ego involvement in the reading process. Pupils often feel that their worth is reflected by the quality and speed of their reading. Unfortunately, parents and even teachers may feel threatened by the performance of their children or pupils in reading.

De Vita, Pumerantz, and Wilklow (2) stress ways in which middle school teachers can be effective counselors by providing an accepting atmosphere:

> The cardinal rules for effective middle school guidance are inherent in the desire to provide pre-teen youngsters with an atmosphere for constructive thinking and exploration without fear of being ridiculed. An awareness of the youngster's social problems associated with his peer

groups and growth pattern is vital for his well being and security. Finally, there are features in a continuous progress program to meet his daily needs while providing him with the opportunity, motivation and knowledge to make sound decisions.

As counselors in their area of specialization, middle school reading teachers can extend this supportive atmosphere by planning with each pupil a reading program that will enable him to fulfill his own needs. For instance, a disabled reader may need to learn basic skills taught in the primary grades. A program can be planned with this pupil that includes specific activities, provision for regular feedback, and a record-keeping system that he maintains himself so that both he and the teacher can keep track of his progress. Similarly, an accelerated reader may wish to improve his reading speed and perform at higher levels of comprehension. Such a program can be planned with this pupil to include appropriate activities, feedback, and a record-keeping system.

Ideally, the reading teacher as counselor can help pupils to assess their own needs, set appropriate and realistic goals, and assess their own performance. The entire sequence will be revised when appropriate. Such a program places the emphasis upon individual improvement and eliminates the meaningless competition between pupils performing on a fourth grade level and pupils performing on an eleventh grade level.

THE READING TEACHER AS A RESOURCE PERSON

Reading is a functional tool that must be applied to a wide variety of activities. In order for pupils to read widely, appropriate materials must be available to them. The reading teacher must function as a resource person in selecting these materials.

The first consideration in the acquisition of materials is the range of instructional reading levels among pupils. A pupil should be taught with reading materials which match his instructional reading level. This is the level at which pupils read with 95-98 percent accuracy and comprehend with 75 percent accuracy. Unfortunately, the materials pupils use for reading instruction are often the only books which meet this criteria. Books in the content areas are usually written on a higher level of difficulty. The reading teacher, as a resource person, may be able to help content area teachers select alternative reading materials at more appropriate reading levels.

Another function of the reading teacher as resource person is to acquire practice materials needed by the individual pupil. Some middle school pupils may need practice on word attack skills taught in the primary grades. These pupils need materials that provide practice but are oriented to the interests of older pupils. Other pupils may need to improve their study skills. Appropriate reference materials and guides should be available for these students.

Evidence suggests that one's learning style is affected by his personality. Introverts prefer to work alone, extroverts prefer to work in groups. Similarly, sensing pupils work better with concrete, factual information while intuitive pupils are more creative and work better with theories and ideas (8). The middle school teacher of reading should experiment with available methods and materials to determine which approaches to reading instruction are most effective with individual pupils and should then serve as a resource to other teachers regarding the implementation of these approaches.

It is essentially true that all teachers are teachers of reading. But reading teachers are the only teachers who have been adequately prepared in reading. Consequently, the middle school reading teacher can function as a valuable resource for content area teachers by making available the following: 1) information regarding the instructional reading levels of pupils; 2) strengths and weaknesses of pupil's in word attack and comprehension skills; 3) pupils' goals for reading improvement; 4) lists of books at various readability levels to be used in content areas; 5) displays of games, materials, literature, and hardware designed to improve particular reading skills; and 6) demonstrated lessons for development of word attack vocabulary, comprehension, study, or flexibility skills.

THE READING TEACHER AS MANAGER

In proposing the various instructional activities for the middle school reading teacher, the writer does not suggest that the teacher will personally perform every activity. Today's middle school will utilize competent paraprofessionals. Innovations such as team-teaching, individualized instruction, reading resource centers, and cooperative approaches to reading instruction call for the use of aides who can work effectively under the management of the reading teacher.

A suggested list (3) of reading tasks that the paraprofessional could be prepared to perform follows:

1. Constructing materials
    a. Adapt Bingo, Lotto, checkers, and other games in which players move a piece over squares to reach a goal; to teach letters, vowel and consonant sounds, diphthongs, digraphs, blends, and sight words. Devise word games, games requiring motor skill activities, puzzles, riddles, and matching games designed to improve recognition or comprehension skills.
    b. Help pupils design and complete bulletin boards and other displays relating to the development of reading concepts.
    c. Reproduce and assemble experience stories created by pupils into individual booklets that may be used as teaching materials.
2. Organizing field trips
    a. List various community resources that might be visited.
    b. Confirm field trip dates and arrange for transportation, guides, permission slips, and parent helpers.

c. Work with teachers in planning with specialists for art, music, literary, and physical activities to help the field trip become a vital learning experience.

3. Working with individuals
   a. Assist individuals in practicing reading skills taught by teachers.
   b. Supervise pupils working with hardware or equipment.
   c. Work with pupils in the library, other parts of the building, or in the community.

4. Observing behavior
   a. Observe and record the behavior of individual pupils in particular situations.
   b. Systematically observe the interaction of pupils and teacher at the teacher's request.
   c. Tabulate positive reinforcement of particular pupils by the teacher.

5. Reading to pupils
   a. Read poetry or stories to the class or to small groups of pupils.
   b. Read information to pupils practicing various types of listening activities.
   c. Read directions for specific lessons, exercises, or activities and be sure that pupils understand what they are to do.

6. Keeping records
   a. Administer, score, and record diagnostic or reading survey tests for pupils.
   b. Keep records of pupils in an individualized reading program and mark progress on record forms.
   c. Make appropriate entries on pupils' cumulative record folders.
   d. Record pupils' scores in teacher's record book.

7. Evaluating performance
   a. Score worksheets, practice exercises, and tests completed by pupils.
   b. Analyze standardized or informal inventories and record areas of strength and weakness.

In addition to managing the paraprofessionals in the program, the reading teacher must also be a record keeper. With the increased emphasis upon accountability in education, the reading teacher should establish a skills checklist or other management system to be maintained daily by each student. The system should reflect the hierarchy of skills leading to accomplishment of the goals set for himself by the student. A test should be available for each skill listed. When the pupil successfully passes the test on each skill, he should indicate this fact on the appropriate form. By checking each pupil's management form regularly, the teacher can keep track of individual progress.

As each goal is accomplished, the student and teacher agree upon additional goals. A management system containing a hierarchy of skills will then be developed, insuring the continued improvement of reading skills.

THE READING TEACHER AS PROGRAM PLANNER

The middle school reading teacher must collect, analyze, and interpret research data from many different areas, because the middle school reading program must articulate the aims and objectives of the primary reading program with those of the high school. Because reading is a schoolwide concern, the middle school reading teacher must also provide help in planning and evaluating reading activities in the content areas.

Logan, Logan, and Peterson (7) support this position by stating:

Knowledge of the developmental sequence in reading will enable a school staff to organize a program in terms of the needs of the children enrolled in a particular school situation. Further, knowledge of the process of development in reading implies an understanding of the objectives of reading, of the sequential development of skills in the reading process, and ways of providing for the individual differences to be found in every school, in every educational level, and in every class. In the elementary school, the teacher will find children at all stages of development as they progress toward maturity in reading. It is only as teachers, individually and together with other teachers and educators on a school staff, recognize landmarks on the road toward maturity in reading that they are able to plan and carry out a program of reading activities and linguistic experiences that will guide each child toward his highest potential, not only in reading but through reading. With such a knowledge, it is possible to organize a sequence of reading experiences commensurate with the needs, abilities, interests and aptitudes of children, whether the administrative organization is based on grade levels, reading levels, or growth gradients.

In order to evaluate the effectiveness of a middle school reading program, the reading teacher must determine how well the program fits into the K-12 guidelines for the school system. If the school system has not adopted such a system of guidelines, the middle school reading teacher should solicit cooperation in doing so.

In Alachua County, Florida, a committee of teachers, administrators, supervisors, and university professors developed such a set of reading guidelines (4):

1. Reading instruction will be concerned with the social and personal development of each student as well as his growth in the skills, understandings, and attitudes necessary for successful reading.
2. Reading instruction will include schoolwide and individual teacher plans for:
   a. A sequential program of specific instruction in basic skill development based on a continuum of skill objectives until

students demonstrate proficiency in skills needed to succeed in curricular areas and life situations.

b. A systematic introduction to contemporary and classical literature.

c. An individualized program of recreational reading that utilizes all kinds of printed material.

d. The application of skills to content area with instruction related to special skills and vocabulary; instructional materials at the appropriate reading level; and opportunities to develop concepts by means other than reading.

3. Each school will formulate procedures for disseminating reading diagnostic information to all appropriate professional personnel.

4. Teachers will design learning objectives based on continuing assessment of needs and interests.

5. Students will be instructed at a level at which success is guaranteed and growth is evidenced.

6. Readiness for reading including visual, auditory, motor, social, emotional, conceptual development, and language development will be considered prerequisite to reading success and will be taught as needed.

7. The initial reading program will offer balanced instruction in the use of word attack skills, including configuration clues, structural analysis, phonetic analysis, and context clues.

8. Organization for achieving instructional objectives in reading requires flexible grouping of students into skill groups, interest groups, task groups, and social groups.

9. A variety of instructional materials appropriate in terms of interest, readability, and learning style will be used to implement the reading program.

10. Instructional plans will include a balance of purposeful oral-silent reading activities.

11. A record of materials used and competencies acquired will be maintained in pupils' cumulative folders.

12. Reading achievement will be reported to pupils and parents in terms of individual progress.

With a similar set of guidelines adapted to his particular school needs, a middle school reading teacher would have a basis for evaluating his reading program in terms of the overall guidelines of the school system.

The middle school reading teacher must accept the responsibility for using and evaluating recently published materials and equipment in terms of pupil performance in specific skills. Research indicates that it is fruitless to attempt to label any approach to reading instruction as "good" or "bad." It is more reasonable to survey the materials to determine what skills can be developed efficiently through using the materials and what skills cannot. The middle school reading teacher should exert leadership in this type of research.

Research should also be conducted to find what particular approaches to skill development are most effective for individual pupils. This type of research has been found to be most effective in improving pupil reading performance in behavior modification models. Once this information has been found, it can be disseminated by the reading teacher to other teachers and counselors with whom the individual pupil has contact.

SUMMARY

Because of the unique nature of the middle school, the reading teacher must play many roles. He must diagnose pupils and place them at the appropriate place in the K-12 reading skill sequence. He must achieve the close relationship between reading performance and self-concept and strive to provide a supportive environment that insures many successes in reading activities. He must help other teachers obtain the materials needed for developing reading skills in the various content areas. He must provide a maximum amount of individualized instruction for pupils in reading by using efficient management systems for scheduling and record keeping and by developing differentiated staffing to reduce the teacher-pupil ratio. Finally, he must do research regarding the most efficient materials and equipment to meet specific needs.

It is not possible, of course, for the reading teacher to emphasize each of these roles equally. He establishes priorities according to the particular needs of the school and the staff and he emphasizes one role or another to insure an efficient and effective program. Only by playing a variety of roles can the reading teacher insure that the middle school will help children achieve their maximum potential in reading.

References

1. DeBoer, John J., and Martha Dallman. *The Teaching of Reading.* New York: Holt, Rinehart and Winston, 1970, 501.
2. DeVita, Joseph C., Philip Pumerantz, and Leighton B. Wilklow. *The Effective Middle School.* New York: Parker, 1970.
3. Fillmer, H. Thompson. "Professional Reading Activities for Paraprofessionals," *Reading Teacher,* 26 (May 1973), 806-809.
4. Fillmer, H. Thompson, and Sue Griffith. "Guidelines for a Systemwide Reading Program," *Elementary English,* 50 (March 1973), 455-458.
5. Hansen, John H., and Arthur C. Hearn. *The Middle School Program.* Chicago: Rand McNally, 1970.
6. Harris, Albert J. *How To Increase Reading Ability.* New York: David McKay, 1968, 220-221.
7. Logan, Lillian, Virgil G. Logan, and Leona Peterson. *Creative Communication: Teaching the Language Arts.* New York: McGraw-Hill, 1972, 366.

8. Myers, Isabel Briggs. *The Myers-Bridge Type Indicator: A Manual.* Princeton, New Jersey: Educational Testing Service, 1972.

9. Stradley, William E. *A Practical Guide to the Middle School.* New York: Center for Applied Research in Education, 1971, 177-178.

10. Wilson, Robert M. *Diagnostic and Remedial Reading for Classroom and Clinic.* Columbus, Ohio: Charles E. Merrill, 1972, 37-38.

CHAPTER SIX

ASSESSING
READING PROGRESS

Richard W. Burnett
University of Missouri at St. Louis

Previous chapters of this book have built a strong case for the uniqueness of both the middle school itself and its reading program. It must be pointed out, however, that some educators are skeptical about isolating particular aspects of reading instruction and discussing them simply as they relate to the middle school. There are those who are not impressed by efforts to isolate reading instruction into neat compartments such as reading in the first grade, reading in the second grade, reading in the inner city, or reading in the junior college (4). Such fragmentation very often seems arbitrary and artificial.

THE MIDDLE SCHOOL AND READING ASSESSMENT

Admittedly, the intrinsic reading needs of pupils remain identical whether they are enrolled in traditional school structures or in the more recently emerging middle school structures. What is different is the way in which these needs might be met in a middle school in contrast to the ways they might be met in a self-contained classroom or in a departmentalized junior high school. The unique characteristics of the middle school are meant to include such things as the following (1):

1. more time for cooperative teacher planning and preparation,
2. greater scheduling flexibility because of the number of teachers,
3. more variety in the curriculum because of the varied backgrounds of teachers,
4. differentiated staffing features because of the availability of specialists to work with teaching teams, and
5. the possibility of operating alternative schools or approaches to instruction within the total structure of the school.

Strategies for assessing reading needs in the middle school then, must be developed to contribute to, as well as take full advantage of, the uniqueness of the middle school concept of educating children from grades five to eight. As is so often the case in educational innovation, the very strengths of a new approach contain the seeds of potential weakness and failure. The strength of the middle school rests in the bringing together of numbers of teachers to work in a coordinated team effort with pupils who, in other structures, would have been taught for the major part of the day by one teacher or for each period of the day by different teachers, each of whose efforts were relatively uncoordinated with the others. Any worthwhile strategy for assessing pupils has to contribute to effective communication among teachers. For a brief and highly readable discussion of strategies for meeting reading differences see Smith's *Correcting Reading Problems in the Classroom* (5). Of particular use for middle grade teachers are the inventory checklists which cover word attack, comprehension, oral reading, and growth in attitude toward reading.

Each middle school faculty member must be committed to contributing to the optimal development of reading skills. No teacher can properly hold the opinion (so widespread in junior and senior high schools) that somebody else takes care of teaching reading. At this stage of pupil growth and development, no teacher is justified in assuming that all he need do is assign work to be done and shrug off any responsibility for those pupils unequipped to perform the tasks. When teachers accept this broader responsibility, however, they are entitled to expect considerable support in the areas of analyzing reading needs and providing differentiated instruction.

What diagnostic procedures and devices should be used in the teaching of reading in the middle school? The broad, general answer to that question must be that the best diagnostic procedures and devices to use at any given time in a middle school are those procedures and devices which provide the information most likely to be understood and made use of by teachers in giving direction to their instructional planning. Such an answer implies that reading tests and other assessment devices have to be chosen relative to the needs of the teachers, as they recognize and accept these needs.

The reading testing program of a middle school should not remain unchanging or static over a period of time. If tests results are useful and help teachers better understand the instructional needs of pupils, the teachers grow and develop in their abilities to differentiate instruction and meet assorted individual needs. When this happy circumstance occurs, teachers will demand and be able to utilize increasingly more subtle and precise test results. In other words, a good assessment program can and should contribute to the growth and development of the faculty.

AREAS TO BE ASSESSED IN READING

There are three general areas of concern in reading instruction which call for definite assessment measures: 1) mechanical skills which encompass word recognition proficiency as well as fluency and rhythm in both oral and silent reading performance; 2) cognitive skills which encompass meaning vocabulary, literal comprehension, interpretive or inferential reading, critical reading, general work-study skills, and applied reading in specific content fields; and 3) affective factors which include the quality and variety of reading done, attitudes toward reading and those derived from it, and the development of enduring, lifelong reading habits.

Mechanical Skills

During the middle school years, many pupils are in transition from acquiring the basic mechanical skills to the point of automatic application of these skills in using reading to serve their entertainment and learning needs. For a variety of reasons, a sizable minority of fifth and sixth graders from the best of elementary school learning situations will still be deficient in basic word recognition skills. One major reason is that many primary age children are unable to pick up the word analysis principles because they are developmentally unready in the first two or three years of school — the years when the basic sounding skills receive their heaviest teaching emphasis. These pupils become the hard core underachievers if the instructional offerings in grades above the primary do not provide for review and reteaching of phonic analysis skills and the opportunity for constant reinforcement in applying these skills in reading materials at appropriate levels of difficulty. Therefore, the assessment provisions in the middle school must be such that these pupils can be identified, the degree and nature of their skill deficits determined, and a periodic appraisal of their reading subskills made in order to insure that continual improvement is being recorded.

Occasionally, a reader who appears to do well in general reading will level off in reading growth and suddenly turn up as weak in word analysis skills. This pupil may be one who was able to cope with the primary experience where most of the words met in reading were introduced in such a way that he could pick them up as sight words. With the increased vocabulary load at the middle grade level, he is unable to maintain his general reading performance because his repertoire of word recognition techniques is incomplete. For this reason, readers of average and above average achievement cannot automatically be assumed to be beyond the point of concern for continual monitoring of their word recognition skills. However, the greatest amount of time and energy in assessment in the basic mechanical skills area probably should be spent with those readers in the lower quartile in reading achievement by the time fifth grade is reached. The more advanced word recognition skills including syllabication in multisyllable words, structural analysis, and accent principles are normally programed into grades five and six, so assessment of growth in these areas should be made for all pupils. Finally, the use of the dictionary in word recognition must be assessed as a vital, but often overlooked, aspect of learning.

Cognitive Skills

The cognitive area, including vocabulary development and the improvement of literal comprehension, tends to receive emphasis in middle grades, regardless of the type of school structure. Especially in departmentalized settings, however, two aspects of vocabulary growth need to be assessed; general vocabulary should be monitored by the reading and language arts teachers, while technical vocabulary is tested through informal devices constructed by the social studies, science, mathematics, and other content teachers in their classes. Similarly, in comprehension skills the reading and language arts teachers may measure growth in general reading comprehension, while the content teachers attempt to assess whether concepts taught in their classes enable the middle grader to read more effectively in the technical materials peculiar to the subject.

Care must be taken not to overlook general work-study skills such as using the dictionary as a study aid; effectively utilizing tables of contents, indexes, and glossaries in texts; obtaining data from maps, tables, and graphs; locating information in reference books; proficiency in outlining an article or chapter; differentiating main ideas from supporting details and restating long selections in accurate but brief summary form. These work-study skills along with the higher level comprehension skills — including the ability to infer meaning, to appreciate the style in which an idea is expressed, to apply ideas picked up while reading to resolve different problems, and to critically evaluate ideas — are learnings that can best be assessed through informal or subjective testing strategies. Each content teacher who feels these reading abilities are important in his class needs to be helped to develop and use informal tests that appraise these skills. Standardized tests tend to have their greatest value in surveying reading skills in a general way. Some, however, also attempt to assess study skills and specific aspects of comprehension. A listing of published tests appropriate for middle school use can be found in Karlin's *Teaching Reading in High School* (*3*). Included in that source are both elementary and high school reading and study skills tests with publishers and addresses.

Affective Factors

Children in the middle grades tend to do more outside reading for entertainment than at any other point during their schooling. Any middle school should include in its reading assessment strategies a record of library utilization, the degree to which periodicals and newspapers are incorporated into instruction, paperback book club sales, and other indicators of the nature and extent of reading done by its pupils. The reading habits of the pupils outside of school, where they are free from coercion and from the need to account for their actions, are the best index of the quality of reading instruction in the total school program. Such data, when it can be collected in a low-keyed and voluntary way, can help in assessing the impact that the reading instructional effort may be having from year to year.

SPECIFIC READING ASSESSMENT TECHNIQUES

The use of group administered standardized tests is a necessary element in a middle school reading assessment program, but their use must be seen as only *one* element. Informal devices and criterion-referenced tests can also be used in certain circumstances.

Standardized Tests

Standardized reading tests serve two functions. One is to insure that measurable growth is occurring over a period of time, both for the total group and for individuals within the group. The second function is to help identify those pupils who are achieving significantly behind the group norm or who fail to show expected gains.

The use of reading survey tests or the reading subtest from an achievement battery is only the beginning of assessment, however; and in no instance should major educational decisions affecting a pupil's class placement be based on group reading test results alone. Grade equivalent scores (GE scores), when they are provided on tests, should be examined relative to the accompanying percentile scores, and those GE scores below the twentieth percentile should not normally be used as points of comparison in subsequent testing. These low GE scores are often misleading because the floor of the test, or the lowest GE score possible, is unrealistically high, being 3.0 for fourth, fifth, and sixth graders, and as high as a 4.0 or 5.0 for seventh and eighth graders. In addition, items answered correctly by chance will tend to inflate the GE score of low achievers when they take a test which is overly difficult for them.

Since standardized test scores, when below the twentieth percentile, tend to be chance scores, it is difficult to interpret tests given a semester or a year later, as these too may result in scores dictated by chance. For this reason, when it is determined that the test for their grade placement is too difficult, the lower achievers in a middle school setting should be retested using a lower level of the test, one which elicits reading responses that are not merely random responses. Growth over a semester or a year should be assessed by using the same level test for retesting or posttesting purposes.

Informal Techniques

Profiles of group test results can be studied and some gross judgments can be made. Low scores in vocabulary comprehension should always be looked at as a possible indication of poor word attack skills rather than assuming immediately that a vocabulary meaning deficit exists. The answer sheets for tests should be kept in the pupil's record folder and a reading teacher should ask each pupil who is considered for special reading help to respond orally to vocabulary comprehension items on a blank copy of the test. The examiner in this situation can readily detect whether items were missed because of inability to pronounce a word or because a word was pronounced, but its meaning was not apparent to the pupil. An experienced reading teacher using this strategy can readily determine the word analysis skills which the pupil can apply and those which he is unable to use. On some of these tests, the vocabulary and comprehension items are presented in a graduated difficulty. In such situations, the examiner can determine whether there are points at which the pupil can perform adequately, as well as approximate points where his skills tend to break down. The same approach can be used to find out why a certain pupil scored poorly on the comprehension items on the test and whether his failure was related to poor word attack or poor vocabulary rather than a weakness in comprehension.

This strategy of individual spot checking test responses can partially eliminate the need for administering more time consuming and expensive individual test batteries to problem readers. In contrast, the practice of administering tests, shipping the answer sheets away for centralized scoring and processing, and filing the printout results away is a ritualistic practice that has no justification at all in a middle school setting. The practice of mailing profiles home to parents, in instances where teachers have not previously attempted to interpret the profiles in terms of suggestions for altered teaching strategies, is another exercise of doubtful value.

Group administered diagnostic tests of reading subskills such as the Bond-Balow-Hoyt Silent Reading Diagnostic Test (Lyons and Carnahan), or the Stanford Diagnostic Reading Test (Harcourt Brace Jovanovich), while appropriate to use with those showing low achievement on the survey tests, tend to be tedious to administer and score. Some reading teachers prefer to use more informal devices, but the use of group administered standardized tests to provide diagnostic information can function to help teachers sharpen their own abilities to assess skills in a less formal manner.

There are also available a number of published word recognition inventories that are designed to be individually administered. A middle school staff of well-trained reading teachers may prefer to use informal tests of word recognition and maintain a record file system that enables them to periodically check the word attack skills of selected pupils and keep track of changes in status. The Wisconsin Design for Reading Skill Development (Interpretive Scoring Systems, Minneapolis) offers a published program with tests and record materials of possible value to middle grade teachers. At the very least, its rationale and structure is one with which middle school reading specialists should become familiar.

Criterion Referenced Tests

There has been some suggestion that so-called "criterion referenced" tests offer an alternative to norm-based standardized tests. At the present time, criterion-referenced tests do not present a genuine alternative but do offer promise as supplements to standardized tests. The issue to consider in appraising tests for adoption is whether the test results translate into valid teaching implications in the estimate of those teachers who use them. True criterion-referenced tests have to relate to teaching objectives; assessing mastery or degree of mastery of those skills, behaviors, or habits which teachers in a given course or program are attempting to develop with a group of learners. In turn, the teaching objectives lead to a competency that is by consensus held to be a desirable outcome of schooling.

The middle school would seem to be an ideal situation for teams of teachers to set up short range objectives and longer range goals and develop criterion-referenced instruments to assess the degree of progress toward these objectives and goals. The objectives at the middle school level are concerned with instilling in pupils a positive attitude toward the acquisition of further learning and developing and refining skills so the students can engage in further learning. Since reading is a process or learning tool to be refined in the middle school, the effort of teachers in content classes to measure reading as it relates to their field can help them to develop a process orientation which may help dispel the perception many teachers have of themselves as "dispensers of facts or knowledge." The reading specialists in a middle school setting should be expected to spend a good share of their time in helping content teachers develop inventory techniques to appraise the abilities of pupils in their classes in reading related to the subjects being taught.

Reading specialists should work in tandem with content teachers in constructing questions that sample the abilities of their pupils in literal comprehension, drawing inferences, and the application of what has been read in one situation to resolving problems met in other situations (2). Tests available from publishers to sample these processes in specific content areas, have little claim to being superior to informal tests that any teacher team might make. Furthermore, the involvement of the teachers in the process of assessment outweighs any advantages that might accrue from gathering computer printouts to file away.

CONCLUDING STATEMENT

The middle school represents a dynamic attempt to bring to fruition, in a single school structure, the advantages of the self-contained classroom without the accompanying disadvantages, and the advantages of a large school organized into departmentalized content specialties without the accompanying disadvantages. For this grand scheme to represent a true breakthrough in instruction for the fifth to eighth grade range of pupils, teachers must individualize instruction in a demonstrably better way than is generally exhibited in self-contained classroom settings or in departmentalized junior high school structures. A reading assessment program in a middle school must be effective in assessing the mechanical skills area as well as the cognitive and affective dimensions of reading. An adequate assessment program in reading should combine the use of standardized tests and teacher-designed informal measures. Without such assessment, the middle school is unlikely to refute the accusation that it is just another junior high school that has moved down a grade or two because of overcrowded building pressures within a school district.

References

1. DeVita, Joseph C., Phillip Pumerantz, and Leighton Winklow. *The Effective Middle School.* West Nyack, New York: Parker, 1970.
2. Herber, Harold L. *Teaching Reading in Content Areas.* Englewood Cliffs, New Jersey: Prentice-Hall, 1970.
3. Karlin, Robert. *Teaching Reading in High School.* Indianapolis, Indiana: Bobbs-Merrill, 1972.
4. Kline, Lloyd W. "Editorial," *Journal of Reading,* 16 (October 1972), 6-7.
5. Smith, Carl B. *Correcting Reading Problems in the Classroom.* Newark, Delaware: International Reading Association, 1969.

CHAPTER SEVEN

INVOLVING
CONTENT TEACHERS
IN THE READING PROGRAM

Lois A. Bader
Michigan State University

Writers in previous chapters have stated that it is crucial to involve content area teachers in the middle school reading program. This does not mean that they should be responsible for the total reading development of the students they instruct, but that they should guide their students' reading of the printed material required for the content class. Even youngsters who read quite well require a statement of instructional purpose on the part of the teacher, preparation in concepts and vocabulary, insight into the organization of the material, and assistance in developing study skills.

The goal is difficult to achieve. The term "content teacher" suggests a secondary education background and, since few secondary teachers are prepared to teach reading, they generally resist any responsibility in this area. Even middle schooteachers having elementary school certification require assistance in teaching reading.

The best approach for involving content teachers in the reading program is embedded in the philosophy of the middle school itself. The structure of the middle school, with its emphasis on the team approach, lends itself to cooperative instructional planning which makes effective use of the contributions of both the content teacher and the reading specialist. Each one has his area of expertise and both can work together to achieve the goal of effective reading instruction throughout the middle school.

A major portion of the responsibility for initiating and maintaining such a team approach, however, lies with the reading specialist, who must systematically involve the content teachers through preinstructional activities, instructional activities, and schoolwide reading committees.

The International Reading Association offers several inexpensive publications dealing with areas such as content area reading, informal open-book inventories, inservice training, and classroom organization. The reading specialist should find these useful in carrying out the functions described in this chapter.

PREINSTRUCTIONAL ACTIVITIES

The content teacher can be made aware of various aspects of reading as they relate to his particular class if the reading teacher involves him in various kinds of preinstruction activities. These include student assessment, analyzing materials, and determining objectives.

Student Assessment

Once the content area teacher has determined his concept, process, and affective goals, the reading teacher can help him determine the entry level of achievement of his students. While standardized test scores can be useful, informal tests are necessary. With regard to concept mastery, for example, the reading teacher may ask, "What concepts about colonial America do you intend to teach in this unit?" The teacher and the specialist can then construct an informal test. Those students who have mastered the concepts can be given different instructional experiences than those who have not. With regard to process mastery, the following questions may be asked: "What reading-reasoning skills will be used in this unit? Will students read to compare, to evaluate, to analyze. . . ?" An informal test can be constructed cooperatively to determine whether students can read for the purposes the unit requires. And finally, regardless of whether the teacher's objectives are process or concept oriented, the reading specialist can help prepare an informal pretest on the technical vocabulary of the content, since word meaning is basic to comprehension in any discipline.

Analyzing Materials

As a first step in helping the content teacher analyze his materials, the reading teacher may introduce him to a simple readability formula, such as the Fry (*1*) or the SMOG (*2*). Aides or volunteers can also obtain, through such a formula, an estimate of reading difficulty of all available materials under consideration.

As a second step, the reading teacher can show the content teachers how to consider the formula estimate along with the following five factors to make a final determination of level of difficulty.

1. Length and complexity of sentences. Long, fact-laden sentences are difficult to read.
2. Syntax involved sentences. For example, "Will and Sam went to the game." is easier to comprehend than, "Will, who is a friend of Bill, and Sam went to the game." When asked, "Who went to the game?" after reading the latter sentence, many poor readers will respond, "Bill and Sam."
3. Abstractness of concepts. The statement, "A rose is a rose is a rose," when tested by a reading formula which only counts words of three or more syllables, would be considered primary level material, while the idea to be comprehended is of a much higher level.
4. Specialized vocabulary. Although a student may be able to pronounce certain words and understand the meaning in one context, he may be unfamiliar with the specialized meaning of the words in a particular content area. Examples include the words *property* in science and *bank holiday* in social studies.

5. Experience background of the students. Previous courses, reading habits, hobbies, home background, media, and other stimulation or lack of it contribute to the student's ability to comprehend ideas expressed in content material.

When the difficulty of the material has been estimated, the reading teacher might ascertain the spread of students' achievement and graphically compare student ability with the difficulty level of the materials they are expected to read.

In addition to determining level of difficulty, the printed material to be used in teaching should also be analyzed according to its possibilities for use in achieving the course objectives selected by the teacher. To help a teacher clarify his thinking in this regard, the reading teacher might ask if he has concept objectives, process objectives, and/or attitude objectives as his instructional goals for the material. With this information as a foundation, the reading specialist can show the content teacher how students, with appropriate instruction in background and terminology, can obtain concept objectives by literally comprehending material that is fairly difficult for them. However, if the teacher has reasoning process objectives such as evaluation or comparison, the specialist can show him how to prepare his students for this activity. In addition, the specialist can show the content area teacher how he can individualize by having different students pursue other process or concept objectives, depending on the material.

Finally, the specialist might use a device such as the following to illustrate how the content teacher can analyze materials for teaching:

Identification of Comprehension Skills

Required for the Achievement of Instructional Goals

1. List implications of the selection for the discipline
   a. Instructional goals in using the material
   b. Reasoning processes required of students
2. Summarize main idea
3. List key concepts
4. List vocabulary
5. Describe organization of the selection
6. Describe author's tone
7. State purpose or purposes for reading which students would be given.

In determining objectives during student assessment and material evaluation, the tentative objectives of the content area teachers influence the nature of the evaluation. This is appropriate. The reading teacher must defer to content area specialists in selecting objectives. The reading teacher can influence the selection of objectives to the extent that he provides information to the content teacher regarding the abilities of students and the nature of the printed material to be used. In addition, he provides assistance in tailoring the objectives to the child's abilities as instruction proceeds. However, the final determination of objectives is made by the content area teachers.

INSTRUCTIONAL ACTIVITIES

In addition to involving the content teacher through preinstruction activities, the reading specialist can do much to involve teachers in the middle school reading program by assisting them in instructional activities. This means that the reading specialist should not confine himself to helping remedial students but should also be in the classrooms demonstrating, assisting in the development of materials, and otherwise involving content teachers in the reading task. The specialist can do this in a variety of ways.

Group Instruction

The reading teacher may work with the teacher helping him to assign students to groups, prepare teaching outlines, and select materials. He may also teach a group to demonstrate particular instructional techniques.

In this regard, emphasis should be on flexible grouping. The basis may be prescriptive at times; Mike, Sue, May, and Sam could be asked to work together because they need to develop a particular skill. At other times, however, interest and other forms of grouping are desirable.

Independent Learning

The reading teacher may work with the content teacher to prepare learning packets for independent learning. He may analyze the material for instruction, create guided-reading questions, and make criterion-referenced tests.

Attention should be given to oral language development when children are working independently. In some independent learning programs in mathematics, children often perform rote operations at the expense of concept development. The reading specialist should show the content teachers how to avoid such pitfalls in independent learning.

Tapes for Nonreaders

For very poor readers, the reading teacher may coordinate a program of volunteers or aides who will tape material. Just as a directed format is used to guide reading, a similar sequence should be used with the tapes; i.e., key terminology should be explained, curiosity aroused, a purpose for listening given, and final discussion or an extended activity provided for closure.

Library

The reading specialist can also bring together the content teacher and the librarian to compile materials of appropriate levels for students and prepare instructional outlines for reports. For a thematic unit, materials may take many forms: short stories, novels, news articles, and essays. For an informational unit, materials on many levels of difficulty can be found to answer the same set of general questions. These materials can be placed on reserve in the library or borrowed for the classroom library. Because this is a time consuming chore, teaming is necessary. Once the unit lists have been completed, they can be used again in subsequent years.

Tutoring

Tutoring by volunteers or aides, cross-age tutoring, and team learning have all been found to be effective in producing learning. Most research indicates that success is related to the amount of structure given to the tutorial element by a professional. This would indicate that the reading teacher could be useful to the content teacher by helping to develop guides for the tutors and by assisting in the supervision of their tasks.

Reading Guides

To help stretch available reading material over several grade levels, the reading teacher may create multilevel reading guides. These have differing amounts of structure. For example, the poorest readers may be asked to "Read page 17 and list the three major causes of forest fires," while the best readers may be asked to "Read Chapter 2 and summarize the economic effects of forest fires." Or the reading teacher may help to create margin-reading guides; guides that may be aligned with reading material. Explanations of terms and concepts may be given, or the reader might be directed to attend to such elements as main ideas or logical fallacies.

Language Experience

If the team has opted to use language experience sequences in which the students dictate, write information, and then read their own material, the reading teacher may coordinate volunteers or aides as they print, type, and, if desired, duplicate such material. This strategy may be more useful for the poorest readers, as they can report on their experiences or taped lessons while also creating their own reading material.

Learning Center

Finally, the reading teacher can make the learning center available to the content teacher either on a drop-in basis or on an assigned basis. Students may work in the center in some of the ways listed or they may be given individual or small group instruction by the reading specialist. In any case, the center is a useful place for the content teacher to test materials and instructional techniques. In effect, the teacher uses the center as an instructional laboratory.

SCHOOLWIDE READING COMMITTEES

A less direct but important involvement of the content area teacher is participation on the Reading Committee. Here, program areas of evaluation are selected, schoolwide needs are determined, and priorities chosen.

Every content area should be represented. Division chairmen should be invited, but membership should be open to all teachers. The committee might consider such areas as:

1. *The Testing Program.* Are crucial areas being evaluated by the tests? Is the timing of test administration useful? Are test results disseminated in a helpful fashion?
2. *Parental Involvement.* How can parents encourage reading interest? How can parents be helped to understand the goals of the program?
3. *Purchase of Materials.* What is the reading achievement range of students? What is the range of readability levels of materials in each content area? What are the content areas most lacking in reading materials to meet the achievement range of students?
4. *Development of Reading Centers.* Is there a need for classroom libraries within content division areas? Is there a need for a paperback book room? If so, how might it be organized and supervised? What services are most desired of the learning center?
5. *Reading Needs of Special Groups.* Are the needs of slow learners, gifted students, and second language speakers being met throughout the school day?
6. *Articulation K-12.* What is the nature of the reading programs of feeder schools? Does information helpful in planning programs for special students follow those students to the middle school? Is the information used? What is the secondary reading program?
7. *Reading Progress of Students.* What are the strengths and weaknesses of the reading and study skills of the students? Is there evidence of growth in all areas? What should be the instructional priorities?

In planning, discussing, and evaluating the total reading program, content area teachers come to feel that the program is their own, not one devised by the reading teacher or the administration. As such, they become involved in the program, support it, and attempt to achieve its goals.

CONCLUSION

If the middle school is to meet its potential in reading, the content area teachers must be involved in the reading program. The responsibility for obtaining such involvement from content teachers lies largely with the reading teacher who must use tact, skill, and resourcefulness in drawing teachers into the program. This goal can be achieved if the reading teacher consciously and persistently draws content teachers into reading by helping them with preinstruction and instructional activities and by involving them in the decisions made by the school reading committee.

References
1. Fry, Edward. "A Readability Formula That Saves Time," *Journal of Reading* 11, 7, 513-516, 575-578.
2. McLaughlin, G. Harry. "SMOG Grading – a New Readability Formula," *Journal of Reading,* 12, 8, 642-645.

CHAPTER EIGHT

SELECTING MATERIALS
FOR A MIDDLE SCHOOL
READING PROGRAM

John E. Connelly
New York State University College at Fredonia

The selection of instructional materials, a crucial problem faced by those organizing a middle school reading program, is particularly perplexing because there is no single material that will work with all students. In the middle school, where the students' emotions, attitudes, and interests change from day to day, it is impossible to get concensus on what materials are best.

Despite the problems inherent in selecting materials, however, it is possible both to formulate principles which can guide personnel who are organizing middle school reading programs and to provide a source list of representative materials.

GUIDING PRINCIPLES

All too often, materials for reading programs are selected in a random manner. Such should not be the case. Rather, the selection of materials should be guided by principles which take into account the uniqueness of the middle school population, the principles of teaching reading, and the particular problems associated with the school in which the materials are to be used.

The Middle School Student

As has been pointed out in previous chapters, the middle school student population represents a wide variety of interests and abilities. The material selected for the reading program should reflect these differences.

In selecting materials, one should concentrate first on materials containing interesting reading selections. Too often we "phonic them to death" or we teach skills, skills, and more skills without allowing them to read. Particularly in the middle school, where student interests are divergent and mercurial, it is essential that a wide variety of highly interesting material be selected.

There must be a concern for the variety of ability levels found in the middle school. Every teacher, including the content area teachers, should have an assortment of textbook materials which spans five or six reading levels. Without such variety, the teacher is unable to place students in books which match their reading ability and either frustration or boredom results.

The Nature of Reading Instruction

In addition to considering the uniqueness of the student population, the supervisor of the middle school reading program should select materials with a view to the nature of reading and the process of reading instruction.

In this regard, the first principle to remember is that the development of students who do read is the ultimate goal of reading instruction. A sizable portion of the materials selected should be of a recreational nature, designed to entice students into developing a reading habit. Too often, the materials purchased are strictly for skills instruction — workbooks, kits, and textbooks. While these are crucial in any reading program, they must be supplemented by purchases of trade books, paperbacks, magazines, and other materials which will involve children in the reading act itself.

While recreational reading material can include a broad spectrum of randomly selected materials which reflect the tremendous variety of interests and abilities found in the middle school, instructional materials should be selected carefully and evaluated individually. Such evaluations should be based upon a set of criteria or standards. It is best that such a criteria be developed by the teachers who will be using the material, but as an initial guide the standards developed by Goodman (*3*) and Sartain (*5*) can be used.

The best source for specific criteria for the selection of recreational and instructional reading material is *Choosing Materials to Teach Reading* by Goodman. This convenient handbook presents and examines an inclusive set of principles from which educators can select when choosing and analyzing reading materials for middle school students. It offers teachers, reading specialists, librarians, principals, and other curriculum workers principles that can enable them to efficiently and effectively analyze materials and advises them to apply their selection criteria consistently. The principles are discussed separately under these chapter titles: "Psychological Principles," "Sociocultural Principles," "Educational Principles," "Linguistic Principles," and "Literary Principles" and the text can be used as an intensive reference to formulate standards which can guide personnel who are organizing middle school reading programs.

Finally, regarding instructional material such as workbooks, a distinction should be made between instructional materials and practice materials. Some materials do not teach the reading skills themselves; they only provide the practice and repetition needed to make habitual a response taught previously (*1*). Such instructional materials should be thoroughly investigated prior to purchase to determine whether they are truly instructional (whether children can learn from the materials alone) or whether they are practice materials (to be used only after the teacher has directly assisted the student in learning the skill). Once the materials are purchased, the supervisor of the reading program should insure that they are used correctly.

The Particular School Setting

While the principles regarding the nature of the middle school student and the nature of reading instruction tend to be universally useful in selecting materials, consideration should also be given to the particular school situation in which the materials are to be used.

For instance, if the school draws upon a particular ethnic or minority group, the materials for the reading program might be selected in terms of their appeal to these groups. Similarly, if the school has a high proportion of disabled readers, the emphasis might be upon purchasing materials of high interest but low readability, such as those that have been listed by Duffy and Sherman (1).

The financial capability of the school might also pose some limitations. For instance, reading machines such as the controlled reader and the shadowscope, tape recorders, and cameras provide excellent motivation when used wisely in a reading program. Where resources are limited, however, it might be wiser to choose more economically so that a greater variety of material can be purchased for the amount of money available.

Summary

When selecting materials for the middle school reading program, the purchaser should make his choice on the basis of the uniqueness of the middle school student, the demands of reading itself, and the particular problems associated with the school. It must be remembered that materials are not limited to commercial materials; while they are convenient, no reading program is complete that does not also include teacher-made materials tailored to the particular needs of the students being taught.

SOURCES OF MIDDLE SCHOOL READING MATERIALS

While the above list of principles can be useful in guiding the selection of reading materials for a middle school program, a source list is often helpful in getting started. Each major publisher readily will supply a list of developmental reading textbooks and anthologies that are available for use in systematic programs. Most teachers also will need a list of materials for practice and remedial work. The following list, compiled by the author and Sharyn Emmett (2) is meant to be representative rather than exhaustive. The materials listed are appropriate for the middle school because of their motivational, recreational, remedial, or enriching aspects and can be used for individualizing, reinforcing, or motivating in the reading program.

The list is compiled alphabetically by publisher. It includes the name of the material, publisher, reading and interest levels, description, and main purpose(s).

Reading and Interest Levels (Grade equivalent)

Name of Material	Publisher	RL	IL	Brief Description	Main Purpose (s)
Reading Development Kit A (K)	Addison-Wesley Publishing Co.	1.7-3.9	5-Adult	75 lessons divided into 3 progressively harder series. Each lesson is on a 4 page folded card. Includes vocabulary development, the story, and comprehension exercises. Contains instruction manual and	Remediation for older students through high interest controlled readability material and development of vocabulary, word skills, and comprehension.
Reading Development Kit B (K)	Addison-Wesley Publishing Co.	4.0-6.0	5-Adult	placement tests. Stories contain practical information on topics such as Law, Health, etc.	Remedial and/or developmental exercises for older students through high interest controlled reading material and development of vocabulary, work skills, and comprehension.
Reading Development Kit C (K)	Addison-Wesley Publishing Co.	7.0-10+	7-Adult	65 self-instructional lessons in 4 series; each lesson on 6 page folded card and has 3 parts: vocabulary and critical reading, story, critical thinking and comprehension.	Provides developmental and/or enrichment reading for older students. Emphasis on developing independent critical thinking and reading skills.
Fitzhugh PLUS Program Perceptual Training (WB)	Allied Education Council	Pre K-3	Pre K-3	3 workbooks on Spatial Organization- special yellow marker turns green under correct answer instant feedback, diagnostic placement guide to place child.	Supplementary readiness and primary vocabulary and skills material for children with learning disabilities. May also be used in severe or primary remedial and/or
Fitzhugh PLUS Program Language Concepts (WB)	Allied Education Council	Pre K-3	Pre K-3	3 of 6 workbooks in the Language and Numbers series. Special marker for instant feedback. Introduction to alphabet, nouns, and basic grammar.	preparatory programs for all students. Problem oriented, self-teaching, individualized instruction.
Mott Basic Language Skills Program Semi-Programmed Series 1301-1306 (WBs)	Allied Education Council	1.5-4.5	4-12	Individualized program teaching remedial reading to older children from skills approach. Each of 14 workbooks is self-correcting, supplying immediate feedback. Set up in progressive skills development, and on a	Developmental and/or remedial; teaches cursive writing, beginning comprehension, and word attack skills.
Semi-Programmed Series 1607-1610 (WBs)	Allied Education Council	5.0-6.7	4-12	diagnostic prescriptive basis. Includes teacher manual and placement guide.	Developmental remedial and/or enrichment. Includes readings of high student interest, vocabulary building, beginning grammar, the American scene. Includes practical everyday situations.
Semi-Programmed Series 1911-1914 (WBs)	Allied Education Council	7.5-9.5	6-12	Same as above description.	Developmental remedial and/or enrichment; includes fundamentals of grammar, vocabulary study, spelling, oral and written usage, library skills, and American scene.
Mott Basic Language Skills Program Classroom Series 300 Series (WBs)	Allied Education Council	1.2-5.0	4-12	6 workbooks provide a group approach to teaching basic Language Skills.	Developmental and/or remedial; teaches reading, writing, and comprehension skills at easiest levels.

Name of Material	Publisher	Reading and Interest Levels (Grade equivalent)		Brief Description	Main Purpose (s)
		RL	IL		
Mott Basic Language Skills Program Classroom Series 600 Series (WBs)	Allied Education Council	5.0-8.0	4-12	Ideally suited to reading class that can be grouped into three reading groups. Can be used in conjunction with semiprogramed series.	Developmental, remedial, and/or enrichment; includes readings of high interest, controlled readability, word study, skill lessons, everyday words for practical vocabulary building and the American scene - readings on contemporary life.
Classroom Series 900 Series (WBs)	Allied Education Council	8.0-10.0	6-12		
Mott Basic Language Skills Program Comprehension Series 301-304 (WBs)	Allied Education Council	2.7-4.5	4-12	4 workbooks containing about 25-30 short stories each. Structured, self-correction format, designed to coordinate with skills development in semiprogramed 1300 series.	High interest, controlled readability material to develop comprehension skills and reinforce word attack skills. Can be used as remedial developmental, and/or enrichment material.
Comprehension Series 601-604 (WBs)	Allied Education Council	5.0-7.2	4-12	Same as above except coordinates with skills developed in semiprogramed 1600 series.	To be used for diagnosing, prescribing, and/or evaluating student placement and progress in the Mott Program.
Mott Basic Language Skills Program Auxiliary Materials Book 160-Word Attack Skills (WB)	Allied Education Council	1.2-5.0	4-12	A workbook containing exercises and 76 word attack skills and 19 additional skills necessary for good reading.	
A Head Start for Reading (WB)	Allied Education Council	1	1-12	A workbook to develop prereading skills such as left to right and top to bottom eye movement.	To be used in severe remediation cases or with students who have perception problems.
Word Bank (WB)	Allied Education Council	3-5	4-12	A workbook containing 12-25 word units of photo association with upper and lowercase print, and cursive writing. Vocabulary also used in short stories.	A self-help workbook for students to develop written vocabulary, reinforce instant word recognition, and spelling skills.
Consumer Buying - Basic Numbers and Money (WB)	Allied Education Council	3-5	4-12	A programed workbook of word problems based on actual newspaper ads. Provides real life situations in basic arithmetic and reading.	To help person read and understand newspaper ads and give assistance in using numbers and handling money. Gives practical use of math and reading.
Reading Success Series 1-6 (WBs)	American Education Publications / Xerox	2-6	5-12	Comic book format using short, fast moving stories to teach basic phonetic and structural analysis skills.	To introduce and reinforce basic reading skills for the older remedial student through high interest, low readability material.
Know Your World (NP)	American Education Publications	2-3	4-12	Weekly newspaper containing current events, comic strips, science news, recreational reading, and fun exercise to reinforce basic skills.	Permits severe remedial cases to read about current events and offers pleasurable means of reinforcing basic skills. High interest, low readability material.
You and Your World (NP)	American Education Publications	3-5	7-12	Adult type newspapers at low reading level. Contains current events, job and money guidance, fun quizzes, and crossword puzzles.	To create interest in reading about current events while reinforcing comprehension and work study skills. High interest, low readability material.

Reading and Interest Levels (Grade equivalent)

Name of Material	Publisher	RL	IL	Brief Description	Main Purpose (s)
Specific Skill Series Complete Specimen Kit (K)	Barnell Loft, Ltd.	1-6	1-12	Set of 50 exercise workbooks. Each book contains 1 of 8 skills on 1 of 6 reading levels, 8 skills are: following directions, using the context, getting the facts, locating the answer, working with sounds, getting the main idea, drawing conclusions, and detecting sequence.	To provide remedial and/or developmental intensive practice in 8 reading skills at 6 different reading levels.
Language Master Cards Vocabulary (OM)	Bell and Howell	4-12	4-12	Intermediate and advanced vocabulary cards to be used with Language Master.	To develop (4-12) or remediate (9-12) vocabulary.
The Dan Frontier Series (B)	Benefic Press	K-4	K-7	Series of 11 books about frontier life. High interest, low readability material; boy oriented.	To provide supplementary remedial and/or at-level reading material to reinforce skills through recreational reading; to advance social studies concepts.
Mystery Adventure Series (B)	Benefic Press	2-6	4-9	Series of 6 mystery and adventure books; high interest, low vocabulary. Young adult boy and girl central characters; introduction to various ethnic groups.	To provide supplementary remedial and/or at-level reading material of high interest, low vocabulary.
Sailor Jack Series (B)	Benefic Press	K-3	K-6	Series of 10 books about adventures aboard an atomic submarine with an underlying note of anecdotal humor throughout; boy oriented.	To provide supplementary remedial and/or at-level reading material of high interest, low vocabulary.
Space Science Fiction Series (B)	Benefic Press	2-6	4-9	Series of 6 books about adventures of men of the future. There are extension enrichment reading sections at back of book.	To provide supplementary remedial and/or at-level reading material of high interest, low vocabulary.
Sports Mystery Series (B)	Benefic Press	2-3	4-9	Series of 4 books of high interest; combination of sports, mystery, and school environment; appearance and illustrations appeal to older students.	High interest, low readability supplementary material offering high degree of identification with characters by reader and reinforcement of family and social concepts.
Tom Logan Series (B)	Benefic Press	K-3	K-6	8 books about the adventures of a young man growing up on the old frontier. Boy oriented.	To provide supplementary remedial and/or at-level reading material of high interest, low vocabulary. To advance social studies concepts.
World of Adventure Series (B)	Benefic Press	2-6	4-9	8 books of high adventure stories featuring adult characters. Each book contains a story map, news article, and tall tale for further teaching aids. Boy oriented.	To provide supplementary remedial and/or at-level reading material of high interest, low vocabulary. To help develop interpretive skills.
First-Sixth Reading Helper (WB)	Book-Lab	K-3	K-6	6 workbooks containing exercises on 6 progressively harder levels of skills needed in reading in K-3 grade. Workbooks for tutor and tutee.	To remediate K-3 reading skills by using 1 to 1 peer tutoring.
Play the Game Series (B)	Bowmar	2.5-4.0	3-9	4 books containing short stories based on exciting incidents in the lives of great athletes; multiethnic.	To provide high interest, controlled readability supplementary reading material for remedial and/or developmental classes.

| Name of Material | Publisher | Reading and Interest Levels (Grade equivalent) | | Brief Description | Main Purpose (s) |
		RL	IL		
Reading Incentive - Part I (K)	Bowmar	3	3-12	16 kits on 16 different topics such as snowmobiles, minibikes, and horses. Each kit contains a filmstrip, cassette, 10 soft-covered books, and teacher manual. Same pictures on filmstrip are used in book.	Use of multisensory approach and high interest, controlled vocabulary reading material to develop independent reading and communication skills.
Flash - X Discs: Basic Accuracy - Numbers (OM)	Educational Developmental Laboratories	K-2	2-12	Includes 12 discs, 480 exposures of from 3 to 8 digits. To be used with Flash - X, a tachistoscopic device.	To provide practice for at-level or remedial development of perceptual accuracy. Gives practice in concentration and attending to order.
Basic Accuracy - Letters (OM)	Educational Developmental Laboratories	K-2	2-12	12 discs, 480 exposures of from 2-7 letters. To be used with Flash - X, a tachistoscopic device.	To provide practice for at-level or remedial development of perceptual accuracy. Gives practice in concentration and attending to order.
Advanced Accuracy Letters and Numbers	Educational Developmental Laboratories	9-Adult	9-Adult	12 discs, 480 exposures of 9 digits or 7 letters. To be used with the Flash - X, a tachistoscopic device.	To improve seeing habits of the advanced student and adult. Encourages minuteness of scrutiny and careful ordering of the material.
Study Skills Listening Materials Sight Vocabulary Grades 1, 2, 3 (OM) 4, 5, 6 7 - 13	Educational Developmental Laboratories	1-3	1-9	12 discs, 480 exposures for each grade level of basic sight words most commonly used in 10 leading basal reading series. To be used with the Flash - X coordinated with controlled reading films and vocabulary workbooks.	To provide practice in and reinforcement of instantaneous recognition of the most commonly used words in all reading material.
Adventures in Space Series (B)	Fearon Publishers	2.5-3.5	4-12	4 groups each of which contains 3 paperback books of 32 pages each. Each booklet is complete in itself; 3 booklets complete a story. Serial element produces high interest.	To provide high interest, low vocabulary supplementary reading material to stimulate student interest in independent reading. To be used with educable mentally retarded, slow learners, or enrichment and/or remedial cases.
Pacemaker Classics (B)	Fearon Publishers	2.1-2.8	6-12	7 paperback classics abridged and adapted by professional writers to lower the reading level while keeping the high interest novel intact.	Same as above description.
Pacemaker Story Books (B)	Fearon Publishers	1.9-2.6	4-12	4 sets of 6 paperback books, 48-64 pages each. Each story contains teenage boys and girls involved in a mystery and/or adventure, dealing with realistic life problems.	Same as above description.
Pacemaker True Adventures (B)	Fearon Publishers	2.0-2.5	4-12	11 paperback books, 32 pages each, containing 3 true stories. Titles include *Tales of Escape, Shipwreck, Spies,* and *Flying.* Each story highlights some important character trait that has enabled a person to overcome difficulties.	Same as above description.

Name of Material	Publisher	Reading and Interest Levels (Grade equivalent)		Brief Description	Main Purpose (s)
		RL	IL		
Checkered Flag Classroom Audio-visual Kit A and B (K)	Field Education Publications		6-12	4 filmstrips, 4 records, and 4 tapes or cassettes to correspond to books in Kit A or B. On the scent color photographs, sound effects, and professional narrations highlight these materials.	To motivate the "turned off" older student through multisensory means to read the corresponding books.
Checkered Flag Series Classroom Reading Kit A and B (B)	Field Education Publications	2.4-4.5	6-12	8 books in this series; each kit contains 6 copies of each of 4 titles. Stories revolve around cars and motorcycles in competition of some sort with background element of mystery, sabotage, and adventure.	To provide high interest, low-vocabulary supplementary reading material for the slow reader in the upper grades.
Deep Sea Adventure Series (B)	Field Educational Publications	1.8-5.0	3-11	12 exciting novels with teacher manual (controlled vocabulary) on such topics as: captured sharks and whales, pearl diving, submarine rescue, frogmen, salvage, and smugglers.	To provide high interest, controlled readability supplementary reading material for older students.
Jim Forest Series (B)	Field Educational Publications	1.7-3.2	1-6	12 high interest, controlled vocabulary books about a young boy and his uncle, a forest ranger. Action filled and suspenseful stories about great outdoors.	To provide high interest, controlled vocabulary supplementary reading material. Also provides sound conservation concepts.
Kaleidoscope Readers (WB)	Field Educational Publications	2-9	7-12	8 books using contemporary content on secondary-adult interest level (short stories, paragraphs, and poems) to lead into exercises to develop reading skills. Teacher manual for each book and placement test.	To remediate or develop reading skills (word attack, vocabulary, comprehension, study skills) through material of interest to secondary student.
Morgan Bay Mysteries (B)	Field Educational Publications	2.3-4.1	4-11	8 high interest, low vocabulary mysteries dealing with deserted houses, surfing, missing emeralds and sleuthing. 1 teacher manual for series.	To provide high interest, controlled vocabulary supplementary reading material for the older student.
Dolch Basic Sight Cards (O)	Garrard	1-3	1-6	Small flash cards for each of the 220 Dolch Basic Sight Words.	To provide practice in instant recognition of commonly used words in reading material.
Reading Attainment System 1 (K)	Grolier Educational Corporation	3-4	7-12	120 reading selections with comprehension checks, 120 skills cards on word attack and vocabulary, 120 answer keys, 30 record books, instructor manual, and pronunciation wall chart.	To provide a remedial program through high interest, controlled vocabulary reading selections to promote functional literacy in secondary school students.
Reading Attainment System 2 (K)	Grolier Educational Corporation	5-6	7-12	Same as above description.	Same as above description.

Name of Material	Publisher	Reading and Interest Levels (Grade equivalent)		Brief Description	Main Purpose (s)
		RL	IL		
Teenage Tales Books A, B, C Books 1, 2, 3 (B)	D.C. Health	3, 5-6	7-12	6 books, each containing about 30 short stories on exciting teenage adventures. Discussion questions in back of book.	To provide high interest, controlled vocabulary supplementary reading material for secondary students.
Reading Skills Lab Level 1 Box A=Diagnostic tests Box B=Lab books (K)	Houghton Mifflin	4	4-6 7-12	Diagnostic tests; self-teaching, self-correcting lab books on Unlocking strange words, Overcoming meaning difficulties, and reading for different purposes; achievement tests; and teacher manual.	A self-help program to develop the skills necessary to read and study independently in middle grades. Can also be used to remediate these skills at higher grade levels.
Level 2 Box A=Diagnostic tests Box B=Lab books (K)	Houghton Mifflin	5	4-6 7-12	Same as in level 1; titles of lab books are overcoming Meaning Difficulties, Reading for Different Purposes, and Using Reference Aids.	Same as above description.
Level 3 Box A=Diagnostic tests Box B=Lab books (K)	Houghton Mifflin	6	4-6 7-12	Same as in level 1; titles of lab books are Studying Informative Materials, Using Reference Aids, and Reading Critically.	Same as above description.
Criterion Reading (WB)	Random House Singer School Division	K-12+	K-12+	3 workbooks on each of 5 levels; contains a hierarchy of over 450 skills arranged from simple to complex. Each level contains teacher manual, student book of process skills and learning evaluation, and a book of diagnostic outcome assessments.	To diagnose individual strengths and weaknesses in reading skills, prescribe teaching program based on diagnosis, and evaluate student progress after teaching.
Random House Reading Program Reading Pacemakers (BO)	Random House Singer School Division	1-12	2-12	6 units of 50 hardcovered books each, color coded to determine reading level of books. Each book contains packet of 5 cards on inside cover. Includes survey, vocabulary detail, comprehension, and activity cards, as well as answer key. Teacher manual contains synopsis of all books and questions to be asked in book conferences.	To individualize reading progress by letting child pick books of interest at his reading level, use cards to increase reading skills, have immediate feedback by correcting own work, and let teacher evaluate progress through book conferences.
Random House Reading Program Skipacers (K)	Random House Singer School Division	1-12	2-12	Each of 6 Pacemaker units has a corresponding kit of cards that relate to skills required on cards in packets of the books. Each kit contains instruction card and a number of practice cards for 15 different comprehension skills (literal, study, skills, creative, critical).	To remediate the comprehension skills needed to work independently in the Pacemaker books.
Sights and Sounds Unit C only (K)	Random House Singer School Division	K-4	K-6	8 copies of 10 different books and a cassette tape of the narration of each of the 10 stories. Teacher guide included.	A motivational supplementary program to create interest in listening to stories and reading on the student's own. Also used to develop vocabulary, comprehension, and left to right eye movement.

Name of Material	Publisher	Reading and Interest Levels (Grade equivalent)		Brief Description	Main Purpose (s)
		RL	IL		
Adult Readings (K)	Reader's Digest Educational Division	1-4 4-9	7-12+	4 copies each of 12 booklets each containing 6 stories identified as Reading for Pleasure and Comprehension. 3 copies each of 60 leaflets on Reading for Information. Practical information about consumerism, health safety, government (4-9 RL). Leaflets make use of reader listening vocabulary obtained through media such as TV.	To provide high interest, low readability material of pleasurable and practical use for the adolescent and adult remedial reader.
Reading Skills Library Reading Skill Builders Audio Lessons (K)	Reader's Digest Educational Division	1-10	1-12	2 copies each of 24 books of short stories with vocabulary comprehension and word analysis exercises following each story, 4 self-help reading improvement books, 12 cassettes containing 24 narrations of 24 stories found in books on 1-6 reading levels.	To provide motivation to read and provide help with vocabulary and word recognition through the audio lessons; to develop and reinforce reading skills and desire to read through high interest, controlled readability material. Can be used as a reading program in itself or supplementary to other programs.
Reading Skill Practice Pads (WB)	Reader's Digest Educational Division	1-6	1-6	4 workbooks that supplement reinforce, and offer practice in basic reading skills taught in the Reading Skill Builders or in any reading program.	To provide remediation or reinforcement of word analysis skills, literal and critical comprehension study skills, and vocabulary skills.
Science Readers (WB)	Readers Digest Educational Division	3-6	3-9	4 books of short stories on modern science concepts with comprehension and vocabulary exercises at the end of each story. Each book covers 4 major areas: the earth, living things, matter and energy, and astronomy and space.	To strengthen reading skills in the content area of science with high interest, controlled readability material. To introduce modern science concepts, problems that confront scientists, and methods used to solve problems.
Help Yourself to Improve Your Reading (WB)	Reader's Digest Educational Division	7-10	6-12+	4 books, each containing different types of writing (narrative, essay, biography.); tips on how to preview and read for different purposes. Self-correcting exercises.	Supplementary enrichment material for secondary students; to increase comprehension skills on individual basis.
Reader's Digest Readings (WB)	Reader's Digest Educational Division	1-6	7-12+	6 books, each containing short stories of low vocabulary. Many illustrations, footnote definitions of new words, and self-correcting exercises on comprehension and vocabulary.	High interest, low readability material for secondary students and adults learning English as second language. Also good remedial material.
Reading Skill Builders New Reading Skill Builder (WB)	Reader's Digest Educational Division	2-8	2-12+	24 books of short stories at different reading levels. Each story has word analysis vocabulary and comprehension exercises at its end.	To motivate each child with high interest, controlled readability material based on real life content at his reading level and to develop skills at that level.
Action (K)	Scholastic Book Services	2-3.1	7-12	1 record, 20 books each of 3 Unit books, 1 short story anthology, 1 book of short plays, 6 posters, spirit masters for word attack skills, and teacher guide.	To develop vocabulary, comprehension, and word attack skills through high interest, low vocabulary material. To motivate student to read for pleasure.
Action Library I (K)	Scholastic Book Services	2-4	7-12	4 copies each of 5 novelettes and 50 spirit masters (10/book) to introduce and/or reinforce vocabulary.	To provide high interest, low vocabulary supplement reading material for the secondary student.

Name of Material	Publisher	RL	IL	Brief Description	Main Purpose (s)
		Reading and Interest Levels (Grade equivalent)			
Scope/Skills (WB)	Scholastic Book Services	4-6	7-12	7 workbooks, 3 with reading selections and comprehension exercises, 1 on speed reading, 1 on study skills, and 2 with word games and crossword puzzles to develop vocabulary and word skills.	To develop skills through high interest, controlled readability material and fun games and exercises. Pictures, games and cartoons provide high degree motivation.
Scope/Visuals (WB)	Scholastic Book Services	4-6	7-12	3 workbooks containing dittoes and transparencies of each lesson: 1 book on 8 comprehension lessons, 1 book of 16 vowel crossword puzzles, and 1 book of 16 consonant crossword puzzles.	To develop skills (comprehension and phonics) through visuals, games, puzzles, and high interest, controlled readability material.
Diminsions in Reading – an American Album (K)	Science Research Associates, (SRA)	3-8.9	4-12	300 four page reading cards on the anecdotal history of America. Each card has a comprehension check. There are answer keys and teach guides.	To stimulate interest in independent reading through high interest, controlled readability material. Useful supplementary material in reading and social studies classes.
Dimensions in Reading – Manpower and Natural Resources (K)	SRA	4-11.9	7-12	300 four page reading cards of high interest, informative material from popular magazines and books on conservation and occupational skills.	Supplementary material for the special needs of students soon entering the working world. Independent reading for high school developmental reading, guidance, occupational, and adult programs.
Pilot Library IIb (K)	SRA	3-8	4-6	72 16 - 32 books; each book is an excerpt from a full-length book chosen for its interest, appeal, and reading level. Each book has comprehension exercises and is correlated with a power builder in a specific SRA Reading	To provide supplementary reading material of high interest, controlled readability to stimulate independent reading. To lead student from excerpts to reading full length books.
Pilot Library IIc (K)	SRA	4-9	5-9	Lab. This correlation and synopsis of each is in teacher guide.	Same as above description.
Pilot Library IIIb (K)	SRA	5-12	6-12	Same as above description.	Same as above description.
Reading for Understanding (General) (K)	SRA	5-12+	5-12+	400 exercise cards, student placement tests, record books, answer keys, and teachers guide.	To create interest through an individualized approach and to diagnose, develop, and/or remediate interpretive comprehension and critical thinking skills.
Reading Laboratory IIb (K)	SRA	2.5-8	4-6	Power builders (4 page readings develop vocabulary, comprehension, and word attack skills). Listening skill builders (develop listening skills) and rate builders (timed	To provide skill building materials for individualized reading instruction and to provide for many ability levels found within a single classroom.
Reading Laboratory IIc (K)	SRA	3-9	4-9	exercises develop speed and comprehension). Includes teacher guide and answer keys.	Same as above description.

Name of Material	Publisher	Reading and Interest Levels (Grade equivalent)		Brief Description	Main Purpose (s)
		RL	IL		
Reading Laboratory IIIa (K)	SRA	3-11	7-12	Same as above description.	Same as above description.
Reading Laboratory IIIb (K)	SRA	5-12	7-12	Power Builders, 4 page readings develop vocabulary, comprehension, and word attack skills. Listening Skill Builders develop listening skills and Rate Builders - time exercises - develop speed and comprehension. Includes	To provide skill building materials for individualized reading instruction and to provide for many ability levels found within a single classroom.
Reading Laboratory IVa (K)	SRA	8-12+	9-12+	teacher guide, answer keys, and record books. Also has Listening – notetaking Skill Builders.	Same as above description.
Synchroteach M₃Xᵗᵐ IIIa (OM)	SRA		7-12	4 reel-to-reel tapes and teacher guide correlated with Reading Lab Kit IIIa. Presents step-by-step instructions for using the kit. Introduces each part on the Listening Skill Builders.	To allow student to work completely on his own, make up missed lessons, free teacher from giving class directions, and for use in in service training.
Vocabulabᵗᵐ III (K)	SRA	@4-9	7-9	150 Vocabu-builders (reading selections at 6 different levels) and exercises on words, word elements, and word histories. Also an introductory record and 20 word wheels (build words – root, prefix, and suffix).	To improve vocabulary through multilevel, individualized instruction.
New Linguistic Block Series - Set 1L (K,G)	Scott, Foresman	K-3	K-3 4-6#	21 one inch plastic blocks with letters, timer, workbook, and teacher guide.	To motivate and increase understanding of our language through games of manipulating letter and word cubes. To strengthen awareness of
New Linguistic Block Series - Set 1W (K,G)	Scott, Foresman	K-3	K-3 4-6#	30 one inch plastic blocks with sight words and endings, timer, workbook, teacher guide.	phonemic-graphemic relationships, spelling, and sentence patterns. Ideal remedial way to learn basic sight words.
Reading for Concepts (WB)	Webster Division, McGraw-Hill	1.6-6.8	3-12	8 books containing short, contemporary nonfiction stories and narratives. Each contains fundamental ideas about living. Comprehension exercises develop critical reading (interpretive and literal).	To provide informative reading material while developing literal and critical comprehension skills. To be used in remedial, corrective, and/or developmental classes.
Magic Teacher Puzzle Plans (G)	Wilcox + Follett	1-2	K-3 4-6#	Puzzle pieces contain sight words to be matched with heading word that has same vowel sound.	To teach basic long and short sounds of vowels through games as motivation.

* severe remedial cases

Additional Materials

Benefic Press materials, including high interest, low level series such as *Invitation to Adventure, Cowboy Sam*, and *Button Family Adventure.*

Bowmar materials, including multisensory, high interest materials such as *Play the Game, Reading Incentive Series, Bowmar Language and Communication Program, ABC Serendipity, Highway Holidays Series*, and *Motorcyclopedia.*

Field Educational Publications materials, including *Wildlife Adventure Series* and *Cornerstone Readers.*

Speech to Print Phonics materials published by Harcourt Brace Javonovich.

Harper and Row series on *Reading in the Subject Matter Areas.*

BRIM Student's Kit — Teacher's Overview, published by Baldridge Reading Instruction Materials.

McGraw-Hill materials, including *Dr. Spello, Reading Clues, Reading for Concepts*, and *Conquests in Reading.*

Macmillan Reading Spectrum and *Decoding for Reading*, published by Macmillan.

Be A Better Reader series, published by Prentice-Hall.

Human Values Series, published by Steck-Vaughn, Austin, Texas.

The Name of the Game, published by New Dimensions in Education.

Encounters: Reality in Reading and Language Series, published by Cambridge Book Company.

Improving Reading Skills materials, published by Borg-Warner Educational Systems.

New Fat Cat Fun Books, published by Troubador Press.

NCTE volumes — *Adventuring with Books, Reading Ladders for Human Relations*, and *Book and Non-Book Media.*

American Library Association materials — *A Basic Book Collection for Elementary Grades; Aids in Selecting Books for Slow Learners; Subject Index to Books for Intermediate Grades, A Multimedia Approach to Children's Literature.*

Bibliography of High-Interest, Low-Vocabulary Books for Readers, published by Colorado Department of Education.

Fare for the Reluctant Reader, from Capital Area School Development Association, State University of New York, Albany.

A Place to Start: A Graded Bibliography for Children with Reading Difficulties, published by University of Missouri.

Releasing Children to Literature and *Where the Readers Are*, published by Dell.

Spache, *Good Reading for Poor Readers*, published by Garrard.

Schubert-Torgerson, *Improving the Reading Program*, published by William C. Brown Company.

Trends and Practices in Secondary School Reading, published by International Reading Association, Newark, Delaware.

Nonbook Materials from the Canadian Library Association.

Blueprints for Better Reading, published by H. W. Wilson.

A final source for middle school teachers selecting material for a reading program is the *High School Reading Taxonomy: A Guide to Materials*, available through the New York City Public Schools (6). The middle school teacher who has determined that a student is deficient in a particular skill can use this guide to select materials at the appropriate reading level to correct the deficiency. For example, if the student has difficulty in recognizing and identifying main ideas, the teacher will find in the section on comprehension, a variety of materials listed in the materials column, labeled easy (1.0 - 4.5), medium (4.5 - 6.0), or hard (6+). The teacher can then individualize instruction by selecting the most appropriate material based on both ability and interest.

CONCLUSION

A well-organized reading program in the middle school must have a variety of materials of both an instructional and a recreational nature. Without abundant materials reflecting both the variety of middle school children and the reading needs of the school in which they are to be used, the reading program becomes inefficient and falters.

As a final word, however, materials must be placed in perspective. The materials do not make the reading program. A much more important ingredient is the teacher, for it is how materials are used that is important. As desirable as materials are to the middle school reading program, the fact remains that they are only as good as the teacher who uses them.

References

1. Duffy, Gerald G., and George B. Sherman. *Systematic Reading Instruction*. New York: Harper and Row, 1972, 262, 267-270.

2. Emmett, Sharyn. *Reading Materials Resource List*. Fredonia, New York: Chautauqua BOCES, The Chautauqua Project, 1973.

3. Goodman, Kenneth et al. *Choosing Materials to Teach Reading*. Detroit: Wayne State University Press, 1966.

4. Mandell, Muriel, and Anita Dore. *High School Reading Taxonomy: A Guide to Materials — Project No. 2019*. New York: Bureau of Curriculum Development, 1972.

5. Sartain, Harry W. "Materials for Developing Reading Vocabulary and Word Attack Skills," University of Pittsburgh Conference Proceedings, No. 1811962, 107-120.

CHAPTER NINE

ORGANIZING
A READING LABORATORY PROGRAM

Hellen Ireland Guttinger
University of Florida

"I like reading lab in a-way and in a nother way I donot. Maby to moro I will. One resing is becose it tackes me away from Core* and that is the class I ned to be in the most and a 'nother reson is that I have been doin this all my life and I did not thank I wold have to do it en 6th grad and it never helpt me."

David's first day in reading lab
Spring 1973

The above comment reflects the feelings of many middle schoolers who find themselves in special reading classes. David may have a chance this time, however, because his class is a reading laboratory and, as such, has several unique features.

1. He has had a 45-minute individual reading conference with a teacher-counselor to talk about his reading scores and how he sees himself as reader. Possibly this accepting atmosphere and approach has made it all right to express his feelings (even though they include the negative) in writing.

2. He has set some personal reading goals for himself for the few weeks he will be in the laboratory. These goals are what he is competing against — not every other person in the class.

3. He will not be performing before peers in ways which may be embarrassing to him. Instead, his work is a private relationship involving laboratory materials and the support of trained teacher-counselors.

*Language Arts and Social Studies Class.

4. He is in a laboratory with his total Core class. No one has been identified as needing special help. A basic assumption has been made that all persons are on a continuum in reading that extends through their lives and all can improve in reading skills (*17*).

5. He will see his Core teacher working on her own reading skills while the class is in the laboratory. Hopefully, there will be safety in improving skills when the teacher does it too.

6. He will chart his own progress daily and see it for himself.

7. He will receive positive feedback from teacher-counselors in the laboratory, both verbally during the lab and written in his folder between his visits.

8. He will have an opportunity to teach other learners to use laboratory materials or machines, once he has mastered the technique.

9. Because the laboratory is located in the school's learning resources center, he will have an opportunity to go easily from skill building materials to library books where he can utilize the skills in a meaningful, personal way.

10. He will have an opportunity to choose reading lab as an enrichment activity later this spring and return for other intensive laboratory sequences during seventh and eighth grades. In addition, many of the materials and techniques used in lab will be utilized daily by his classroom teacher during his Core class time.

WHAT DAVID'S PROGRAM IS ALL ABOUT

David attends middle school at P. K. Yonge Laboratory School, University of Florida, Gainesville. His program is the product of several years' work.

The Beginnings

In Spring 1970, in response to a directive from the State University System, P. K. Yonge began a new role in research and development. After extensive diagnostic testing of students, one project was undertaken to design, research, evaluate, and disseminate findings concerning reading at the middle school level.

In designing the program, it was recognized that the needs of adolescents are very different from those of elementary school children. Therefore, it was assumed a program would not work if modeled after elementary type programs. Also, a remedial program for a small group of poor readers was not congruent with the school statement of values, beliefs, and goals specifying that only those activities which enhance a student's self-concept should be included in the school's curriculum. It was felt that an inherent weakness in the remedial approach results when the student's perception of himself as an inadequate reader is reinforced through a public announcement of his deficiencies.

By Fall 1970, a pilot program in developmental, individualized reading, modeled after the University of Florida's Reading and Study Skills Center program for undergraduate students, was initiated for all sixth and eighth grades.

The following is a description of this structured program in reading for middle school students. For many readers, it may represent a model for possible implementation. In the author's personal view, it is a tested model for change and a starting point — until growth indicates that changes are required.

The Reading Laboratory Program

At the beginning of the program, eighth graders were given pretests using the Diagnostic Reading Test (Triggs, upper level, form A). Sixth graders were given the Diagnostic Reading Test (lower level, form A).

After initial testing, teacher-counselors scheduled individual conferences to help each student look realistically at himself as a reader. An interpretation of his reading test scores was given on the basis of percentile ranks within his present grade placement. Grade levels were never used as a point of reference with the student. It was felt students associated *grade level* with *maturity level* and that the use of that term would defeat a primary goal of the school and the reading program — that all students have increasingly positive perceptions of themselves.

Goal-setting by the student was encouraged. He was assisted in developing an individualized program focusing on needs he felt were important. These included areas of strength as well as areas needing improvement. No set curriculum was followed and no grades were given. Responsibility for growth in reading skills was given the student. Care was exercised to insure success on an individual basis.

During the six-week laboratory experience, the teacher-counselors provided continuous guidelines for the effective use of materials and methods needed to implement change. Students corrected their own answer sheets and charted progress daily. Close communication with the student regarding his progress was maintained through personal contacts in the laboratory and written responses in his folder.

Posttests were given using the Diagnostic Reading Test, Form C (upper level for grade eight; lower level for grade six). In addition, each student completed a progress report and self-evaluation. The student's gains in reading achievement and his success in assuming the responsibility for improving reading skills were evaluated during a final individual conference between the student and his teacher-counselor.

The program was staffed by a teacher-counselor and a graduate assistant, both trained in developmental reading laboratory procedures. In addition, many middle school students assisted in the laboratory after they had completed the program and had been given additional special training.

Classroom teachers were in the laboratory with their students. They did not assign materials but became involved in student programs as catalysts or models. Attendance provided an opportunity for teachers to observe attitudes, work habits, and peer relationships as well as to become familiar with laboratory materials and activities. Some teachers participated in their own programs of self-improvement in the more complex skills of reading. Modeling behavior of teachers who chose to participate along with their students in the program was a positive influence.

The laboratory is located in the school's learning resources center and equipped with a variety of media such as cards, folders, programed readers, tapes, pacers, and other mechanical devices. Materials ranging from low elementary to college level are made accessible.

Initial Evaluation

After fifteen hours in the reading laboratory (spread over a six-week period) outcomes included the following:

1. Virtually all students improved their reading speed during the six weeks they were in the laboratory. Reading rates changed from an overall average of 274 words per minute to 337 words per minute, a 23 percent increase. At individual grade levels, increases ranged from 52 to 90 words per minute. Based on an institutional cycle design, these gains were three to five times mean annual gains. These are five to nine times the annual gains reported in the 1967 *Diagnostic Reading Test Norms.*

2. Seventy-two percent of all students significantly improved their comprehension and vocabulary skills (at least five months' progress gained during the eight weeks between testing).

3. Sixty-four and six-tenths of the below-average P. K. Yonge students gained 1.0 or more grades in reading comprehension.

4. Students who went through a second cycle of the program, after not doing well the first time, did not improve appreciably if the second cycle followed closely after the first one but did improve if there were a lapse of several weeks between cycles.

5. A year and one-half after participation, pupils had gained two years in comprehension and vocabulary.

RATIONALE

Each year approximately 50,000 pupils repeat grades in Florida's public schools at a cost of approximately $40 million (*13*). According to the U. S. Office of Education's *Digest of Educational Statistics* for the year 1970, one in four students entering the fifth grade in the United States fails to complete high school (*16*). One study of high school dropouts shows that 45 percent of those pupils who drop out are reading below sixth grade level (8). Penty's comprehensive study (11) of pupils not completing their high school career indicated that 90 percent had reading problems.

Other studies report large numbers of college students with reading difficulties (15). About 70 percent of the students entering community colleges have been identified as needing remedial help in language arts, of which reading is the major component (12). At the University of Florida, where almost no entering freshmen are below the seventieth percentile on statewide senior placement tests, hundreds of students seek help from the University Reading Clinic each year.

These data indicate that there is a need for planned continuation of a comprehensive and systematic developmental reading program for all pupils beyond elementary school. Formal instruction beyond the sixth grade is a need that has been recognized by persons who were not specialists in the area since the early sixties (14). The availability of federal funds in the mid-sixties stimulated growth and development of many reading programs through the middle and high school levels.

Much information is available concerning experimental practices in secondary reading (3, 4, 10). There is a remarkable diversity of programs now in operation. One survey (6) of practices in California schools in 1968 indicated the following trends:

1. Schools are becoming increasingly aware of the need for structured programs beyond the elementary grades.
2. Most efforts are initiated by the English departments.
3. Organization patterns are to establish a special reading class which meets daily for predetermined times.
4. Pupils are selected by test scores and teacher recommendations;
5. There are serious shortages of qualified personnel;
6. Practically nothing is being done to assist with the refinement of reading skills in the content areas.
7. Approximately one-third of the programs have a course of study; the remainder are described as haphazard or piecemeal.

At the present time, some state departments of education, national groups, and individual school systems are attempting to improve reading and reading instruction by preparing voluminous lists of behavioral objectives. While these are useful guides from which inferences can be made, this movement neglects one ingredient which has often resulted in successful teaching and learning. That ingredient is capitalizing on the purpose of the learner.

Studies, going back to Dewey's Laboratory School at the University of Chicago (9), Colling's *Experiment with a Project Curriculum* (5), the well-known eight-year study of thirty innovative secondary schools (1), plus a number of others, have all shown that when pupils have an opportunity to act on their own purposes and are guided by appropriate teaching, they exhibit marked superiority in learning over pupils taught by methods which require acting on the purposes of others. Further, even though good evaluation studies were seldom found, Alexander et al. (2) reported pupils of all ability levels, in most subject areas, and in grades seven through twelve have successful experiences with independent study where they are pursuing their own goals.

Recognizing that guideposts of research and objective data on individualized, developmental programs are needed before large-scale programs are implemented in middle schools, the pilot program developed and tested during the past three years at P. K. Yonge Laboratory School has attempted to meet this need. First year findings were reported to middle and high schools in the state of Florida in an April 1972 monograph (7). Since that time, 47 of Florida's 67 county school systems have sent representatives — including administrators, reading supervisors, teachers and counselors — to one-day, drive-in conferences and/or four-day workshops designed to assist schools interested in implementing similar programs.

The Need for Future Research

On the basis of interest expressed by many county systems, there is a need to test the effectiveness of this individualized developmental reading program with larger numbers of students in public school settings, and to seek additional or different means of improving the reading skills of those pupils who did not make significant progress during their laboratory period. One of these needs was met during the 1974 school year when four middle schools in Florida (approximately 2,000 students) were involved in field testing the P. K. Yonge reading laboratory model.

CONCLUSION: Whatever Happened to David?

David did not solve all of his reading problems during the six weeks of reading laboratory experience. In fact, he struggled through the posttest and asked permission to be retested because he "knew" he had improved more than his test indicated! For research purposes, the first test will be used. For David's purposes, he will take another test. In addition, David has chosen to continue to come to the reading laboratory as an enrichment activity for the remainder of this school year. While he is at the laboratory, reading personnel will continue to 1) focus on his purposes, 2) assist him in setting and carrying out his goals, 3) help him assume responsibility for his own growth in reading skills, 4) involve him in helping relationships with his peers, 5) assure his involvement in successes, and 6) assist him in charting and evaluating daily progress.

David wrote this evaluation of this progress following a post conference:

"readen lab tock up a lot of my time but it helpt me."

References and Notes

1. Aiken, Wilford M. *The Story of the Eight Year Study.* New York: Harper, 1942.

2. Alexander, William M. et al. *Independent Study in Secondary Schools.* New York: Holt, Rinehart and Winston, 1967.

3. Bamman, Henry A. et al. *Reading Instruction in the Secondary School.* New York: Longmans, Green, 1961.

4. Caldwell, Margueritte J. "Who Speaks for Reading?" *English Journal,* 56 (February 1967), 245-248.

5. Collings, Ellsworth. *An Experiment with a Project.* New York: Macmillan, 1923.

6. Graham, Harold Vernon. "Present Practices in Reading Programs in Secondary Schools in California with Suggestions for their Improvement," unpublished doctoral dissertation, University of Florida, 1968.

7. Guttinger, Hellen I., Vynce A. Hines, and Janet J. Larsen. "An Experiment in Developmental, Individualized Reading: An Alternative to Performance Contracting," Research Monograph I. Gainesville, Florida: P.K. Yonge Laboratory School, 1972.

8. Keppel, Francis. "Research: Education's Neglected Hope," *Journal of Reading,* 8 (October 1964).

9. Mayhew, Katherine Camp, and Anna Camp Edwards. *The Dewey School.* Appleton Century, 1936.

10. Newton, J. Roy. "Organizing and Scheduling a Developmental Reading Program," in J. Allen Figurel (Ed.), *Vistas in Reading,* 1966 Proceedings, Volume 11, Part 1. Newark, Delaware: International Reading Association, 1967, 153-155.

11. Penty, Ruth C. *Reading Ability and High School Dropouts.* New York: Bureau of Publications, Teachers College, Columbia University, 1956, 73-74.

12. Raygor, Alton L., Past President, National Reading Conference, University of Minnesota.

13. *St. Petersburg Times,* St. Petersburg, Florida, January 19, 1972.

14. Smith, Helen K. "Better Read, Comments on Development Reading in High School," *Curriculum Report #7.* Washington, D.C.: National Association of Secondary School Principals, 1965.

15. Smith, Nila Banton. *American Reading Instruction.* Newark, Delaware: International Reading Association, 1970.

16. *Statistical Abstract of the United States.* Washington, D.C.: United States Bureau of Census, 1972, 128.

17. Strang, Ruth. *Reading Diagnosis and Remediation.* Newark, Delaware: International Reading Association, 1968.

PART THREE

Teaching Reading in the Middle School

CHAPTER TEN

PROBLEMS AND PRINCIPLES IN TEACHING MIDDLE SCHOOL READING

Jane H. Catterson
University of British Columbia

As the previous chapters suggest, successful organization of a middle school reading program requires effective supervision and administration. Once the reading program has been organized, however, the teachers must utilize instructional strategies to make it work. These strategies are the focus of this and the following chapters.

There are numerous problems associated with reading instruction in the middle school. These can be classified into two categories: the problems that are old and have been with us for a long time and the problems that seem to be genuinely new and spring from real changes both in the content of school programs and in our understanding of the reading process. This chapter summarizes the most prevalent of these problems and elicits some principles of instruction which can serve as a foundation for the teaching of reading in the middle school.

OLD PROBLEMS

Old problems include 1) the central argument about whether reading is a tool or a basic subject, 2) certain prejudices among teachers about what constitutes suitable instruction at certain grade levels, 3) a tendency to substitute ritual use of commercial materials for programs with a sound conceptual base, and 4) an impatience with the characteristics of the age group.

Reading as a Tool or a Subject

The quarrel over whether every teacher should be a teacher of reading goes back essentially to the more basic problem of deciding whether reading is taught to improve achievement in content areas or because it forms a basic target for education. Those who take the "tool subject" stance look first at goals in social studies, science, and mathematics and select reading instruction goals which suit the content areas. Those who take the other stance look upon the content areas as no more than sources of material for teaching in reading. Thus far, it seems the tool subject proponents are in the ascendancy and it is out of that frame of reference that most present programs above the primary grades are being developed. But one should be aware of the fact that content area teachers are, at least subconsciously, aware of the other point of view and are very sensitive to any slight to their subject areas. Such implied slights account to some extent for the reluctance of many content teachers to learn how to help students in reading.

Prejudices Regarding Reading Instruction

The second common problem of middle school instruction in reading are the notions of teachers about what can or cannot be done with post-primary pupils. There seems to be a kind of folklore in the educational world that categorizes certain types of instruction as "primary grades."

One of these notions centers around the idea of "adjustment to level" of curriculum materials. Teachers will listen with some degree of interest to suggestions about how to help children read in a text teachers have placed on a reading list. But they frequently become stone deaf when the suggestion is made that certain books are totally unsuited to the reading level of the pupils they teach and should be dropped, at least for a specific group of pupils. Content teachers often feel that the selection of an easier text will so subvert their curricular goals that they refuse even to consider such an option. If pupils cannot cope with the selected materials, the teacher may lecture, or give notes, or make a filmstrip using the materials, rather than seeking appropriate substitutes.

Another concept, labeled primary school practice, is the "grouping" idea, at least if it implies a difference in curriculum for different parts of the same class. A teacher may encourage group projects where the final target behavior is about the same for each group. But the idea that groups within the same class might have different curriculum goals selected for them seems to be anathema to many teachers. They imagine that pupils expect goals to be the same for everyone and teachers become uncomfortable with having to explain a different standard for each group within a class.

Commercial Programs vs. Programs with a Conceptual Base

A third old problem results from lack of early program planning. Unfortunately, many reading programs are started too hastily; they limp along for awhile and then fail from sheer lack of point and direction. Generally speaking, such programs are products of staff anxiety to get started. The programs may have an unadequate conceptual base, with meagre information about reading and reading programs or the age group to be served. Such programs may start with a base in commercial materials without proper rationales for existence.

The reason for inadequate development of programs may be due to the shortage of trained reading personnel; the administrator – not fully aware of what he is doing and not entirely convinced of the need for careful planning – may use a kind of press-gang approach to staffing developmental reading classes. The unfortunate teacher assigned to this task may be new to teaching and have no specific knowledge of how to teach reading. This teacher may go to a reading conference armed with a list of skills culled from texts on reading and buy whatever materials appear to match his skills listing. This reading teacher, when asked about the goals of the reading program, may offer as an answer his list of commercial materials.

In contrast, good programs are discussed in terms of goals selected from across the curriculum. It would be foolish to suggest that there are easy solutions. It is probably untrue that "something is better than nothing." A hastily begun, ill-conceived program not only may do no good, it also may turn students against future reading programs.

Characteristic of the Age Group

It is always difficult to decide which of a number of problems is the most important, the most basic, or the most troublesome. Among the top contenders in the "instructional problem sweepstakes" is teacher impatience with the middle school age group – which is by turns volatile, restless, angry, lazy, quiet, relaxed, peaceable, sweet-tempered, and energetic. The middle school teacher naturally may long for the relative dependency of the younger child or the relative independence of the senior secondary school student and may attempt to persuade middle school pupils into one stance or the other. The fact is, however, that teacher attitude and motivation are very important variables in the achievement of school pupils. If a teacher thinks a pupil can learn, the pupil will learn. Alternatively, if a teacher is convinced that a pupil is poorly adjusted or hopelessly weak in basic skills, any instructional program may be foredoomed to failure. A teacher may be coaxed into trying new techniques, he even may be captivated by obvious pupil improvement and become a convert. But this experiment may be dangerous and anyone trying to persuade a reluctant teacher to participate in a new reading program should be aware of the potential dangers.

Summary of Old Problems

A close look at the four old problems discussed makes it evident that they are all aspects of the same problem; that is, each implies a view of the primary grades as a place to teach basic skills and as the place where there is time to be less than serious about the business of education. In this view, once a child is nine- or ten-years-old he is ready to start the serious, content-oriented business. The United States teacher of reading often is surprised to find the strict academic view of education surviving after thirty years of what has been called the "democratization" of the schools. Canadians are not surprised, for the broadening of the curriculum that seems to go with technological development began with them only ten or twelve years ago and the struggle has barely begun. If the United States' experience is an example, the struggle in Canada has many more years to go.

It must be added that one should probably not wish too hard for the time when the "hard line" disappears entirely from education. We are often accused of throwing out the baby with the bath water and of teaching more and more about less and less. The accusation is not unfounded.

NEW PROBLEMS

Not all problems of instruction have a long history. Two problem areas have appeared in the past ten years: problems that arise from major changes in content area teaching, and the problems of doubts about how to utilize recent research in the areas of linguistics and psychology. Actually, each of these problems has several facets.

Changes in Content Area Teaching

Changes in content area teaching have been tremendous in the past ten years, with both texts and methods affected. Since the advent of discovery learning, school children have been inundated with printed material when once they had a single text to master; and they are expected to read widely in many books in an independent learning approach, where once they were guided, structured, and drilled in the acquisition of a basic set of facts and skills. Add to this the fact that many books are written in language patterns quite different from the patterns in which social studies and science books were written a few years ago and one realizes that the new curricula present quite new problems in the teaching of reading.

Consider that content books are being written in new patterns. Until recently, both social studies and science books were written in a simple informational pattern. For this logical exposition pattern, reading specialists recommend reading by the Survey-Question-Read method — Robinson's technique (12) designed to search out main ideas first and details later. Although some adjustments are suggested to accommodate experiments to be read in the science texts, on the whole the SQR technique works well for information-oriented materials.

Mathematics presents a different set of reading problems, with both explanations and problems requiring reading guidance. In the past, teachers seemed to present explanations orally and leave only word problems to be dealt with by the children independently. Reading specialists, therefore, developed a set of guide questions (see Chapter 16) to fill the bill and to be used with the word problems of the science books. This greatly changed set of materials in science, math, and social studies posed new problems for those providing reading guidance. New science, with its proposition-proof kind of writing pattern does not yield its meaning well within the SQR method; no one has developed a systematic way of getting at a lab text; the bulk of the problems in new math are not word problems; and even the social studies book, although it retains its information-centered pattern, has a new look and presents much more graphic material than it did formerly. Does this graphic material reduce the reading problem or increase it? Certainly it *changes* the problem and such changes must be taken into account in the teaching of reading in social studies.

Printed material to be used has also changed. Consider the change in the curriculum materials as "discovery learning" has become the accepted target behavior. At one time, mastery of a single text was considered a desirable goal. Reading specialists said that children should be helped to read a single text, be given vocabulary practice, be guided in silent reading, and be helped with study notetaking. Now many texts are made available for children to read; the information is to be used in discussion periods or for reports and research papers. New problems which result may concern what vocabulary should be taught, whether one should obtain at least one text from which to teach the basic reading skills, whether study notetaking is worth teaching, and how much time should be given to guiding the production of reports and research papers. Teachers may be torn between their desire to put students into contact with many interesting topics and their suspicion that it is foolish to continue to assign wide reading and reporting when students are unable to perform these tasks adequately. The teachers may ask, How much time should be devoted to teaching the skills of discovery learning and how much to discovery learning itself? Are they different?

A third problem relates to the fact that schools have signed only an uneasy truce with the discovery method idea. At an ASCD Conference, Bruner (*3*) seemed to suggest that he was "backing off" from the discovery approach, having concluded that the approach assumes certain student motivation middle-class values not apparent in all schools. Ausubel (*1*) seemed to be convinced from the beginning that discovery as a broad overall approach is inefficient for older pupils. We must be aware, then, that although certain curriculum changes may be new, more may come shortly. Reading teachers would do well to be flexibly ready.

Utilizing Recent Research

To add to the problems of new curricula, we have the problem of new research which is difficult to put into practice. The bulk of this research has been in linguistics and psychology. Some linguists are suggesting that a child's oral language is so basic and close to him that rejection of his language represents rejection of the child himself. It is proposed, therefore, that books and other instructional materials be prepared in the reader's natural language. While the idea has appeal, we must ask certain questions. Would we be preparing certain segments of society to read specialized forms of writing that would be unlikely to be accepted by the scholarly community? Would we be shutting some people out from the formalized language of literacy which, at the upper levels, is quite unlike natural spoken language? Can we utilize the linguists' research on oral language in an instructional program?

The area of transformational grammar is an area of linguistic theory little used by reading people. Chomsky's work has had an impact on the field of writing and some research has been done in exploring the implications for comprehension of the deep structure notion. Fagan (6), Robertson (11), and Smith (14) concluded that exercises directed at analyzing written sentence patterns would be valuable in improving reading comprehension of sentences. However, that research has not yet been reflected in the teaching materials on the market.

Similarly, Pike (10) and Christensen (4) have been working in the field of rhetoric — structures in English beyond the sentence — as an avenue to improving composition, but only a little work has been done by reading specialists to explore the significance of their work in teaching comprehension of paragraphs.

Some research in the area of psychology and measurement may mislead us. Certain standardized reading tests yield scores that may be seriously misleading when taken literally and applied as having valid relationship to materials used at particular grade levels. We have discovered that standardized test scores seem to overestimate reading level by at least a full grade (8) and some researchers suggest that only cloze tests (9) will give us answers about student performance in specific books. But can we, given discovery learning and multiple tests, hope to utilize such information in the average school situation?

Obviously, this listing of recent research could be much longer. The items included are selected as being among the most interesting and perhaps most in need of attention.

FUNDAMENTAL PRINCIPLES OF INSTRUCTION

What principles for good instruction can be elicited from the foregoing statement of problems? It is proposed that the instructional problems in middle school reading will be reduced to a manageable minimum if the program is based on the following principles. Instructional programs should 1) be research based, 2) be problem centered in the content areas, 3) adhere to a principle of planned obsolescence, 4) discard all preconceptions about what is suitable for any specific population, 5) adopt a stance that regards the characteristic volatility of the age group as a strength rather than a weakness, and 6) implement instruction which is both differentiated and enriched.

A Research Base

If programs are to have a sound conceptual base, they must be built on what we know from research about the reading process, existing good practice and programs, the characteristics and needs of the age group, and national curriculum goals for the age group. Added to broad-based research must be local research and assessment of existing practice and programs in the local schools, the characteristics and needs of the local age group, and local community goals for the age group. Without both kinds of basic knowledge, the foundations of a program are likely to be shaky.

It will be obvious that what is being urged is a serious attempt by both teachers and administrators to look at the literacy problem full-face and recognize it as a problem that cannot be solved with cosmetic half-measures. Proper funding, trained teachers, and energetic leadership involved in constant study of the field are demanded.

Problems Centering in the Content Areas

The second principle states that programs should center around real problems in the content areas, use real books as vehicles for instruction and include intradisciplinary planning with all subject area teachers. The problem of limiting instruction to commercial packages has already been discussed. Such packages have a role to play in helping content teachers become accustomed to teaching reading and to structuring their thinking as they guide students through instruction. Once teachers have become familiar with strategies and have had some practice in using them, they can teach reading in their own selected texts and gradually move away from the need for canned exercises. Unless real books become the vehicle for teaching and real tasks become the focus of instruction, students will fail to make the connection between reading and study processes.

Equally important is an ongoing dialogue between and within subject areas. Berkey (2) reported that in her situation, it was decided that English teachers should do basic teaching in outlining first and that other teachers would capitalize on the skill later within certain guidelines all had agreed upon; and Gates (7) reported on interdisciplinary teaching of the novel. Such concerted action makes a distinct impact on students and the cumulative effect is greater than might be expected.

Planned Obsolescence

A third principle for instruction, and probably the hardest to adhere to, is that it should be based on a principle of planned obsolescence. It should use current materials, focus on current problems, and avoid expenditure of large sums for equipment or materials that may not be of long range value. Actually, this principle is based on awareness of the fact that changes in information in all of the subject fields come rapidly and printed materials may be outdated in a short time. Add to this the fact that discovery methods already have had some doubts cast on them and one becomes aware that reading programs must keep in mind the past, the present, and the future.

Discarding Preconceived Notions About the Suitability of Certain Ideas

The notion that certain types of instructional practice belong to the primary school can be a handicap in developing post-primary programs. Good middle school programs will operate on the principle that no practice belongs to any specific level of education but should be utilized if it seems to produce a desirable result.

Capitalizing on the Characteristics of the Age Group

As a final principle, it is suggested that the volatility of the age group should be considered a strength rather than a weakness. The budding and maturing adolescent has problems enough in coping with society without being faced with school instruction that seeks to curb his energy and narrow his focus. Planners of the instructional program should utilize the uniqueness of the age group and channel its energizing force into creative instruction. Participating teachers should become acquainted with their middle school children and learn to enjoy working with them; no less involvement will do.

Criteria for Practice

Teachers need a kind of matrix of factors to consider in rating their daily lessons and no model seems more complete or more clear cut than the one presented by Durrell (5).

Essentially, Durrell's scheme is based on the idea that, given an interested teacher and a suitable choice of content, lessons should provide for either differentiation of instruction or enrichment of instruction or both. He enlarged on these two basic ideas in this pattern:

A. Differentiation of Instruction
 1. Adjust to level of skills ability
 2. Adjust to strength and weakness in skills learning
 3. Provide for self-direction in selecting practices
 4. Provide for varied progress rates

B. Enrichment of Instruction
 1. Assure understandings: facts, concepts, principles
 2. Integrate learning into thinking and action
 3. Develop initiative and independence
 4. Assure growth in personal-social abilities

Scribner (13) used the above scale as a basis for directing teachers' attention to possible strengths and weaknesses in their daily classroom lessons and found that, over the space of a year, it helped greatly in the improvement of instruction. The scale apparently gave point and direction to teacher-consultant discussion of instruction while reducing the emotional loading that can interfere with discussion when personality, manner, dress, or voice are factors in evaluation.

CONCLUSION

Reading instruction in the middle school is fraught with difficulties and problems. However, if teachers remain vigilant for the problems and implement the basic principles described above as well as the strategies described in subsequent chapters, reading will be taught effectively in the middle school.

References

1. Ausubel, David. "In Defense of Verbal Learning," *Readings in School Learning*. New York: Holt, Rinehart and Winston, 1969.
2. Berkey, Sally. "Reading and Study Skills in a High School District," *Reading Teacher,* 16 (November 1962), 102-103.
3. Bruner, Jerome S. "The Process of Education Reconsidered or Ten Years After," paper delivered at ASCD Conference, 1971.
4. Christensen, Francis. "A Generative Rhetoric of the Paragraph," *Notes Toward a New Rhetoric.* New York: Harper and Row, 1967, 68-69.
5. Durrell, Donald D. "Challenge and Experiment in Teaching Reading," in J. Allen Figurel (Ed.), *Challenge and Experiment in Reading,* Proceedings of the International Reading Association, 7, 1962. New York: Scholastic Magazines.
6. Fagan, William. "Transformations and Comprehension," *Reading Teacher,* 25 (November 1971), 169-173.
7. Gates, Patricia. "Interdisciplinary Novel Reading," *Reading Teacher,* 15 (February 1962), 361.
8. Lockerbie, David. "The Relationships Between Three Methods of Measuring Readability," unpublished master's thesis, University of Saskatchewan, Saskatoon, 1968.
9. Pennock, Clifford D. "Selecting Instructional Materials to Meet Students' Reading Performance Levels," *Alberta Journal of Educational Research,* 19 (March 1973), 30-36.
10. Pike, Kenneth S. "Beyond the Sentence," *The Study of Units Beyond the Sentence.* Champaign, Illinois: National Council of the Teachers of English, 1964.
11. Robertson, Jean. "Pupil Understanding of Connectives in Reading," *Reading Research Quarterly,* 3 (Spring 1968), 387-416.
12. Robinson, Francis P. *Effective Study.* New York: Harper and Sons, 1961.
13. Scribner, Harvey B. "Construction and Evaluation of a Scale to Rate Teaching Services in Grades Four, Five, and Six," unpublished doctoral dissertation, Boston, University, 1960.
14. Smith, W. L. "The Effect of Transformed Sentence Structures on Reading," in Carl Braun (Ed.), *Language, Reading, and the Communication Process.* Newark, Delaware: International Reading Association, 1971, 53-62.

CHAPTER ELEVEN

HELPING THE
DISABLED READER

Richard W. Burnett
University of Missouri at St. Louis

A great and continuing American educational tragedy is that our schools are continuing to release large numbers of pupils at all levels who read below the minimal levels of functional literacy. This tragedy is compounded when these same pupils perceive their schooling as a waste, become alienated, and finally contribute to a dissonance which may interfere with the school's efforts to educate students at all levels. Perhaps the middle school concept can be a positive factor in alleviating the problem. This chapter explores ways in which the middle school, because of its unique nature, can come closer to delivering on the promise of American educators to teach every individual to read.

THE DISABLED READER AND REMEDIAL EFFORTS

Historically, the disabled reader has been defined as one who functions significantly below his expected level of reading achievement as related to relative mental abilities and past opportunity to learn. Two texts that provide the major classifications of reading problems, as well as techniques for diagnosing and remedying them, are Harris' *How to Increase Reading Ability* (2) and Bond and Tinker's *Reading Difficulties: Their Diagnosis and Correction* (1).

Many attempts have been made to understand why certain pupils from all socioeconomic groups become underachievers in reading. In the middle 1950s, it was loudly trumpeted that reading failure was largely due to inadequate approaches to beginning reading instruction. Pupils simply were not taught properly in grade one. Extensive studies done in the 1960s tended to negate that belief, since it was demonstrated that a sizable minority of pupils fell behind their peers in measured reading performance regardless of the approaches used in beginning instruction.

The Cause of Reading Disability

A great percentage of the disabled readers in American schools might be described simply as normal children who have fallen behind the norm at which most children master the word recognition skills in reading. Perhaps these disabled readers are developmentally incapable of responding to instruction in the visual or auditory aspects of word recognition. Unfortunately for them, heavy emphasis is placed on the mechanical skills of teaching reading in the primary grades, with emphasis decreasing past grade one. Furthermore, the stigma of inadequacy or failure is attached to these learners at an early stage in their school experience and upon reaching middle grades, they must compete with more able learners who already have mastered the mechanical aspects of reading and are automatically utilizing basic skills in reading for pleasure and information. The slower developer may be called "disabled" and may be singled out for special remedial help. Soon he is aware of his deficiencies and becomes sensitive to his inability to meet teacher and parent expectations. Ironically, since reading is the key element in so many areas of the curriculum, this child's reading deficit may result in a form of punishment through low grades due to failures to do tasks which were quite impossible in the first place because of his reading deficit.

Principles of Remediation

Whatever the reasons for the existence of the reading problem initially, by the time a pupil is in the intermediate grades, there is good evidence that he will show continued reading growth if he has continuing instruction in reading. The basic strategy for improving his reading status is not particularly complicated. It calls for placing in his hands material that 1) is of interest to him, 2) is written in a vocabulary that does not overtax his word recognition proficiency, and 3) contains concepts within his range of understanding. While the learner is reading to satisfy some need or to accomplish a purpose such as enjoying a good story or securing information, the teacher strives to improve the learner's word recognition skills, expand his vocabulary, and develop his ability to comprehend or understand what he reads. The intent is to provide ample opportunity for the learner to read and be reinforced in desirable habit patterns while reading.

Some general principles of remediation follow: 1) accept the reader at his level of performance; 2) utilize the reader's intrinsic interests when presenting reading-related learning tasks; 3) insure immediate learner success and maintain a favorable balance of successes and failures; 4) illuminate, perhaps even magnify, each gain the learner makes; and 5) avoid unfavorable comparisons of the learner's performance with that of other pupils.

Remedial reading teachers know that offering remedial assistance in an isolated setting is not effective. Helping the disabled reader in any significant manner calls for an interrelationship between the remedial help the pupil receives and the instructional program he experiences throughout the school day. The frustration in remedial reading is that often the positive features outlined above can be applied only for the limited time the pupil is in the remedial setting, while the rest of the school day is spent in classes where: 1) he is expected to perform at grade level in reading; 2) the type of reading he is asked to do is not of interest to him; 3) he is directed to complete reading and writing assignments that he is not equipped to complete; 4) every task he attempts turns out to be incomplete or incorrectly done; and 5) the quality of his work is compared unfavorably with that of others.

THE MIDDLE SCHOOL — NEW OPTIONS

In principle, the middle school should provide the ultimate learning situation which every remedial reading teacher seeks. Characteristics include: 1) a focus on the needs of the pupil as an individual rather than a focus on arbitrarily determined content areas; 2) flexibility in staffing and scheduling that enables pupils with learning problems to be in smaller groups and receive instructional attention from specialists; 3) provision for staff planning time and intercommunication to encourage close coordination of all instructional efforts for problem learners; and 4) assessment and record keeping that enables teachers to evaluate pupils on the basis of their individual patterns of growth rather than on normative comparisons.

The middle school is a type of structure where the arbitrary lockstep or graded-ladder concept can be played down by those teaching in the school. Subject matter specialists, since they are working with younger children and instructing in coordinated team situations with reading teachers, can modify their grade level normative reading expectations and provide differentiated reading and writing assignments consistent with what their individual students are able to do. In the middle school, the concepts which are important to a particular subject area can be presented by a specialist using demonstration techniques, films, filmstrips, field trips, and various activity projects. The traditional self-contained classroom teacher often feels he must depend on his students, reading the available textbooks because he either does not know the field well enough to use other devices or he lacks time to prepare and use other instructional devices. The middle school teacher need not be dependent on textbooks and on the lecture-discussion approach in presenting his course. The middle school teacher's orientation (if he understands and accepts the middle school guidelines in contrast to the traditional secondary school's mode of operation) is to utilize his expertise in his content discipline to develop students' awareness of their own world and to develop their general language and reasoning abilities. The content teacher in a middle school should be aware that pupils will be exposed more than once to the content areas. The teachers' first concern, then, should center around the processes of science, social studies, or mathematics. These processes are of consequence to ten- to fourteen-year-olds as they attempt to understand themselves in relation to their current experiences in a complex world.

The middle school pupil usually is not career oriented nor is he ready to single out and pursue an area of study through senior high school and college. A ten- to fourteen-year-old's perception of his world may change rapidly. He becomes susceptible to peer pressure, and peer group interests are easily influenced by current fads and media-related topics of interest. The middle school boy may exhibit excessive interest in ice hockey during the hockey season. The middle school girl may become obsessed with a current teeny-bopper singing idol. In terms of susceptibility to peer pressure and media determined interests, disabled readers do not differ from the high achiever.

SUGGESTIONS FOR THE MIDDLE SCHOOL READING TEACHER

Too often middle grade pupils are singled out because of reading difficulties and assigned to special class sections where they spend their time working with kits of reading materials and sets of skill building workbooks. Such reading classes are based on a distorted understanding of assumptions that have some validity.

Use of Materials

One such assumption is that disabled readers need to practice reading in materials at "their level." Science Research Associate's *Reading Laboratories*; Barnell-Loft's *Getting the Main Idea, Drawing Conclusions*, or *Using the Context*; and Teacher's College Press' *Standard Test Lessons in Reading* are all examples of skill building exercises that can be fitted to the reading level of disabled readers at middle grade levels. Unfortunately, when such materials become the *total* program, the principle of reading at level is completely overbalanced by the material's cold impersonality and lack of relevance to the world the reader sees around him.

The Role of Oral Reading

A second related assumption is that by the middle grades, readers should be doing all silent reading because silent reading excellence is immeasurably more important to the mature reader than oral reading proficiency. Here again, a valid assumption may be used to justify practices that are detrimental to reading improvement. The disabled reader, whose problem is likely to be grounded in inefficient word recognition skills, is often reinforced only in bad habit patterns as he reads silently in skill building materials. His ability to answer multiple choice questions and to keep a record of an acceptable percentage of correct answers to these questions may not be related at all to the fluency, rhythm, and accuracy of his actual reading.

Reading teachers should be advised that oral reading, judiciously practiced, is an indispensable tool to use in instruction of the poor reader who needs to establish a workable pattern of word recognition approaches. Oral reading rhythm and fluency are valid indicators of silent reading performance. Some able learners can dispense with oral reading practice as they acquire silent reading skills. Disabled readers in the middle school range, however, cannot dispense with directed oral reading activities. To do so may limit them forever to hit-or-miss patterns of inaccurate silent reading performance.

Often, the disabled middle grade reader cannot maintain attention for long periods of silent reading; and when he is compelled to do so, he resorts to skipping or miscalling words, guessing at answers, and generally reinforcing other undesirable habit patterns. The basic teaching strategy to alter his pattern of behavior is to wean him into the silent reading of increasingly longer segments of material by interspersing oral and silent reading gradually. The teacher should ask carefully directed questions preceding the reading and afterward he should check for reading accuracy. An inappropriate strategy for the reader who is still erratic in word recognition approaches is the old practice of introducing an article to be read silently in its entirety and later to be reread orally in response to specific questions. At low levels of performance, such as a sixth grader with second grade level skills, only a sentence or two read silently may be appropriate.

The nature of teacher directed questioning as it relates to the difficulty of the reading material can also influence the fluency of a given reader. Preceding reading, the use of questions containing the exact words of the excerpt to be read seems to enable the learner to read difficult material with more acceptable fluency than otherwise might be expected.

Choice of Reading Material

The substance of what is read must be considered along with the readability of material. Babyish-appearing books or artificially written, vocabulary controlled materials are not likely to interest middle grade pupils. The reading teacher should appreciate the legitimate value of using popular or library reading material as part of the reading improvement program. Disabled seventh and eighth grade readers who were carefully helped through a paperback version of *Jonathan Livingston Seagull* at the peak of that bestseller's popularity, enjoyed a new status of participation in the "real world of reading" which never could be realized through typical anthologies of skill builders.

Recreational Reading

It is common practice in middle grades to encourage recreational reading during part of the time assigned for general reading improvement. To keep a wide variety of attractive books (especially paperbacks) in the classroom and provide opportunity for reading without teacher intervention, are laudable practices for those readers who have a level of independence and can read accurately and with a high degree of understanding. It is hard for many middle grade teachers to accept the fact that lengthy free-reading periods for severely disabled cases actually may be counterproductive. These learners may not have developed independent reading levels and to encourage them to spend significant amounts of school time in recreational reading is not only to ask them to waste time but also to engage in the very practices that must be eliminated before they can move ahead to mature reading status. Middle grade reading specialists cannot assume that everyone learns to read just by reading; all students do not.

Content Material

Content material from subject matter classes is a source for legitimate learning activities in any reading improvement program, especially in a middle school setting. Reading teachers should solicit vocabulary lists and reading assignments from content teachers to serve as part of the ingredients of the reading class. This is not to imply that the reading specialist should teach the science or social studies concepts, but the use of current topics and assignments from the content classes can be used to demonstrate the interrelationship between the training in the reading class and the reading called for in other settings. After all, science terms call for the application of word analysis principles, and what better words to use for a lesson in structural analysis or syllabication than those from the current science unit? Such an effort keeps the reading specialist alerted to his dual responsibility of helping disabled readers survive with whatever level of skills they possess while also upgrading their overall reading achievement.

Listening as an Instructional Technique

Finally, the reading specialist needs to remain aware of the place of listening training as an adjunct to reading improvement activities for the disabled reader. Although the nature of the students' reading problems necessitates that reading practice focus on his attempts to pick up literal meaning, the areas of drawing inferences and critically evaluating ideas must continue to receive attention. If the reader's mechanical reading skills are very low, critical thinking processes usually applied in reading may have to be presented and reviewed for him through listening avenues. Listening and reading practice materials should be selected at equivalent difficulty levels. Transfer of training is most likely to occur when the two learning situations are similar. Disabled readers very often have difficulty applying a principle learned in one setting to similar situation in another somewhat different setting. The special reading teacher's listening improvement efforts should aim at minimizing problems in transfer. Recording discussions of reading assignments and replaying them so that questions and comments can be classified as to type by the students themselves would be one use of listening to sharpen reading comprehension skills.

SUGGESTIONS FOR THE CONTENT TEACHER

While the reading specialist assumes the greatest amount of responsibility in correcting the reading deficiencies of the severely disabled reader, the content teacher can also help. In cooperation with the reading teacher, the content

Helping the Disabled Reader

teacher can implement several strategies which will give the disabled reader a better chance of surviving and ultimately of becoming a competent reader.

Setting Reasonable Expectations

The subject matter teacher must understand that poor readers are not malingerers when they are unable to perform reading tasks which most children can perform. The content teacher must learn what each student can do and must avoid criticism of his crippled readers. Once a teacher identifies the capabilities of individual pupils, he then can establish performance objectives and expect reasonable standards of accuracy in return. In setting these expectations, the content teacher should make use of a pupil's past experiences as reported by the reading specialist and other teachers. One recommended device in a content class is simply to give, at an early meeting, a reading text assignment with accompanying questions. The teacher calls each individual to his desk to read excerpts quietly from the selection. The teacher can quickly differentiate those who can and cannot cope, at least mechanically, with the reading and he can obtain some estimate of the range of proficiency within the group.

Coordination with the Reading Program

In introducing technical vocabulary, the content teacher should make a concerted effort to use the same diacritical marks that are used by the reading and language arts teachers. He should supply these teachers with vocabulary lists accompanying each unit and explain the nature of the reading assignments. Hopefully, these assignments will be differentiated based on the reading performance of those in the classes; nevertheless, the reading teachers should use them as a basis for correlating the efforts to teach individual pupils, especially those with problems that set them apart from the group norm.

Grouping

Where the reading of certain text material is deemed essential, there is nothing wrong with grouping better readers with weaker readers, asking the fluent readers to read the material aloud, and arranging whole group and small group discussion of the concepts. Other techniques include tape recording a better reader's oral reading of assigned chapters and encouraging disabled readers to read silently along with the tape while listening with headphones. Differentiated assignments for poor readers might require them to read only selected key passages. The important thing is to distinguish between inability to understand the concepts and inability to read the concepts in the first place. A teacher should be clear in his own mind whether he is making an effort to teach a subject-related concept or is attempting to improve the content reading ability of his students. For many of the students, the concept will have to be presented through some avenue other than reading. In addition, varied materials or differentiated levels of questions will have to be given to the class if each individual is to make some gain from the reading task (3).

Encouraging Transfer

The content teacher who is concerned about improving the reading of his middle grade pupils will relate his discussion and other teaching presentations directly to the assigned reading segments, illustrating how the pupils might have gleaned this fact or that principle from a specific bit of reading. Here again, the teacher is not assuming that transfer of training automatically occurs but is continually showing how learnings conveyed in one medium or setting are related to learnings derived through reading sources. The disabled reader, especially, needs this explanation of how sources tie together since this reader's problem often is the inability to relate one learning with another.

Selecting Materials

The content teacher who really wants to encourage reading for reading's sake in his subject area must seek reading materials that vary in readability; he must select some books which are less complex, better illustrated, and which utilize a less difficult vocabulary to convey valid principles. Weak readers may be encouraged to read these easier materials; but the content instructor should remain alert to the fact that there are likely to be some in his classes who will not be able to read any material presented without direct assistance, no matter how easy it appears to the teacher.

Testing

A final area is that of testing or measuring whether concepts have been mastered. Poor readers are also poor spellers and writers. Questions will have to be read aloud for the disabled readers and possible answers will need to be listed on the board or provided on the answer sheet so that spelling does not interfere in the student's answering correctly.

CONCLUDING STATEMENT

A sober look at reality dictates that middle school enthusiasts remain aware that devices such as team teaching and modular scheduling in no way change the nature of the task called for in teaching reading to those who are least able to inductively master the mechanics of reading. The middle school may provide a climate where basic, good teaching practices are more likely to flourish than in other school structures designed for the ten- to fourteen-year-old age range. If disabled readers are better served in the middle school, it will be because skill oriented reading teachers and subject matter oriented content teachers coordinate their efforts so that the best features of each orientation are brought to bear on the needs of problem learners. An empathetic teacher, who exhibits a workmanlike. dedication to meeting the needs of they pupils, cannot be supplanted by complex organizational schemes and lists of good intentions. The middle school concept is still young and a clear record has not yet been established regarding its impact. Happiness is seeing this venture live up to its promise.

Helping the Disabled Reader

References

1. Bond, Guy L., and Miles A. Tinker. *Reading Difficulties: Their Diagnosis and Correction*. New York: Appleton-Century-Crofts, 1973.
2. Harris, Albert J. *How to Increase Reading Ability*. New York: David McKay, 1970.
3. Herber, Harold L. *Teaching Reading in Content Areas*. Englewood Cliffs, New Jersey: Prentice-Hall, 1970.

CHAPTER TWELVE

A TECHNIQUE FOR TEACHING WORD IDENTIFICATION IN THE CONTENT AREAS

Ernest Adams
Mott Institute for Community Improvement, Michigan State University

Difficulty in word recognition — the inability to identify and pronounce words without hesitation, he probably possesses the prerequisite decoding skills middle school. This deficiency must be corrected. Several suggestions are made in the previous chapter and an additional technique is offered here.

BACKGROUND TO WORD IDENTIFICATION

It is difficult to present new statements or data which will assist middle school teachers in instructing their pupils in word recognition techniques. For decades, reading scholars have theorized about word recognition for pre-schoolers, first graders, adolescents, the verbally handicapped, and the culturally deprived. Each theory proposes a new gimmick which teachers saddle and ride with enthusiastic faith. But, as the ride becomes familiar and saddle sores develop, the theories are discarded in frustration and confusion. This leads to turned-off learners who are accused of laziness, innate ignorance, ethnic stupidity, or dyslexic tendencies.

One of the difficulties is that word identification is a complex task involving skills a learner must master if he is to become a proficient reader. These skills can be grouped in the two categories of word recognition and word analysis. As Duffy and Sherman (1) state, "A reader memorizes some words — learns to instantly identify them at sight — and this is a recognition skill. Other words must be examined for known elements and then pronounced. This requires an analysis of words."

Although a significantly large number of students acquire these skills with no apparent difficulty, many others do not develop word identification skills easily. One has to look no further than any given middle school classroom to discover pupils whose eyes are continually cloudy with confusion as they attempt to look at written symbols and provide accurate oral responses.

University libraries are well stocked with research reports in the area of word identification development. The bulk of these efforts investigate various traits of the learner and his level of achievement or the desirability of one method of instruction as opposed to another. However, these attempts have not significantly improved the instructional behavior of classroom teachers as they try to elicit proper responses from their pupils. Nor have the voluminous reports on various methods clarified the issue of which mode of instruction is proper. So many approaches have been billed as *the* way, *the* truth, and *the* life that it is no wonder teachers and pupils are confused.

This chapter does not attempt to provide a detailed report on phonetics, whole word recognition, and the various commercial programs which could be used. The intent is to provide middle school content area teachers with a technique for helping their students identify words, even though these teachers may have little interest in providing instruction in the basic skills. (This is no criticism of content teachers; they naturally tend to be content-oriented rather than skill-oriented.) The intricate details of the various facets of word recognition are avoided because poor readers at the middle school level are often so turned off by their disability that they are unable to give the task the required psychological attention while also trying to learn the content subject. Such students have turned off their "Dick and Jane receptors" and they need specialized help which the content teacher is unprepared to provide.

Many deficient readers are receptive to the content which their teachers present; they are interested in history and science. The conflict arises when the teacher says, "Now, class, turn to page 24 and read . . . ." Since the student is unable to pronounce some of the words on page 24 and subsequent pages, he resists this activity.

While the content teacher cannot eliminate completely such word recognition difficulties, there are psychological elements that can be manipulated to assist pupils in learning the correct association between the printed word and its oral response. These elements are applicable to content area classrooms and are called *meaningfulness* and *familiarization training.*

THEORETICAL ROLE OF FAMILIARIZATION

Simply stated, *meaningfulness* and *familiarization* refer to the degree of meaning or the amount of familiarity which the student associates with what he is to learn. The more familiar he is with a concept, the easier he will learn that concept.

Several researchers support this notion. Underwood and Schulz (*3*), felt that the familiarization process made responses more available during the learning trials that followed, while Mandler (*2*), sees pretraining on the desired response as an exercise that decreases the probability of error as what is to be learned becomes more integrated or familiar to the subject. Such research indicates that familiarization reduces the number of alternatives to the learned one and reduces the separate information elicited by the components of the familiarized item, thereby making them more integrated and available during learning. This is illustrated in Figure 1 in which the words shown within the circle are the ones to be learned by the subject; familiarization training isolates the words to be learned within the circle of the student's memory, excluding all other possible responses. Hence, the learning is facilitated.

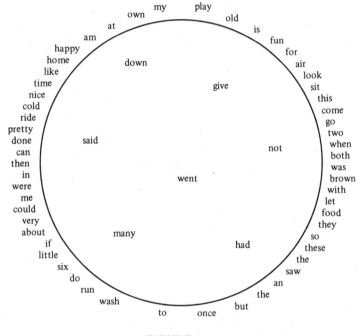

FIGURE 1

The theory indicates that stimulus items to be learned become more distinctive as they become familiar. This conclusion leads one to hypothesize that a student might learn to identify a written word more readily if he were familiar with the shape or meaning of the word. This hypothesis, tested by the author in 1969, indicated that words which are highly meaningful are learned more readily than less meaningful words and that familiarization training resulted in familiar words being learned with greater ease than mere unfamiliar words.

APPLICATION IN CONTENT CLASSROOMS

The experiment cited suggests that words which generate the greatest number of associations — or that are most meaningful or most familiar — will be identified most easily in print. What is the implication of this for the middle school content teacher who wants to help a poor reader to identify more words in his reading?

One immediate implication would seem to be that the teacher should encourage the student to talk. The meaningfulness or association value of a word rises and falls to the degree that the learner has had experience with the word and one good way to gain such experience is to talk about it.

A student who has had little or no verbal background regarding the word *density* cannot be expected to give a maximum psychological effort to remembering that the letters *d-e-n-s-i-t-y* produce the sound of the word density. How many verbal situations can be invented to increase a given word's association value for a given middle school student? The answer depends upon the individual teacher's creativity in developing as many different associations as possible for new words. Before he creates associations, the teacher must first decide which words are to be learned. This usually can be done by selecting those words in each content unit which in the past have proved to be the most difficult for students to learn. Once the words are selected, the teacher must devote some time and effort to planning how he will elicit associations with the words in order to familiarize students with them.

Eliciting such responses can be as elaborate or as simple as the teacher wishes or as the occasion demands. In the most elementary form, familiarization training only involves telling the student orally what he is to be presented in writing, saying, "John, tomorrow you are going to learn to read the words *condense, tripod*, and *violate*." At a higher level, a discussion could be developed in which the many implications of each word are cited by the student as a means for tying many associations to the word. The teacher can further enhance the process by demonstrating how something is condensed or by showing the student a tripod or by illustrating the word *violate* through role playing. At still a higher level, the words to be learned can be put on tape so that students can preview and become familiar with the words to be learned the next day. A tape which simply lists words one after another, however, will probably not hold the student's attention. It is more helpful to include background music, ridiculous comedy, or other devices which will excite the middle school student. An example of the script for one such tape follows:

> "This is the control tower. Ready yourself for take-off." (sound of airplane) "The words for today are *tripod* and *violate*. Ok, now we're airborne. Isn't it neat? Oops! Watch out! Grab your tripod holding the gun and shoot back. Wow, I really never thought that Oklahoma would actually violate the air space of Texas!"

Ridiculous? It certainly is. But nevertheless, it is familiarization training which is fun while it is being done and which is profitable the next day when the students are asked to learn to identify these words in their reading.

CONCLUSION

Word recognition is a real problem for the content area teacher since students in his classes often cannot read basic textbook words. The problem is compounded by the fact that the teacher has neither the training nor the time to correct such reading deficiencies within the class. Consequently, he needs a technique which is highly effective and can be applied with relative ease.

The concept of familiarization training meets this need. While this technique is not a cure-all for word recognition problems, it does have the advantage of being particularly applicable to the terminology commonly found in the content areas while demanding a little imagination and persistence on the part of the teacher. For middle school pupils who are frustrated and tired of having to learn to read and for the teacher who has about reached the end of his rope with students who cannot pronounce the words in their textbooks, meaningfulness and familiarization training offer some hope.

References

1. Duffy, Gerald G., and George B. Sherman. *Systemic Reading Instruction.* New York: Harper and Row, 1971, 36.
2. Mandler, G. "Response Factors in Human Learning," *Psychological Review*, 61 (1954), 235-244.
3. Underwood, B. J., and R. W. Schulz. *Meaningfulness and Verbal Learning.* Chicago: L. B. Lippincott, 1960.

CHAPTER THIRTEEN

IMPROVING ACHIEVEMENT THROUGH DIFFERENTIATED INSTRUCTION

Gerald G. Duffy and George B. Sherman
Michigan State University

Much has been said in previous chapters about the individual differences found among students in the middle school. In the five classes and approximately 150 individuals he meets in a typical school day, the teacher will find that some students are bored in class, some lack the basic experience background to handle the content, others cannot efficiently identify the words in the textbook, and still others cannot find the answer to comprehension questions even when they can pronounce the words. The implication is that the teacher should differentiate instruction to accommodate these differences.

The middle school teacher, however, is seldom prepared for this task. While he may have heard about individual differences in college, his preservice training focused primarily on subject matter content and rudimentary pedagogical skills such as lesson planning. Rarely was he provided with a strategy or a model for individualizing his content in terms of the student differences confronting him.

This lack of training starts an all too common cycle among middle school teachers. First, because he has not been presented with differentiating strategies, the teacher often uses his favorite university professor as his model, instructing the class as if all middle school students were alike in terms of interest, intelligence, background, and reading skills. Because this method does not succeed, he becomes frustrated, blaming his failure on the students or the elementary school from which they came or the class load or some other factor. Having thus rationalized his failure, he continues to teach as he was taught; he confronts more frustration and becomes more adamant in his rationalizing.

One has to sympathize with teachers caught in this cycle. While the situation may be understandable, it is not tolerable. We cannot ignore those children who do not happen to fit our preconceived mold of what a middle school student ought to be. This chapter presents an alternative. Specifically, the differences which influence content learning in a typical middle school class are identified, a strategy for differentiating instruction in terms of these differences is developed, and a model for organizing and managing such differentiated instruction is provided.

HOW DO MIDDLE SCHOOL STUDENTS DIFFER?

Middle school students differ in numerous ways. They are different sizes, shapes, colors, and personalities. The middle school teacher's major concern, however, is not with these differences but with those which affect learning of the subject matter content. These differences include decoding, background experience, interest, and comprehension.

Differences in decoding abilities. The term *decoding* commonly refers to the student's ability to identify the words on a printed page.* While it is often a shattering revelation to the neophyte teacher, the fact is that some middle school children cannot recognize and pronounce many of the words in the textbook being used. These children may be labeled *nonreaders* by the teacher, although it is rare that such students cannot read at all. The precise difficulty is that they cannot pronounce the words in that particular textbook. Deficiencies in decoding often directly affect the learning of content since, in many middle school classrooms, all students are expected to read a single textbook. Whenever a student is expected to read, ability to decode at the level at which the text is written becomes a prerequisite to effective learning of the content.

Differences in background experience. Some children enter a middle school content class with little or no prior experience with the topic. The concepts studied are alien to them and the basic terminology is completely new. Such deficiencies can result from a limited experience background or from inadequate instruction in previous years, but they usually result from a combination of both. In any case, a student deficient in background soon flounders because the discussions are over his head. If familiarity with basic concepts and terms is necessary for a particular subject, then background experience becomes a pre-requisite to effective learning of the content.

Differences in interests. Middle school teachers frequently complain that lack of student interest inhibits their effectiveness as content teachers. Students are bored, do not find the material relevant to their lives, or see no real purpose in pursuing the topic being studied. As a result, they either daydream in class or seek excitement and diversion by distracting the teacher or causing classroom disturbances. Such student behavior directly affects achievement because attention is required in order that learning may occur. Therefore, because the absence of interest results in a lack of student attention, interest is a prerequisite to effective learning of the content.

*A number of authorities suggest that *decoding* is not complete until meaning has been obtained. They sometimes refer to the translating of the visual symbol (print) into the oral symbol (speech) as *recoding*. – Reviewing Editor.

Differences in comprehension. Despite the presence of decoding, experience, and interest prerequisites, some children still may evidence achievement difficulties in a middle school content area because of poorly developed thinking skills. That is, the students cannot answer teacher questions regarding the facts, relationships, main ideas, or implied meanings in an assigned reading selection. The inability to comprehend inhibits the student's ability to do the thinking required by the teacher. Thus, to the extent that the teacher expects the students to comprehend in specific ways, thinking skills become a prerequisite to effective learning of the content.

Summary. To be effective, the middle school teacher must identify the prerequisites to effective learning of his content. If he expects students to read the textbook, decoding becomes a prerequisite; if he expects children to use certain concepts and terminology learned previously, background experience becomes a prerequisite; if he expects students to pay attention, interest or motivation becomes a prerequisite; and if he expects students to answer specific comprehension questions, thinking skills become a prerequisite. In brief, the teacher must sensitize himself to these differences as they affect his subject matter, and he must be prepared to differentiate his instruction for students deficient in one or more of these areas.

WHY MUST WE DIFFERENTIATE?

We must differentiate for two basic reasons. First, attempts to narrow or eliminate individual differences through the use of various administrative and organizational schemes have failed to free the teacher from the problem and, second, differentiation is the key element in motivating students.

Over the years, educators have devised and implemented many grouping patterns — such as tracking — in an attempt to minimize the problem of individual differences. While it would seem logical that individual differences could be controlled by grouping together those students who lack certain prerequisites, actual experience indicates that such groupings cannot be made precise enough. For instance, when students are grouped according to differences in decoding skills, the classroom teacher still finds himself with children who differ widely in terms of experience, interest, and comprehension skills. Similarly, when children are grouped in terms of previous experience in the content area, the teacher still finds students differing in terms of decoding, interest, and thinking skills. While various organizational plans can narrow the range of differences in a single prerequisite area, it cannot simultaneously eliminate differences in the other three. Consequently, while homogeneous groupings do help the teacher deal with some differences, they do not account for all differences.

While the failure of traditional grouping plans forces us to turn to other strategies, differentiation has the additional positive value of providing the key to motivating students to learn the content. Although much has been researched and said about motivation, it all boils down to the concept that people, whether they be students or adults, want to do what they can do successfully. A basic task of any teacher, then, is to provide each child with the success which generates a positive attitude toward learning. A middle school student does not succeed when he must read materials he cannot decode, learn content for which he has no background, perform tasks for which he has no purpose, or answer questions requiring thinking skills which he lacks. Because he does not succeed, he tries to avoid the situation, exhibiting one or more of the aggressive or withdrawal symptoms associated with unmotivated students. In contrast, the student whose instruction is adjusted in terms of his individual needs does achieve daily success, does receive positive feedback regarding that success, and does continue to pursue the learning. He is the motivated student. Hence, the middle school teacher differentiates instruction to assure the student success which is the essential element of motivation.

We must differentiate instruction for two reasons. First, despite our best efforts to homogenize individual differences through all-school grouping patterns, it is clear that differentiation within the classroom is the only effective way to account for *all* the individual differences affecting learning in a particular content area. Second, we must differentiate as a means to insure the success which is essential to motivation.

BASIC STRATEGY FOR DIFFERENTIATING INSTRUCTION

Differentiated instruction makes four demands of the teacher: he must possess certain attitudes and beliefs regarding his role as a teacher; he must determine how the prerequisites of decoding, background experience, interest, and comprehension affect his content area; he must determine student strengths and deficiencies in each of the four prerequisite areas; and he must devise ways to compensate for these differences in his instruction.

Necessary teacher attitudes. While differentiated instruction has the potential to improve student achievement, teachers who attempt it must possess certain prerequisite beliefs and values about middle school teaching. The absence of such attitudes dooms differentiated instruction before it starts.

For instance, differentiated instruction only works for those teachers who accept individual differences as an integral part of teaching middle school children. Teachers who do not want to be bothered with substandard students will see no need to do anything about individual differences beyond removing such children from their classrooms. Similarly, differentiated instruction requires that middle school teachers view their roles broadly. Teachers who limit their role to the dispensing of content knowledge will resist broadening that role to include concerns with decoding, background experience, interest, and thinking skills. Finally, differentiated instruction requires an abundance of commitment, dedication, and diligence. Teachers who limit their working day to the hours when students are in the building will not have the necessary planning time to make differentiated instruction work.

In short, while differentiated instruction is a potentially powerful innovation, it will not work for the teachers who are looking for easy answers to the problem of individual differences. Supervisory personnel and teachers contemplating the adoption of differentiated instruction would be wise to determine whether potential staff members possess the necessary attitudes before initiating this innovation. If such attitudes are lacking, strategies such as those described in Chapter 4 can be implemented.

Determining the demands of the content. Assuming that the middle school teacher possesses these basic attitudes, his first step in initiating differentiated instruction is to determine what decoding, interest, experience, and thinking skills are required to achieve the subject matter objectives. Only when he knows what is demanded can he know how he must differentiate.

The need to differentiate in terms of decoding will vary according to whether the teacher expects students to obtain most of the content information from a required textbook, from a variety of written materials, or exclusively from a listening situation in which no student reads. Similarly, the teacher who teaches the third course in a sequence of science courses will be more concerned with background experience than will the teacher who teaches the first course; the teacher who teaches a required course will be more concerned with the interest variable than will the teacher who teaches an elective course; and the teacher who expects children to use content as a vehicle for developing thinking will be more concerned with students' comprehension skills than will the teacher who simply expects students to remember the facts.

Only the teacher can determine the demands of the course since only the teacher knows what kind of reading he wants students to do, what he expects them to bring to class from their experience background, what the interest level is for his subject, and what thinking he wants students to do while in the class. Once he has decided on the demands of his course, the next step is to assess the extent to which his students can perform these prerequisite tasks.

Assessing differences. Assessments must be made to determine which students are deficient in prerequisites needed for successful achievement in the course. The teacher determines such deficiencies by collecting data in the following manner. For decoding, the teacher must discover whether the student can pronounce the words in the materials he is expected to read. This can be most efficiently determined by asking each student to read orally a short passage from that material. If he reads smoothly and quickly and if he pronounces most of the words without hesitation, he probably possesses the prerequisite decoding skills to perform the required reading tasks. However, if his reading is hesitant and jerky and if he needs help in pronouncing more than five out of every hundred words on the page, the reading of that material is likely to be a failure situation for him.

Experience background can be determined by looking at a student's previous performance in similar courses and by informally checking his understanding of

95170

fundamental terminology. Most students who have had difficulty in previous science classes can be expected to be deficient in the basic prerequisite concepts needed in the present science course. Similarly, students who cannot adequately explain terms such as *igneous* and *metamorphic* are likely to have difficulty in an earth science class in which the understanding of such terminology is a prerequisite. When deficiencies such as these are discovered, instruction has to be differentiated for the students involved.

Assessment of the interest variable should include an investigation of the student's previous success with that subject as well as an assessment of student preferences and goals. Previous performance is valuable data because students who have been successful in a subject tend to exhibit continuing interest while those who have had difficulty tend to avoid it. In addition, information regarding preferences and goals, obtained either from questionnaires or conversations with the student, helps the teacher decide how content objectives can be matched to the student's stated interests. Both sources of data also provide clues on how to rekindle interests.

Ability to use thinking skills can be assessed by asking students to read or listen to short passages and to answer comprehension questions regarding the content. The type of comprehension questions asked depends upon the kinds of thinking the teacher wants his students to do. The social studies teacher who emphasizes history may assess the ability to answer questions relating to chronology and time sequence; the science teacher who wants children to perform experiments independently may want to determine how well students follow written directions; while the English teacher who is concerned with literature may ask questions which require the student to infer meanings implied by the authors of stories and poems. Compensatory instruction is then provided for those students who cannot handle independently the thinking required by the teacher.

Assessment, then, identifies both the student who will need differentiated instruction and the areas in which this differentiation will occur. While the assessment techniques themselves are not imposing, they have the advantage of being quick and easy for the content area teacher to use.

The basis for differentiating. So far, all the steps detailed have been preparatory to the actual task of differentiating. Once the teacher knows the demands of his content area and the differences which exist among his students, he must then use this information to help each student achieve the course objectives.

In a middle school content classroom, the student's mastery of the subject matter must take precedence over the development of reading skills. The student must learn the content regardless of his reading prowess; consequently, when the content teacher discovers a reading deficiency, he adjusts the instruction to insure that the student will achieve the course objectives regardless of his individual differences.

But upon what basis does the teacher adjust instruction? Since we have already implied that the teacher must help each student learn the content, we cannot change the content itself. We can, however, compensate for individual student deficiencies by adjusting student objectives, learning activities, and evaluations.

The following diagram will be helpful in visualizing the thinking a teacher does when planning differentiated instruction.

Student Differences*

		Decoding	Experience	Interest	Thinking
Tools to be used	Student Objectives				
	Learning Activities				
	Evaluations				

If the teacher finds that he has one or more students who cannot decode the required reading material, he looks down the *decoding* column and asks himself these questions:

> How can I adjust the student's *objectives* to compensate for the decoding deficiency?
>
> How can I adjust the student's *activities* to compensate for the decoding deficiency?
>
> How can I adjust the student's *evaluations* to compensate for the decoding deficiency?

If he has assessed deficiencies in experience background, he follows the same pattern, asking himself how he can adjust the student's objectives, activities, and evaluations to compensate for this individual difference. Similarly, the teacher follows this pattern in planning how he will adjust instruction to compensate for deficiencies in interest and thinking skills.

The diagram is a structure for planning differentiated instruction. The teacher identifies the student's strengths and deficiencies and then fills in the space under the appropriate column with details of how the objectives, activities, and evaluations will be adjusted to insure that the child learns the content.

This structure will remain an empty shell unless the teacher knows what to put in the spaces. Suggested ways to adjust for each category are discussed in following sections.

*In some situations the highly skilled teacher may also wish to consider additional aspects of student differences, such as *work-study skills* and *literary appreciation*. – Reviewing Editor

DIFFERENTIATING FOR DECODING DIFFERENCES

For illustrative purposes, let's assume that we are in a middle school social studies class where a study of ancient Egypt is about to begin. If the social studies textbook contains much valuable information on this topic, the teacher may want all children to read that section. However, five children lack the decoding skills necessary to pronounce many of the words in this book. How can the teacher differentiate his objectives, his activities, and his evaluations to insure that his students all obtain the basic knowledge about ancient Egypt?

Objectives. For the five poor decoders, the teacher can vary his objectives in two ways: he can provide nonreading material which does not require decoding or he can find easier reading material which matches pupils' decoding skills. Thus, the teacher does not alter the ultimate content objective of the study but he adjusts only the medium through which the student obtains the necessary information. He changes his objectives for *how* the students will learn, not *what* they will learn. In short, the objectives are adjusted from that of having all students read the textbook to having some students read the text while others read easier material or listen to material or view material relative to the topic.

Activities. The change in objectives results in differentiated activities. For instance, the teacher may tape the textbook selection which contains the necessary information and, while the majority of the class is reading the text, the students with the most severe decoding difficulties listen to the same material. On other occasions or with other students, the teacher may use filmstrips which the children view, or magazine articles written at a level lower than that of the text, or books which are easier to decode. In any case, instead of having one group in which all children pursue the same objective through the same activity, the teacher differentiates the kind of material, creating different activities in order to compensate for the decoding deficiencies of the five students.

Evaluations. Evaluations can be differentiated in two ways to compensate for decoding deficiencies: first, the teacher should evaluate his poor decoders only on the material they used to obtain the basic information about ancient Egypt and second, the teacher may account for the students' decoding deficiencies by allowing oral evaluations. Many poor decoders respond better to oral evaluations that are not labeled "test" and others will often pass tests with flying colors when the decoding variable has been neutralized.

DIFFERENTIATING FOR BACKGROUND EXPERIENCE DIFFERENCES

While some middle school students may lack prerequisite decoding skills, others may be unfamiliar with basic concepts regarding ancient Egypt. In such cases, the teacher must also differentiate instruction to compensate for this deficiency.

Objectives. Differences in background experience can be accounted for through two kinds of compensatory objectives. If the student's previous social studies experience is inadequate, the teacher creates additional objectives which will provide him with the social studies understandings needed to study ancient Egypt. If the student's difficulty is with the prerequisite terminology, the teacher states additional objectives designed to develop understanding of this terminology. In either case, the teacher's objectives are differentiated to account for differences in experience background.

Activities. The differentiated activities, like the objectives, compensate for deprivation in both general background regarding ancient Egypt and specific vobabulary associated with the study. General experience background is built by providing children with books, films, filmstrips, magazines, and other media which discusses or illustrates fundamental concepts about ancient Egypt. Vocabulary is strengthened by identifying the prerequisite terminology and then either teaching these words directly or leading students to the meanings through study guides or other independent material. In both cases, the student is provided with experiences he can apply in class.

Evaluations. When evaluating pupils, the teacher may differentiate for the experience variable in two ways: he takes into account the compensatory study completed by students and he administers differentiated tests which provide structured assistance with terminology and general background concepts for those who need it while other students, although they are answering the same basic questions, are not provided with such assistance. In any case, evaluations are adjusted to account for the student's individual differences in background.

DIFFERENTIATING FOR INTEREST DIFFERENCES

While differentiating in terms of decoding and experience accounts for some individual differences, still other students need help because they are not particularly interested in learning about ancient Egypt. How can instruction be adjusted to involve these children?

Objectives. There are two basic reasons why a student would not be interested in a study of ancient Egypt: he has had difficulty with social studies in the past and is afraid he will fail again or he sees no personal purpose in the study. For a pupil in the first category, objectives can be altered to allow him to work at an easier level. Utilizing instructional strategies similar to those described for decoding and background experience often results in greater interest simply because the student achieves success. For a student in the second category, the objectives can be expanded to include facets which are of special interest to him, either by designing objectives which entice the student or by allowing students some choices in the selection of objectives.

Activities. When a teacher devises the objectives for individual students, he must sell the student on each objective's relevance. While this approach is better than making no effort at all, in fact the student is pursuing the teacher's purpose, not his own. A second approach tends to be more powerful. Instead of dictating the objectives to the class, the teacher describes the topic generally and then involves all the students as well as himself in planning content objectives. In so doing, the teacher captures interest by allowing the disinterested student to propose objectives which are relevant to him. Motivation results because each student pursues an aspect of the study which is of interest to him.

Evaluations. Evaluations, as well as activities, can be differentiated to accommodate the varying interests of pupils. Rather than limiting his evaluations to a standard end-of-unit test, the teacher may also evaluate the student's work in a particular interest area by attaching to the standard test form a sheet which reflects the student's special interests. Still another technique is to have students make their own evaluation decisions, since the teacher who allows students to individually determine whether their learning will be measured by a test, a report, a project, a debate, a discussion, or by some other means, creates a differentiated evaluation system that significantly raises the student's interest in the content area. Whichever technique is used, the goal is to have evaluations reflect varying student interests.

DIFFERENTIATING FOR DIFFERENCES IN THINKING SKILLS

Some children know how to comprehend and others do not. Those who do will be able to answer the teacher's questions about ancient Egypt and those who don't, will not, Because of these differences, the teacher must help those students deficient in thinking skills.

Objectives. To help the poor comprehenders, the teacher plans compensatory objectives according to the type of thinking he wants the students to do while studying ancient Egypt. If he wants children to pick out main ideas, his objectives must include compensatory help for those children who are unable to do this; if he wants children to classify concepts, his objectives must include special help for those children who cannot do this. Special objectives, then, are created to account for the deficiencies noted in comprehension.

Activities. On the basis of the objective, the teacher forms special skill groups to teach the desired thinking. Specific techniques for teaching comprehension in the various content areas are specified in the following chapters and it need only be stated here that such instruction must include direct teacher assistance in how to comprehend in the specific subject matter.

Evaluations. The teacher must remain cognizant of the differences in thinking when evaluating students. The tests or evaluations must be differentiated so that those who can answer the required comprehension question independently do so on the tests while those who cannot are provided with easier questions or with structured guidance within the framework of the question. In either case, the evaluation is differentiated to give the poor comprehender a reasonable chance of achieving success.

VARIATIONS ON THE BASIC STRATEGY

When taken at face value, it seems that the middle school teacher must simultaneously vary the objectives, the activities, and the evaluations for each of the four prerequisite areas. Such a task would be tremendously difficult and undoubtedly would collapse under its own weight. Consequently, rather than rigidly trying to differentiate in terms of each difference during each lesson, the teacher deals with priorities and combinations. He determines which variable is the most crucial in today's lesson and he combines groupings whenever possible to account for several variables at once.

When a difficult textbook is the only source of good information about a topic, differentiating in terms of decoding becomes a priority task; when the number of new words is particularly heavy, differentiating in terms of background experience becomes a priority; and so on. Similarly, in the interest of efficiency, the teacher combines groups whenever possible. If his study requires both the reading of the textbook and answering certain kinds of comprehension questions, the teacher may bring together in a single group the students deficient in both decoding and comprehension, directly assisting them in both areas while the rest of the class works independently. If he has students who lack both interest and background experience, he may bring them together in a group where he would provide help with both variables through compensatory experiences and purpose-setting activities.

While it would be ideal to accommodate every difference found in children in our middle school content classes, such a goal is difficult to achieve when faced with five different classes a day. To maximize instructional time, the teacher must identify priority needs and combine differentiated groups whenever possible.

ORGANIZING AND MANAGING DIFFERENTIATED INSTRUCTION

In the final analysis, differentiated instruction implies intraclass grouping of one kind or another. Because grouping means different things to different people, however, the organization and management of differentiated instruction in a middle school classroom is illustrated here.

What does a differentiated classroom look like? As described in this chapter, differentiated instruction combines whole group instruction with temporary small groups. Typically, it follows a pattern illustrated in the following diagram.

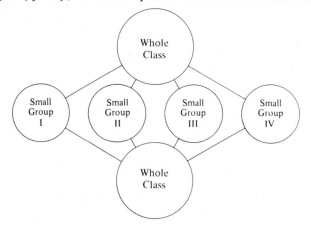

At the beginning of the class period, the teacher works with the whole group, setting purposes for the day's work, describing goals, and giving specific directions for various groups. During the heart of the period, small groups, formed on a basis of common needs, work on various tasks prescribed by the teacher. One group of five children may be listening to a tape of the teacher reading a textbook selection they cannot decode themselves; another may be using various materials provided by the teacher to locate information regarding purposes that are relevant to them; another may be using the textbook and a teacher-prepared study guide to answer specific questions posed earlier; while the teacher may provide the fourth group with directed assistance in answering questions regarding chronology. In the final part of the period, the class again meets as a whole, sharing the information obtained from various sources, achieving the goals set at the outset, and determining the goals for the next period.

This plan, then, requires the teacher to work directly with some children while other children work independently. Such instruction requires efficient management of those students not directly under the teacher's supervision. Several principles can be employed to accomplish this goal.

Independent activities. Inherent in differentiated instruction is the concept that some children work independently while others work directly with the teacher. Such a system succeeds only if students have been trained to work independently and if the teacher clearly explains what students are to do.

Since all middle school children do not naturally possess the work habits conducive to independent study, the teacher must first train them to handle the routines and procedures which are essential to an efficient and smooth organization. Once children know how to work independently, they will tend to continue to do so if they know precisely what they are to do for each activity. The teacher must explain the independent work for each day, either through detailed verbal directions, written directions, or study guides. Most successful teachers employ a combination of these, using verbal directions for the more independent workers and providing written directions and study guides for those who need more guidance.

In any case, the independent activities proceed smoothly only when each child knows how to work independently and when he has been told exactly what it is that he must do.

Safety valves. Children being children, it is safe to assume that no matter how precisely the teacher prepares the independent activities, some students either complete their work sooner than was expected or need assistance in one way or another. This contingency can be handled in two ways. First, the teacher anticipates the need for back-up activities which students can turn to when they finish independent work. These activities, which are always available, may include listening posts, magazine corners, game corners, and various independent learning centers. They differ from the regular independent activities in that they are always there, they are not planned to correlate directly with that particular day's activities, and they tend to be enrichment activities.

The second kind of safety valve is an assistant teacher — paraprofessional, parent volunteer, or student selected from the class — who handles questions and provides routine assistance when needed. This person becomes a buffer between the group the teacher is directly assisting and the students who are working independently. The teacher recognizes that some children will have questions and structures a device in the classroom to help these children without disrupting the group.

Differentiated instruction implies grouping. Any time grouping is employed, efficient organization and management become crucial since some children will not be directly under the teacher's control. Such organization is accomplished to the extent that the teacher trains his students to work by themselves and builds structures to handle special problems which are likely to arise.

A FINAL WORD OF CAUTION

Implementation of the strategy described in this chapter results in student success in the content areas despite differences in reading ability. However, a caution must be observed.

For the content area teacher who has done little differentiation in the past, it is natural to be somewhat overwhelmed by all the elements inherent in this strategy. The difficulties of assessing, grouping, and managing may lead a teacher to the conclusion that all this cannot be accomplished with five sections each teaching day. While it is important to remember that differentiating instruction is a difficult task which cannot be implemented overnight, it is equally important to remember that the strategy can be broken down into smaller pieces and implemented in a gradual fashion. For instance, a teacher may initially wish to differentiate with only one of his five daily classes, or he may wish to differentiate only for one unit of study within one class, or only differentiate in terms of a single variable for a small group of students within one of his classes. The point is that the keys to successful content area teaching lie with the principles described in this chapter. Don't ignore them. Make them work for you, no matter how small you start.

CHAPTER FOURTEEN

TECHNIQUES FOR IMPROVING COMPREHENSION IN ENGLISH

John E. Connelly
New York State University College at Fredonia

Among the content area teachers in the middle school, the English teacher often has the most difficult task. Not only is he responsible for the English curriculum per se but, because reading is one of the language arts, he is also frequently looked to as the resident specialist in reading. Such an added responsibility usually is not any easier for the English teacher than it is for anybody else since, like many of his colleagues, he typically receives no preservice training in the teaching of reading.

In recognition of the problem, this chapter provides some generalized techniques for reading improvement, including suggestions for diagnosis, program planning, motivation, materials, and instruction. These suggestions can be put to work within the framework of a regular English class or, when the occasion demands, can be adapted to developmental reading at the middle school level.

DIAGNOSIS

Diagnosis is the first requirement of an effective reading program, whether it is a developmental reading class or a regular English class. Before effective instruction can begin, information must be gathered regarding each child's strengths and weaknesses. While this topic is dealt with in depth in Chapter 6 of this book, some additional suggestions may be helpful.

The English teacher should use both standardized tests and informal diagnostic devices to assess reading needs. In both cases, he should look for data regarding a student's reading level and his specific strengths and weaknesses as a reader.

In selecting standardized tests, the teacher should base his decision on the type of material used in the English class. Compare the frequency of rare or abstract words, length and complexity of sentences, and complexity of thought.

Once the test has been administered, check to see what items students have answered successfully and compare the difficulty of the hardest item correctly answered with the difficulty of the materials in the English course. Such an examination will provide an indication of which students can handle the material of the course as it is planned and what modifications will have to be made.

Standardized tests also will help you screen out those students who need to be looked at more closely to discover their exact needs. For those who are scoring well below the desired grade level, the teacher can administer an informal inventory to determine his precise reading level and skill needs. The procedures detailed in Chapters 3, 5, and 6 of this book should be used in this regard.

PLANNING THE PROGRAM

Once the diagnostic data have been compiled, the program must be fitted to the needs of the group. In most cases, this will require that the teacher plan a variety of activities using the principles described in Chapter 13. The goal is to make every student feel that he is making progress. Because of the divergency among middle school students, this is not an easy task.

Certain groups will feel that reading is a waste of time, since they are certain that they already know all that is needed concerning reading skills. Activities for these students should require in depth reaction to materials, opportunities to go beyond classroom materials, a more challenging use of the materials in the classroom, and a minimum of basic skills. Writing which requires personal reaction substantiated by definite facts is helpful as is the development of root words, prefixes, suffixes, and vocabulary improvement.

Other groups will be at the other end of the scale. They may feel that they can't do anything, so why try? Here, activities must be worthy of effort while also assuring success. Listening development is helpful here since much of the information we acquire all through life comes through listening. Discussion about common, everyday things will also be helpful, clarifying concepts and providing new words with which to express ideas. Work on learning words and word attack skills can best be approached in game form with these students. The teacher must make sure that the learning which results makes the game worthwhile.

In any case, the program planned by the English teacher must reflect the specific needs of his students. Since the needs in any one class are likely to be wide, the teacher must be willing to differentiate instruction for the various groups and must be skillful at planning a variety of activities to meet the various needs.

MOTIVATION

Motivation is always a crucial aspect in the success of any reading program. Two important elements of motivation are discussed in other sections of this book; the importance of success is detailed in Chapter 13, while the role of interests is described in Chapter 19. These two elements are just as important in English as in other areas and should be given priority by the teacher. In addition, the following techniques might be useful.

1. An important factor in any motivational attempt is to gain the respect of the students. Without this, students often ignore even the most enticing piece of motivation.

2. Never say "no" to anything a middle school student wants to read. One bright student asked to read *Last Summer* by Hunter, for a class report, primarily because he wanted to see the teacher's reaction since the book is about four teenagers involved in a rape. However, the book provides some interesting insights into the effects of this violence on these young people and the boy who read it found much more than just a good dirty story.

3. While the class is doing seat work, give ten minute library passes to two students at a time. Often they come back with books and always they feel as if they've gotten away with something. This is good with slower students who seldom receive passes.

4. Have fun reading. Read with your class every day.

5. Keep an index card file on your desk. As students read books, have them fill out a card with the title, author, a very brief plot summary, and a rating for the book. In this way, students can get others' opinions about books to read.

6. Line your windowsills with paperback books and allow students to use them. If the student wishes to have the book to take home, immediately send him to the library for a copy. That way your books will always be available to all. In addition, many students will bring their own paperback copies after browsing through yours.

7. Place a table in the room with many magazines and at least one daily newspaper on it. Allow your students to browse and read during class time.

8. When you find a class session really dragging, capitalize on a current event which can be related to reading, such as, "Did any of you see 'Go Ask Alice' on television last night?" The ensuing informal discussion is a great way to motivate the reading of a book.

9. Read aloud to your students since even the most advanced classes will enjoy it. Read an exciting part of a selection or in your slower classes, read a chapter a week until you finish the book.

10. Read a lot yourself and mention interesting points about your reading to the students in your class.

11. When asked about a book, never be satisfied just to say that you are not familiar with it. Find it, read it, and get back to the student as soon as possible.

12. Comparing a movie and a novel or play can be fun and stimulating, especially if the class can go together to see it. The next best thing is the videotape from television and next, the record of the sound track. For instance, when reading *David Copperfield*, show clips of W. C. Fields doing Mr. Micawber.

13. One of the best motivational devices for middle school students with reading difficulties is *Scope Magazine*, published by Scholastic Book Services.

14. Casual remarks such as "It's very difficult to read," or "That might be beyond your comprehension," may become automatic challenges to your accelerated students and almost guarantee that whatever you are talking about will be read.

15. Paperback book clubs can be motivating because many of the books offered are high in motivational content but easy to read. In addition, the prices are lower than in book stores.

16. Students who cannot read well, often do other tasks well. Put their talents to use when doing a class reading project. They can dress dolls, make models, draw, design bulletin boards, make clay models, and build models of wood. If the range of projects is broad and the idea is planted when reading is first begun, some students will read with much more interest.

17. Use student projects to decorate the room a few weeks before beginning a class project in a particular book. These help to arouse curiosity and interest. (Most English teachers are not in favor of requiring an entire class to read the same book. However, when the curriculum so deems, one must do something to survive the ordeal.)

18. One alternative to the class book project is having the class work in small groups with each group reading a different novel or story. This can be helpful to students with reading problems since peers are helping them in the small group discussions and they are working with the easier books. With help from the teacher, each group presents a panel discussion about its book. This way, even the poorest reader can be involved and students in other groups can be motivated to read a book they have just heard about.

19. Music is always a great way to get into poetry. Many nonreaders suddenly develop a love for poetry when they hear "Richard Corey" as sung by the Beatles, and some of the most beautiful lyric poetry ever read can be found in Simon and Garfunkel.

20. Study guides which follow the sequence of events in a story or play, but leave blanks for students to fill in while reading, can be very helpful to poorer readers.

21. Cartoons mocking the classics can be used for bulletin boards. It helps to take some of the pressure off difficult reading if people can laugh at it. Students are equally adept at creating these cartoons. Sometimes the car-

toons help in remembering characters or events and, if created by the poor reader, can give him some measure of success with the book.

22. The most important task with a poor reader is to restore self-confidence. Positive, complimentary comments should be made about every piece of work he does. Find his hidden talents and put them to work in your class; if he likes to throw paper airplanes, let him create his own model to use as an introduction to a unit on science fiction.

We often like to pretend that motivation is some kind of mystical thing that some teachers have and others do not. Nothing can be further from the truth, as an examination of the previous suggestions implies. The teacher who motivates is usually the teacher who works hard, who is flexible, and who is willing to do almost anything to insure student involvement in the class.

SOURCE OF MATERIALS

Every middle school teacher of English should have a flexible instructional program that utilizes various types of printed matter (books, magazines, newspapers), and many types of reading (fiction, biography, drama, essays, poetry, informative prose). Suggested lists of such materials are found in most standard works on secondary school reading as well as in Chapter 8 of this book.

In addition to reading matter, the English teacher should be familiar with instructional materials in reading for the middle school level. Of particular worth are Witty's two books, *How to Improve Your Reading* (1) and *How to Become a Better Reader* (2), which are designed for use with middle school and high school students respectively. These books contain chapters on increasing rate of reading, getting the main idea, developing vocabulary, and similar themes, and there are built-in exercises to develop each particular skill. Other books are also available, and most of them are listed in Chapter 8.

INSTRUCTIONAL STRATEGIES

Once the English teacher has diagnosed, planned, motivated, and selected his materials, he must implement the program; he must teach. Several suggestions can be made in this regard.

The Use of Themes

Skillful teachers often use class themes to good advantage. The teacher may build integrated themes on such topics as "remembering what you read," "getting the main idea," or "reading at the right speed." The techniques presented on these topics during skill lessons are then put to use in functional reading situations. Sometimes these might be information-centered selections while at other times they may be stories or poems.

At least once during the semester, a unit theme should be planned for each group in each class. The class and the teacher together determine the topic (or theme), a variety of both easy and difficult materials are collected, and children self-select books within the broad thematic area. Some of the expectations in developing the theme should include writing, engaging in profitable discussion, and making use of information acquired. Choose a topic that is worth spending time on and make sure that you and your students are enthusiastic about the materials collected. Plan carefully so the group realizes what the culmination of the unit is and so that a feeling of accomplishment results.

Vocabulary Development

In the middle school, vocabulary development is an implicit part of every activity. At this level, some individuals develop into "verbalizers"; they use words without really knowing what they are saying. Instruction should emphasize clearness and conciseness of word meanings. The following sentences show the need for constant attention to clear, definite meanings for words:

He send a *telegraphy.*

I will *communicable* with you on the telephone.

He *moralist* the classes every day in school.

Perhaps the first step in improving vocabulary is arousing an interest in words. This may be done through a device such as *Our Word for the Day*, in which an interesting word is highlighted. Sometimes, focusing on word origins arouses interest. In other cases, building from a root word to as many forms as possible may be the key. Magic squares and other word games can also be used.

Finally, the teacher should use expressive language himself and call attention to vivid language or especially clear language in selections. One of the goals for reading instruction should be the certainty that "these words" have been added to the group's vocabulary.

Listening

Listening is a much neglected area in today's schools. We seem to be so busy "talking at" young people that we do far too little to help them learn to listen. English teachers should help young people realize that comprehension includes listening comprehension and should provide instruction in the following types of listening:

1. *polite or conversational listening*, during which one is interested in getting only enough to uphold his part in the conversation;
2. *passive listening* during which the individual lets the flow of sounds wash over him without much of any realization of what is being said (e.g., television commercials);
3. *half-listening* in which the sound is followed while holding fast to one's own ideas so that they can be inserted at the first opportunity;
4. *active listening* which involves reacting to what is said by forming associations and responding with items from one's own experience; and

5. *critical or evaluative listening* which involves actively reacting to the spoken word to discover facts or opinions, emotionally-laden words, author's bias, facts supporting ideas stated, and use of propaganda techniques to influence decisions.

The Directed Reading Activity

The directed or developmental reading lesson, has been around for a long time. Nevertheless, it still has great potential for developing specific reading skills and it can be readily adapted to many content areas, including English.

A developmental lesson is usually taught to a subgroup within the class while the remainder of the class is working on materials specified in advance. The purpose of the developmental lesson is to improve reading ability of the group members and to give the English teacher an opportunity to observe individual reactions such as interest, response, attitude, concepts, needs, and reading habits. A developmental lesson must be carefully planned in every detail to be really successful. The English teacher must know two or three approaches to the information, concepts, or skills that he is developing and he must have a clear, definite, concise purpose for using this particular material at this particular time with this particular group. Vague, general objectives such as "to increase the student's information about fighting forest fires" or "to improve the student's vocabulary" are useless. Instead, two or three specific objectives should be stated and exact plans laid regarding how the materials will be used to accomplish these particular goals.

Normally, the directed reading activity involves four steps:

1. Introduction

The theme is discussed to discover what information students have, to strengthen and clarify needed concepts, to arouse interest, and to stimulate thinking. Pictures, maps, other visual materials, reference to a local event, or any other appropriate opening might be used to involve students.

The words, whose form and meaning must be known for full understanding of the selection, are then presented. Words should be presented in context so that the meaning used in the selection is developed. This part of the lesson presents an opportunity to review any one of a number of skills, including use of context clues, use of dictionary, pronunciation, choosing one correct meaning, and use of suffixes and prefixes. This is also an appropriate place to use the technique of familiarization training described in Chapter 12 of this book.

2. Setting of Purposes

The introduction above should be planned so that some of the purposes grow out of student comments and questions. The teacher may add one or two purposes of his own, but even these should be closely related to the introduction.

Purposes are essential in all reading and listening. One of the greatest services we can perform for young people is to help them realize the importance of knowing why they are doing what they are doing. The closer the purposes are to the student's needs and interests, the better the purposes are. Make sure, however, that there are always reasons for reading.

3. Silent Reading

While usually done independently, silent reading can be done with the teacher once or twice a semester as a means of observing silent reading habits. Always, however, silent reading is completed as a means to achieve the purposes cited above. The teacher may note who finishes first and last, and adjust comprehension requirements as a result.

4. Follow Up

Sometimes the follow up is a discussion but more often it should be a written check. Always, it will be based on the purposes set up previously. Written checks may be true-false to check on details; arranging in proper order for sequence; outlining for main ideas and related details; multiple-choice for relationships, classification, making inferences or drawing conclusions; and open-ended questions for interpretation and reaction.

Specific Techniques to Improve Comprehension

English teachers have the opportunity to improve comprehension in several specific areas. Techniques for each of these areas are described. Reading materials peculiar to English often require special techniques for comprehension. Some of the techniques for helping children to comprehend in English include:

1. when a selection is encountered that involves special reading skills (reading a play, a chart, or a graph), discuss how this may be done effectively;

2. before the reading of a play, the teacher may suggest that students attempt to "set the stage" in their minds as they read, discuss how they think the scene appears and how the characters look;

3. teach students to use appropriate reference materials such as encyclopedias, card catalog, atlases, *World Almanac, Reader's Guide*, biographical dictionaries, and any other special reference aids available for use; and

4. when assigned reading varies in type (a historical background of a period in literature followed immediately by a sample of a short story from that period), the teacher may suggest using the SQ3R approach for the first selection and a quick reading for enjoyment of the short story.

To build adequate concept backgrounds, the teacher may wish to use the following suggestions:

1. call attention in advance to difficult concepts to be encountered if the material itself does not give an adequate explanation and explain these;

2. when a student needs help on the development of a particular concept he encounters in his reading, help him to locate further information in reference books;

3. as a reading assignment in textual material is being made, relate the contents of the selection to what students already know about the topic;

4. use pictures, films, filmstrips, and videotapes to aid in concept development;

5. when important events of significance to the topic being studied are to be televised, such as election returns or a presidential inauguration, make provisions for the pupils to view it if it is scheduled during the school day or encourage them to watch it if it is after school hours;

6. remember that abstract concepts are developed over a period of time and guide the students into building these concepts gradually as opportunities arise; and

7. take students to see activities and places related to their subject matter, such as a trip to court or to see a play.

To help students understand time sequence and the relationship of cause and effect, the following techniques can be used:

1. have pupils retell a story as it was written;

2. present several events in a story or an actual happening in scrambled order, and ask the pupils to place them in the correct order;

3. analyze current happenings in terms of their antecedents, using questions such as, "What events led up to the increase in the price of beef?" or "What important events occurred just prior to the President's address on the Watergate Crisis?"

Students can be helped to draw conclusions and get implied meanings through techniques such as:

1. asking questions that will lead the student to draw conclusions and to read between the lines, leading the student into thinking with the facts;

2. selecting a few paragraphs from a short story, reading them aloud to the class, and asking students to predict what will happen next;

3. writing a short paragraph involving action or feeling, but letting the pupils supply the ending;

4. having the students write a new ending to a story;

5. having the students read the description of a character in a story and having them describe the character more fully, adding other traits they think he possessed; and

6. raising questions that will lead students to put themselves into the boots of someone quite different from themselves about whom they have read, leading them into seeing that in many ways they and the "different" person are very much alike.

Finally, critical reading can be developed by using techniques such as these.

1. Raise questions that will cause children to make judgments about information encountered in reading, using questions such as, "Could this have happened in real life?" "What differences do you see in these two books?" "Did the writer describe accurately life at the time of the story?"
2. Encourage discussion around discrepancies students may note in the same book or in a comparison of two sources.
3. Teach the difference between news stories and editorials in the newspaper.
4. Call attention to the importance of copyright dates on informational books.
5. Teach pupils to separate fact from opinion by presenting a list of interwoven facts and opinions, and ask the children to classify them as "fact" or "opinion."
6. Teach pupils to appreciate intelligent opinion but to recognize it as opinion.
7. Introduce columns and articles in newspapers and news magazines, guiding students into seeing that personal opinions of the writers are often included with the facts.

CONCLUSION

Of all the content teachers in the middle school, the English teacher should be the most sympathetic to the reading needs of students and the most skillful in meeting these needs. The English curriculum should be planned and organized to allow students to read material which is at their instructional level and skill needs should be met systematically. It is hoped that the suggestions for diagnosing, planning, motivating, obtaining materials, and instructing, as outlined in this chapter, will be helpful in achieving these goals.

References

1. Witty, Paul. *How To Improve Your Reading*. Chicago: Science Research Associates, 1963.
2. Witty, Paul. *How To Become A Better Reader*. Chicago: Science Research Associates, 1963.

CHAPTER FIFTEEN

TECHNIQUES FOR IMPROVING COMPREHENSION IN SOCIAL STUDIES

Laura R. Roehler
Michigan State University

Social studies, the curricular channel for introducing students to the past and relating that past to the present, is essential for developing understanding of how people live and interact in cultures, societies, and the world. A student learns social studies in many ways; he listens, observes, interacts with people either directly or through media, and reads people's thoughts in books or other printed materials. While all these learning methods are important, reading is the most important, particularly in the middle school where much content is discovered through written sources. Hence, reading is a fundamental learning tool in social studies.

THE SOCIAL STUDIES TEACHER'S ROLE REGARDING READING

The middle school social studies teacher's first responsibility is to teach social studies. He does so by generating specific content objectives which reflect the knowledge, insights, and judgments to be taught. Each objective is accomplished by matching it with appropriate materials such as textbooks, newspapers, documents, reference sources, journals, magazines, pamphlets, and trade books.

Once the objectives and materials are selected, however, the teacher is faced with a second responsibility. He must insure that each middle school pupil understands what is being communicated. He must help students think. This is where the middle school social studies teacher needs an understanding of reading skills. Specifically, he must know what variables affect comprehension and he must know what thinking skills are required to meet the content objectives of the social studies curriculum.

CONTROLLING THE VARIABLES WHICH AFFECT COMPREHENSION

Certain prerequisite conditions must exist for a student to comprehend what he reads. These variables, which are described extensively in Chapter 13, include the student's ability to decode, his background experience, and his interest in the content.

Ability to Decode

A recent study (4) of the readability levels of social studies textbooks indicates that most books require above average readers, which suggests that the words on the page are too difficult for many students to decode. No meaning is communicated if the student does not know what the written symbols say. Before a student can comprehend specific content, he must have the necessary word recognition or decoding skills. If he does not have them, the teacher must either find easier reading material covering the same content objectives or give the material to the student in a listening situation.

Background Experience

Background experience is the second variable that affects comprehension. If the amount or quality of a child's background experience has been limited, his ability to understand is impaired. For instance, a student from Florida might have greater difficulty understanding life on the polar ice cap than a child who has experienced extremely cold weather. For the child with limited background experience, the teacher must increase that background experience or find another way to relate the child's present experience to the new one. For the student who knows nothing about life on the polar ice cap, then, the teacher could describe what it would be like to live on a frozen lake all year or what it would be like in a large cooler compartment such as is found in supermarkets or food storage areas. The vicarious experience would help the student view life on a polar ice cap more realistically and would increase his understanding of what he reads on the topic. Movies, pictures, slides, and other visual media could be used to accomplish the same goal.

The Child's Interest

The third variable that affects comprehension is the student's interest. Interest determines whether a student will even attempt a task; if no attempt is made, no learning will result. The responsibility for creating interest is the teacher's and can be accomplished either by making the content relevant and exciting or by setting effective purpose.

For instance, a historical study of amnesty for the southern states after the Civil War can be made relevant by relating it to the issue of amnesty for the young Americans who fled to Canada rather than be drafted to fight in Vietnam. The technique of setting purposes creates interest by providing students with a reason to read. Questions are posed ahead of time and, instead of trying to remember all the concepts, the student focuses only on the information that satisfies the purposes. This puts comprehension of social studies material into manageable terms for students and helps focus attention and create interest.

Summary

Controlling the variables that affect comprehension is prerequisite to effective reading of social studies materials. When the middle school student can decode, when he possesses background experience, and when he is interested, the teacher can then turn his attention to specific thinking skills required.

WHAT ARE THE THINKING SKILLS?

The thinking skills that are required to understand social studies can be divided into four major categories: word meaning, structure, literal/inferential thinking, and evaluative thinking (*3*). The category of word meaning includes knowing the meaning of content words that name concepts such as *school, United States*, or *freedom* and knowing the relationships signalled by function words such as *in, and, by*, or *over*. The structure category includes the skills that organize the meaning of the material through perception of relationships and classifications and which reveal the structure of the author's thinking. The literal/inferential category, while drawing upon knowledge of word meanings and structure, focuses on determining the author's purpose, finding the main ideas, drawing conclusions as these are stated and implied, and being aware of factual and inferred information. The last category of evaluative thinking requires the student to pass judgement on accuracy, applicability, and quality of the material he reads.

These four major categories of comprehension are developed in a spiraling hierarchy. The skills build upon themselves and are repeated over and over with increasing complexity and in more difficult material. A second grader uses critical thinking skills but not to the depth that an eighth grader does. As the student progresses, he does more critical thinking in more sophisticated settings.

These thinking skills can be illustrated with the political cartoon (*7*) shown on the next page. Assume that the cartoon has been selected as part of the content material to be used in meeting a social studies content objective. To meet this content objective, the student must think; he must determine the main idea of the cartoon.

In order to find the main idea (methods of transporting the mail are outdated) the student must first think in a literal manner that the postman is old, is riding a rocking horse, and is carrying an overflowing mail bag. He must then classify *pony express* as an old method of delivering mail and *rocking horse* as a mode of travel for youngsters. He must see the relationships among the overflowing bag, the old postman, the rocking horse, and how they all relate to the title, "Pony Express." Further, he must have word meanings for *pony express, U.S. Postal Service, postman, rocking horse, mail*, and *mailbag*. From all this, the student infers that the method of transporting the overwhelming amount of mail is outdated. The inference has required skills of word meaning, classification, relationship thinking, literal thinking, and inferential thinking.

I WROTE MY CONGRESSMAN ABOUT ALL THIS! OH, GOOD MOVE...

PONY EXPRESS

Editorial cartoon by Pat Oliphant. Copyright, *The Denver Post*. Reprinted with permission of Los Angeles Times Syndicate.

ANALYZING SOCIAL STUDIES MATERIAL

The first step in effective middle school social studies instruction is to state content objectives which specify the learning that is to occur. Next, the thinking skills needed to achieve the objectives must be identified. Finally, the student's current thinking skills must be considered. If he can do the necessary thinking, he reads to achieve the content objectives; if he cannot, he must learn the required thinking skill first.

Analyzing material to determine the required thinking is a crucial part of this process. To illustrate, assume that a teacher has chosen a content objective about the humanistic aspects of the judiciary system and plans to use the newspaper article (*8*) shown on the next page as a means to achieve the objective. To understand the article, the student must do main idea thinking so that he can categorize each paragraph as being either central or supporting, and he must know the relationships among them.

The first paragraph (man and family go on vacation before man goes to prison) is the main one because the other paragraphs explain and support it. The second paragraph (man pleading guilty, being sentenced, and admitting crime) supports the first one. The third paragraph (wanting to go on a family vacation before prison sentence) also supports the first one by explaining why the vacation was important. The fourth paragraph about the judge's action on the case again supports the first paragraph by explaining the court's procedure.

Bomber Wins Vacation

GRAND RAPIDS (AP) — A Grand Rapids man will be permitted to take his family on a vacation to Disney World in Orlando, Fla., before he is sent to prison on a bomb charge.

James G. Flynn, 39, pleaded guilty to possessing a bomb with intent to use it and was sentenced to a prison term of two to five years. He admitted planting a pipe bomb at a strike-bound plating company in Grand Rapids last fall. Police removed the bomb intact.

FLYNN TOLD Circuit Court Judge George V. Boucher his family had been planning a two-week Disney World vacation for a long time and wanted to take it before he was sentenced.

Boucher agreed and released Flynn on bond so he can take the vacation.

The ability to relate main ideas and supporting details in this manner depends on the prerequisite skills of classifying the content words in the sentences and seeing the relationships between those meanings. For example, the final sentence has three classifications of content meanings: "Boucher agreed," "released Flynn," and "take vacation." The relationships among these classifications are indicated by *and* and *so*. The ability to use the prerequisite skills of classifying and observing relationships in the last sentence depends, in turn, on understanding the word meanings. The words, *Boucher, agreed, released, Flynn, Bond, he, take*, and *vacation* carry the content meaning while *and, on, so, can*, and *the* signal the relationships.

The analysis began with determining which thinking skills were required to meet the content objective. This was followed by a backward progression through the thinking skills hierarchy from main idea and details to classifying and relationships to content words and function words. By analyzing in this manner, the teacher knows precisely what thinking skills are needed to achieve an objective.

TEACHING THE THINKING SKILLS

The students not possessing the thinking skills required to achieve a particular content objective must be taught these skills before they can read the material with understanding. There are three steps which the teacher can use in teaching the thinking skills: directing the learner's attention, directed assistance, and application.

Directing the Learner's Attention

All the teaching devices and techniques in the world are of no avail if students are not paying attention. Stott (5) has found that the inability to read with understanding is due, for the most part, to inattentive mental behavior. To counteract this, the teacher can direct the student's attention. Two factors play a part in this technique: first, a student may not try because he has learned that failure is bad or because he has learned through failure not to try; and second, a student may not succeed because he does not know what the teacher is trying to teach or because he does not know the important elements of the new skill and consequently pays attention to the wrong things.

When a student does not try because of fear of failure or fear of the unknown, the teacher has to create a climate in which he can try regardless of that fear. This can be accomplished through use of the "psychological attender" (3). Here, the teacher's main purpose is to assure the learner that he is in a situation where failure is acceptable and learning is apt to be difficult. The student must know that the teacher is there to help or to teach. If the student feels that all failure is bad, the teacher should help him realize that some failure is natural. For example, very few people ride a bicycle the first time; it usually takes many attempts. If the student has been subjected to overwhelming doses of failure, the teacher must carefully build the student's confidence in himself and in his teacher by reassurance that he is in a climate where trying will lead to success.

To illustrate, examine the following episode involving a teacher's statement prior to the teaching of a new skill: "This is an easy thing to do. Everyone can do it. If you try, you'll do it."

If the learner does the skill the first time, it is no great accomplishment because it was stated that everyone could do it. If the learner fails the first time, however, that failure is exaggerated because he has been told that everyone can do the skill and yet he just found that he could not.

In contrast, examine this episode: "This may not be an easy thing to do. You may not do it right at first, but that's all right because that is my reason for being here; I'm going to help."

If the learner fails in the first attempt at learning, there is no danger to his self-concept because he was told it might be difficult. If he succeeds, then his self-concept is bolstered because, even though it was difficult, he succeeded. Use of such a psychological attender is powerful in creating climates conducive to learning. It helps to alleviate fear of the unknown and fear of failure.

The next step in directing the learner's attention is the "physical attender" (3) which tells the student what he is going to learn and what he must do to learn it. This sets a purpose for the student and specifies what must be done to reach mastery of the lesson. For example, if the skill to be learned is deciding sequence by use of key words, the student is told that. Then he is told what he has to do; he must look carefully at the words, think about what they are saying, and especially note words such as *first, after*, and *finally* because these words signal the order.

Directed Assistance

In directing attention, the teacher is advised to tell the students that they are in a situation where they will learn. Now the teacher must deliver on that promise. This can be accomplished by directed assistance in which the techniques of modeling and highlighting are used. These techniques are cueing processes in which the important elements of the skill and how they fit together are shown to the students. Modeling can be accomplished by the teacher demonstrating and the students emulating, while highlighting uses visual or auditory emphasis to make the pieces of the skill stand out. Both techniques are, in effect, crutches.

Crutches will fail if they are never removed or if they are removed all at once (1). If they are not removed, the student will depend on the assistance and not learn the skill. If they are removed all at once, the effectiveness is lost because the student has not had time to adjust. Consequently, it is crucial that the crutches be removed gradually as the student shows evidence of catching on to the task. Eventually the students will be using the newly learned skill without any assistance of any type and will have learned the skill. Similarly, it can be said that the teacher has taught because the students were shown how to do the skill rather than being left to their own devices.

The first of these directed assistance techniques (modeling) has been shown by Bandura (2) to be a powerful strategy. Many aspects of the culture, such as talking, are learned primarily through modeling. It is the strongest of the directed assistance techniques since the teacher literally gives the students the answer. For instance, the teacher can model how to recognize the propaganda device of "glittering generalities" by literally verbalizing the steps. Since it is a modeling technique, the students must emulate the teacher's procedure by verbalizing those same steps immediately following the teacher's example. Because modeling is a strong directed assistance technique, it should be the first crutch to be gradually eliminated in an instructional setting.

Highlighting by visual or auditory means is also a powerful strategy. In written selections, highlighting can be achieved through color, underlining, frames, or voice emphasis. For example, if cause and effect relationships are being learned, the words that signal the relationships are highlighted; if the objective is to recognize propaganda devices, words that signal bias are highlighted; if the students are to find the literal purposes of the author, that part of the selection is highlighted; and if the objective is to find glittering generalities, those particular words in the selection are highlighted.

Visual and auditory highlighting can be used separately or together but both techniques must gradually be eliminated. If color is used, it is diminished until a dot of color remains and it is finally eliminated altogether. When underlining is used, the underline gradually fades; when frames are used, sections of the frame are removed gradually until they disappear entirely; when voice emphasis is used, the auditory emphasis is gradually lessened until a normal tone of voice is used. The assistance is diminished as the students respond correctly.

When a student can perform a skill with no directed assistance, he needs opportunities to practice. Practice solidifies skill and it becomes habitual, enabling the student to use it as needed with any selection written at the appropriate difficulty level.

Application of the Skills

The final step is to insure that students can apply the skill to the social studies lesson in order to complete the content objectives. For instance, if the students have learned that *before, during*, and *after* are key words that signal sequence and if they have practiced this skill, they are now ready to apply it to written social studies materials. Continued application insures that this transfer to the content occurs and avoids the dangers of isolated skill instruction.

Summary

The middle school social studies teacher's responsibility in reading includes being able to analyze the content material for the required thinking skills, teaching these thinking skills, and, finally, giving the students many opportunities to apply the skills in the content material while meeting content objectives. The remainder of the paper provides illustrations for teaching each of the four major thinking skills.

EXAMPLES OF TEACHING THINKING SKILLS

Word Meaning

Word meaning is the basic skill in the thinking hierarchy. Unless a student understands the meaning of the content words and the function words, he cannot follow the structure of the selection. For example, the following sentence was included in material that the middle school social studies teacher selected when the students were learning about state governments (*8*):

> Allegations were made that the job was a political payoff to obtain Del
> Rio's support for Milliken in the 1970 gubernatorial campaign.

An analysis of the above sentence yielded the unknown content words *allegations, gubernatorial, payoff*, and *campaign*, based on the teacher's assessment of students' background.

In teaching these word meanings, the teacher follows a three step procedure. First, the characteristics of a word are given; a background is built for the word. The students then use those characteristics during the second step to develop a concept of the word. Finally, the students label the characteristics with the name of the concept, the word.

In teaching the meaning of the words *allegation, gubernatorial*, and *payoff*, the teacher uses a psychological attender and directs attention specifically.

One example would be:

> This morning you are going to learn the meaning of new words. You
> may find this difficult but I'll help you and that should make it easier.
> In order to learn the meaning of this word, you must look carefully at

the characteristics listed and think about how they can describe the word.

During the actual learning, directed assistance may include modeling and both visual and auditory highlighting. For instance, to teach the meaning of the word *payoff*, the teacher might first role play situations in which a payoff is made and list characteristics of each situation. Then, groups of sentences can be given to the students in which *payoff* is used with key words or phrases underlined. The students decide which key words fit the previously listed characteristics of *payoff*, aided by the teacher modeling during the first few sentences. Finally, the characteristics and examples for the word are tied together by the teacher as the meaning of *payoff* is stated. The students emulate the teacher at first and use the word more independently in subsequent responses. The process is repeated for the other words and the student is then ready for practice in which he determines the meaning of the words *allegations, gubernatorial, payoff*, and *campaign* in multiple sentences. Following practice, the learner applies his knowledge of word meanings in reading content material similar to that in which the words originally appeared.

Structural Skills

Structural skills help the reader follow and understand the author's thinking in written material and require the prerequisite skills of word meanings.

The middle school social studies teacher's first step in teaching structure is again to analyze the reading material in terms of the content objectives. For instance, the following sentence was included in material to be used in meeting the content objective of listing the good points and bad points of Nixon's administration (9):

> But sources familiar with the inner workings of the Democratic Party contend that the overheard conversation could have been valuable, if, as has been alleged, the Watergate raid was part of a far flung operation aimed at disrupting the Democratic presidential campaign.

After analyzing the material, the teacher decided the key word *if*, which signalled a cause and effect relationship, was a structure skill needed by some students.

In the teaching episode, the teacher directs the student's attention as illustrated below:

> Today you are going to learn a new skill which might cause some difficulty. If we run into trouble, it will be my problem; and I'll have to find a way to get us out. The skill is interpreting cause and effect relationships by using the key word *if*. To learn this skill, you will have to listen carefully to the sentences, especially noting the *if*, watch how the relationship is set up by the word *if*, and think about how one group of words is the cause and the other group is the effect.

Improving Comprehension in Social Studies

The directed assistance techniques include modeling the procedure and visual highlighting. Using an overhead projector, one teacher showed the following sentence (9): "If the crisis is not resolved soon, it could end the careers of both Brezhnev and Kosygin."

In this example, both the cause and effect elements can be underlined and labelled; the key word *if* will be circled and an arrow will be drawn from the cause to the effect.

The teacher modeled by saying, "This part of the sentence [underlining 'the crisis is not resolved soon'] is the cause, so I'm going to underline it and label it 'the cause.' Now, you do the same."

(Students did the same with a copy of the sentence at their desks.)

"This part of the sentence [underlining 'it could end the careers of both Brezhnev and Kosygin'] is the effect, so I'm also going to underline it and label it 'the effect.' Now, you do the same. The key word *if* signals this relationship so I'm going to circle it. Now, you do the same. Since the cause results in an effect, I'm going to draw an arrow from the cause to the effect. Now, you do the same."

In subsequent sentences, the directed assistance techniques would be gradually diminished. Modeling would be removed first, then the labeling, underlining, drawing the arrow from cause to effect, and circling of the word *if*. When students can identify cause and effect relationship with no directed assistance, they will be ready for practice.

Practice using sentences similar to the above might require students to label the cause and effect and to draw an arrow from the cause to the effect. Following practice, the students should use the cause and effect relationship skill while reading the content material.

Literal and Inferential Thinking Skills

Literal and inferential thinking requires using prior skills of structure and word meanings. Once the students have those prerequisite skills, they can begin to think factually and inferentially about the content of the material, including determining the purpose of the material, the main idea and supporting details, and the conclusions to be drawn.

Whether literal or inferential thinking is required depends on the way the material is written. However, a student must be able to comprehend literally before he comprehends inferentially. Literal skills are taught first because the students interpret only the actual words, while inference requires that the students use the words as well as their background experience to interpret the material.

Assume for instance that the following article was part of the materials being used to achieve a middle school social studies objective of knowing the steps the state government has taken to assist non-English speaking citizens (6).

Driving Manual Now In Spanish

The Michigan secretary of state's office is making available for the first time a Spanish translation of its official driver manual "What Every Driver Must Know."

Secretary of State Richard H. Austin said today copies of the 80-page booklet on Michigan driving laws and rules of the road should be available to Spanish-speaking persons within two weeks.

He said they could be obtained at all driver licensing bureaus and the Bureau of Field Services of the Michigan Department of State.

Austin said only 20,000 of the Spanish booklets, entitled "Lo Que Todo Conductor Debe," have been produced and they could run out quckly.

An analysis of the article indicates that the thinking skill of finding the literal main idea was required to meet the content objective.

To teach this skill, the teacher might start by saying:

> In order to understand these paragraphs, you will have to listen and look carefully at the sentences I point out and think about what they are saying. This probably won't be easy but I will help you. Let's get started and try out this new skill. We are going to learn how to find the main idea of paragraphs.

The directed assistance techniques might include circling the main idea and underlining the supporting sentences, with arrows drawn back to the main idea to show the relationship between the main sentence and the supporting sentences. The teacher uses voice emphasis to highlight the main idea and models aloud the thinking process used to determine the main idea with the students emulating the teacher's steps.

In subsequent paragraphs, the teacher gradually removes the directed assistance as the students respond correctly. After students have used this skill at least once with no assistance, they practice the skill in a repetitious pattern. Finally, application occurs when the students read the original news articles to achieve the content objective.

Critical Thinking Skills

This highest level of thinking makes use of word meaning, structure, and literal/inferential thinking, together with the reader's thoughts or feelings about the material.

Critical (evaluative) thinking skills require students to make judgments regarding the content of the material, answering questions such as Is it fact or opinion? Are there elements of validity? Is the author biased? What is the author's viewpoint? Is the portrayal of characters plausible? The skills in the category are: 1) recognizing and gathering data on special author techniques of communication, 2) interpreting the techniques or collected data, and 3) judging all or part of the written materials according to criteria set by the class or higher level sources. Recognizing special author techniques includes recognizing fact and opinion, persuasive techniques of propaganda, biased words, and denotative/connotative words. Some writing will also require evaluation of such literary devices as plot development, point of view, symbolism, mood, style, figurative language, and personification.

To illustrate this skill, consider a social studies objective relating to busing for integration. The following sentence was part of the material used to meet the content objective (*10*): "The school's job is to teach the kids their subjects, not mix up the races," said one antibusing father.

Critical analysis of the above sentence requires possession of the critical thinking skill of recognizing the glittering generalities propaganda technique.

The student's attention was directed as follows:

> This afternoon we are going to try something different. You are going to learn how to recognize glittering generalities. This will require you to look at the sentences on the board, listen to what they say and think how certain parts of them are alike. It may be difficult because you haven't done it before so I'm going to help you.

The directed assistance techniques used include modeling, visual highlighting by underlining, and auditory highlighting by voice emphasis. The following sentence is used as a starter: "There isn't a place on earth where the air is purer, where body health is more lavishly bestowed." Through a series of questions, the teacher leads the students to explain why phrases like the ones above are glittering generalities designed to sway people's opinions. In subsequent sentences the teacher gradually drops the directed assistance techniques, allowing students themselves to identify and explain the generalities. A practice situation follows and leads to application in which the skill of recognizing glittering generalities is used in the content material.

SUMMARY

The middle school social studies teacher is charged with the primary task of teaching social studies concepts. For students to learn such concepts while reading content material, however, they must possess thinking skills. Using the content objectives as a guideline, the social studies teacher assesses the materials to account for the variables that affect comprehension, decides which thinking skills are necessary, assesses the students for the thinking skills, teaches the thinking skills to those who need them, and finally, provides for an application of the thinking skills in the social studies material being used.

While social studies teachers may not want to accept the responsibility for basic reading instruction, they can hardly dodge the responsibility for developing thinking skills within the framework of social studies. Such an emphasis is particularly relevant to the middle school where the emphasis is on process. And what is the process of social studies if it is not thinking?

References

1. Allington, Richard. "An Evaluation of the Use of Color Cues to Focus Attention in Discrimination and Paired-Associate Learning," unpublished doctoral dissertation, Michigan State University, 1973.

2. Bandura, Albert. *Principles of Behavior Modification*. New York: Holt, Rinehart and Winston, 1969.

3. Duffy, Gerald et al. *How To Teach Reading Systematically*. New York: Harper and Row, 1973, 81-91, 193.

4. Johnson, Roger E., and Eileen B. Vardian. "Reading, Readability, and Social Studies," *Reading Teacher*, 26 (February 1973), 483-488.

5. Stott, D. H. "Some Less Obvious Cognitive Aspects of Learning to Read," *Reading Teacher*, 26 (January 1973), 374-383.

6. *The State Journal*, Lansing, Michigan, March 9, 1973.

7. *The State Journal*, Lansing, Michigan, March 11, 1973.

8. *The State Journal*, Lansing, Michigan, April 15, 1973.

9. *The State Journal*, Lansing, Michigan, April 22, 1973.

10. *The State Journal*, Lansing, Michigan, April 24, 1973.

CHAPTER SIXTEEN

TECHNIQUES FOR IMPROVING COMPREHENSION IN MATHEMATICS

Jane H. Catterson
University of British Columbia

Superficially, mathematics would seem to be the one middle school curriculum area which places diminished importance on reading skills. Careful analysis, however, reveals that this is a misconception. To learn mathematics efficiently, the middle school student must use a textbook which uses special patterns of rhetoric. Students who cannot comprehend these patterns of writing often have difficulty in mastering the mathematics content. It is essential, therefore, for the middle school mathematics teacher to analyze the rhetoric of the textbook and to provide instruction which helps children interpret these crucial language units.

Before discussing these essential elements, two assumptions made by the author must be explained. First, although no mention of word skills is made in this chapter, it must be remembered that word meaning forms the basis of reading comprehension in all subject areas, including mathematics. Every study of comprehension to date indicates that vocabulary is the single largest factor consistently isolated in comprehension (5). In fact, it seems likely that at least 50 percent of any person's ability to understand connected prose is based on his knowledge of the word meanings within the material. That figure can conceivably go far higher in the field of mathematics where symbols often become the vocabulary and play a crucial role in bridging the gap between verbal language and mathematical concepts. The mathematics teacher must, therefore, teach word meanings thoroughly as a first step in insuring comprehension in the subject matter area.

Second, this chapter has been written in terms of the student who has average ability in dealing with mathematics concepts but who has problems in translating print into mathematical images. It is important that the teacher grasp the importance of creating such images in mathematics for, as Paige and Simon (10) found, contradictions in algebra problems were detected less often by students who used verbal, rather than internal, physical representations of the problems. In fact, it is possible that a teacher may compound a math weakness by stressing the verbal where iconic* might be more suitable. An excellent discussion of this, within an extensive review on language factors in mathematics, can be found in Aiken (*1*).

With these assumptions as a foundation, the essential elements of rhetoric found in mathematics can be discussed and suggestions for teaching comprehension of these patterns can be detailed.

ANALYZING THE TASK: THE RHETORIC OF MATHEMATICS

Chapter 8 of this book, as well as other sources (*4*), discuss the importance of a reader's knowing something about the common written language patterns of a subject before he begins to read. A writer of prose in any area chooses a pattern of rhetoric (or form of discourse) that suits his subject matter and his purposes in writing. In addition, he divides his prose into such normal linguistic units as sentences and paragraphs, and may use chapter subdivisions to set off one main idea from another. An understanding of common patterns of rhetoric and the ways they are structured may be the single most important mind organizer a reader can bring to the reading task. Teachers in any subject area, particularly mathematics, must be very conscious of patterns of rhetoric as they train children in comprehension tasks.

In 1964, an examination of patterns of rhetoric was reported by Smith (*12*). Although still useful, it must be pointed out that parts of this analysis have been outdated by new types of writing in certain content areas. New math and new science have changed not only in content but in the written language in which they are presented and we must study that language and its regularities if we are to teach comprehension of it.

Recent mathematics textbooks seem to use two major language patterns and three language units.

Major Language Patterns

The two language patterns that seem to be important in school math texts are the explanation pattern and the problem pattern.

The explanation pattern is usually several paragraphs long and is designed to present a specific mathematical concept to the student. Often it is followed by a set of exercises or problems designed to test the students' understanding of the

---

*The term *iconic thinking* is used in art circles as a contrast to *verbal thinking*. Recently, Helen Diemert of the Fine Arts Faculty, University of Calgary, and I explored the possibilities within the term *iconic* for designating various levels of ability in visual thinking. We came up with *dysiconic* for the person seriously handicapped; *hypoiconic* for the person with weak abilities; and *hypericonic* for the artist or mathematician who thinks entirely in images. The discussion was carried on facetiously at first, but we have since come to think that the terms are meaningful and possibly useful to point toward the right kind of remedial action.

concept before they proceed to another explanation within the same chapter. Within a chapter, there are usually several explanations each followed by illustrative problems. All are linked as subtopics under one general topic.

The problem pattern may be either a word problem or a concept testing problem. The former is usually fairly wordy and can create problems for the poor reader. However, wordiness may at times have an advantage in that it fleshes out an idea. Word problems may then be easier to work with than the concept-testing problem which goes very succinctly to the heart of the mathematical situation. There are those who suggest that difficulties with concept testing problems are difficulties of mathematics, not of reading.

Language Units

Whatever the pattern of rhetoric being employed, the reader must comprehend three linguistic units beyond the word.

The first is the sentence, both the sentence that occurs in isolation as in a concept-testing problem, and the sentence that occurs within an explanation or word problem paragraph. Which kind of sentence is harder would be difficult to say. The single sentence certainly carries a heavy load of meaning, yet the sentence within a paragraph has its own pitfalls because its meaning does not stand alone but in relation to the other sentences within a paragraph. It may refer back to a sentence before it, it may refer to an idea to come, or it may simply be a bridge between two parts of a paragraph.

The second unit is the paragraph, both the paragraph that occurs within an explanation and the paragraph of a problem.

The final unit is the chapter segment which focuses on the development of a particular mathematical concept and is usually followed by a set of sample problems designed to test the student's understanding before he proceeds to the next chapter segment.

Summary

In analyzing his textbook, the middle school mathematics teacher must be concerned with both language patterns and language units. The language patterns found in the math text can be described as patterns of explanation and of problems. The units within these patterns, in addition to the individual words, include the sentence, the paragraph, and the chapter segment. To effectively help the student comprehend in mathematics, the teacher must plan instruction which helps students interpret both explanations and problems.

TEACHING COMPREHENSION OF EXPLANATIONS

For children who have difficulty comprehending in mathematics, it is often necessary to provide specific, isolated drills which develop the skill needed to interpret explanations. The following are samples of such exercises for sentences, paragraphs, and chapter segments.

Explanation Sentences

At least four types of exercises can be used to help students interpret explanation sentences. The first is the "phrase and clause meaning exercise." In this practice, students are asked to indicate the meaning of an underlined part of a sentence by telling whether it tells *how, when, where,* or *which.*

Example: Tell whether the underlined part tells how, when, or where.

1. Since the factors 2, 3, and 5 appear <u>in all factored forms,</u> each of these belongs to the GCD.

2. In every term, the factor 3 appears <u>with exponents.</u>

The second type is the "structured cloze" exercise. In this exercise, the student is supplied with a sentence having deletions and with words, numbers, or symbols that are to be fitted into the deletions.

Example: Use the words and symbols below to fill in the blanks.

1. The_____and the_____are called the terms of the fraction_____.

    (a) 2/3   (b) 2   (c) 4   (d) 3

2. The_____number in a fraction is called the_____.

    (a) denominator   (b) top   (c) bottom

A third exercise is called "understanding deep structure." This exercise is prepared by selecting sentences from math books and asking students to demonstrate their understanding of the deep structure (meaning) of the sentence by indicating whether the short statements placed below the longer sentence are true or false.

Example: Choose the statements that tell the meaning of the sentence.

1. You know that a mathematical sentence, like an English sentence, expresses a complete thought.

    (a) An English sentence expresses a complete thought.

    (b) A mathematics sentence expresses a complete thought.

    (c) You know a mathematical sentence.

The final exercise is for determining the main idea of a sentence. This practice is, to an extent, the reciprocal of the first example above. The student is asked to strike out all but the main thought of the sentence, deleting qualifying phrases or clauses.

Example: Cross out all but the main idea of the following sentence.

1. ~~From the first division we can say that~~ the quotient correct to the nearest tenth is .9.

Explanation Paragraphs

The student needs also to learn ways to focus his attention on the meaning of paragraphs. This comprehension process depends on recognizing that paragraph meaning is the product of both the cumulative meaning of the sentences and the interaction between the sentences. Paragraphs are not simply sentence beads strung on a string. The following exercises may be helpful in developing paragraph comprehension.

The first focuses on the main idea of the paragraph. This exercise, often used with information material, needs attention in math as well. It requires the student to sum up a paragraph in a single statement. Since it is difficult to begin by having students create their own main idea sentence, many exercises should be prepared in which the students must simply choose the correct main idea sentence. A variation of this is to have them choose 1) a title *or* 2) the question answered by the paragraph. Only after they become adept at this kind of exercise should they be asked to create their own sentences.

Example: Choose the main idea.

1. If your name is Richard, your friends may call you Dick. Your mother may call you Sonny and your sister may call you Bud. In much the same way, we have found in this course that a number may have many names.

    (a) Your friends may call you Dick.
    (b) A number may have many names.
    (c) We have found out many things in this course.

The second exercise focuses on understanding references. This paragraph meaning exercise requires the reader to refer to the previous sentence read to get the meaning of the sentence. The words *it, they,* and *this* often cannot be understood unless the reader looks to the previous sentence.

Example: What does the underlined word refer to?

1. We have said before that a line does not end in either direction. To show this, we have used arrows.

    (a) a line   (b) that a line does not end   (c) in either direction

2. The number line in Chapter 3 was really a ray. We named the point at which it began "zero."

    (a) Chapter 3   (b) a ray   (c) the number line

A final exercise is called "following the thought." In this exercise, a word or more is left out of the last sentence of a paragraph and the students are asked to show they have understood the paragraph by completing the blanks.

Example: Complete the blank in the last sentence of the paragraph.

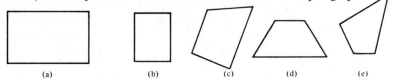

(a)   (b)   (c)   (d)   (e)

Four of the figures above have at least two sides which are parallel. There are some quadrilaterals which do not have parallel sides. Figure _____ is an example of a quadrilateral that has no parallel sides.

Chapter Segments

Normally, a school mathematics textbook does not provide whole chapters of material to be read through as do books of narrative or information. One usually finds some explanatory material at the beginning of a chapter and then segments of such explanatory material alternating with exercises or problems to be done before the student moves ahead to new ideas. Although some teachers of math prefer to provide initial explanations themselves in an oral presentation and let the students work alone only on the exercises or problems, it seems unfortunate that pupils should be taught always to rely so heavily on the teacher for new learning. With proper guidance, the average pupil can be shown how to involve himself in self-teaching and so acquire much more independence in learning. A number of approaches seem appropriate.

One is the directed reading lesson. A frequently used technique is that of asking students to read narrative materials and later answer oral questions directed from the teacher. Usually called guided silent reading, it has been unnecessarily maligned. Used as a single method, it can become boring, but basically its approach is sound. Children need to form the habit of reading to answer questions, and they learn what questions are appropriate for each subject area as questions are prepared and posed by their teachers. The passage on "Decimals" (6) illustrates.

Another technique is the use of a reading study guide. Instead of guiding students orally through the reading of math explanations, a teacher may supply a study guide to allow students to work through such material at their own pace.

The following are some suggested variations:

1. Directed reading lesson. Here questions are printed rather than asked orally (see previous sample).
2. Matching sentences to paragraphs. In this format, "main ideas of paragraphs" sentences are supplied (some correct and some incorrect). The student is asked to match sentences to paragraphs.

Many variations of the reading study guide can be suggested, as well as many organizational patterns for using it. Team learning (6, 9) has been employed successfully with children working in twos and threes to solve common problems.

A third technique is to provide some form of advance cognitive organizer. Ausubel (2) has been interested in exploring the effect of introducing, prior to the presentation of new ideas, some material that will provide "ideational anchorage" for the new ideas. He has called such material "advance organizers" and suggests:

These organizers are introduced in advance of the learning material itself, are formulated in terms already familiar to the learner, are also presented at a higher level of abstractions, generality and inclusiveness.

DIRECTED READING LESSON

Decimals

$$4.2 \times 10^6 = 4,200,000$$

$$\frac{.08}{.002} = 40$$

$$.25 = \frac{25}{100} = \frac{5}{20} = \frac{1}{4}$$

$$.9999\ldots$$

$$2/3$$

$$\frac{3}{16} = .1875$$

Decimal Notation

8.1 DECIMALS IN MODERN LIFE

The adjective "decimal" has two meanings. (1) It may refer to a system of numeration using base 10. Thus, we refer to our present-day system of *decimal* numeration, to the *decimal* system, or to a *decimal* numeral. (2) It may refer to a particular form used to write a fraction. Thus, we refer to 3/5 as the *common* fraction form of a rational number which can also be expressed in the *decimal* fraction form as .6.

For convenience in everyday affairs, we generally use the noun "decimal" to designate a decimal fraction, just as we say "fraction" to mean a common fraction. Thus, when we speak of adding, subtracting, multiplying, or dividing "decimals," we mean, of course, decimal fractions.

In this chapter we shall learn how to work with decimals. In modern times we find that decimals are very useful in our daily lives as well as in science and in engineering. The following statements illustrate some of the uses of decimals:

Mr. Thomas paid $2,478.65 for his new car.
Sheet aluminum used in airplanes is .032 inches thick.
The odometer on Mr. Bell's car read 14,382.7 at the start of his vacation trip.
On a cold day, the outdoor thermometer reading was 16.4

GUIDED SILENT READING – QUESTIONS

1. The Title

(1) What is the topic of the chapter?

2. The Diagram

(2a) What kinds of numerals do you see?

(2b) What does the graph mean?

3. The First Topic

(3a) What is the first aspect of decimals dealt with?

4. The First Subtopic

(4) What aspect of decimals in modern life is dealt with?

5. The First Paragraph

(5) What are the 2 meanings of adjective "decimal"?

(5a) Give examples of how the word decimal may be used in the decimal system.

(5b) What is the difference between the fraction 3/5 and the fraction .6?

6. The Second Paragraph

(6) What word do we use commonly instead of "decimal fractions"?

7. The Third Paragraph & Sample Problems

(7a) In what general ways are decimals useful?

(7b) Name specific ways in which decimals are useful.

On the whole, Ausubel's experiments have been concerned with the acquisition of meaningful verbal material, specifically of the information type. Herber (9) and his students, however, have been interested in the idea of advance organizers applied generally to the school content fields in which reading may be used as an avenue to learning. Directed by Herber, Barron (3), Estes (8), and Earle (7) have reported attempts to use variations of the advance organizer in the content subjects. Although minimally successful in improving mathematics learning, the approaches are interesting and warrant more study.

One interesting variation on the advanced organizer was the "structured overview," introduced in Earle's study. This was a diagramatic representation of the structure of mathematics constructed out of the basic vocabulary of the subject (using words, not symbols). In two experiments, the specially developed diagram was presented to junior high classes before the introduction of a new math topic and referred to periodically during the period of teaching the new material. Such a technique would seem to have potential for improving comprehension of chapter segments.

The table of contents might also be used as a cognitive organizer. Study of the table of contents of a math book just prior to beginning a new topic and periodic review might clarify the relationships of all topics to each other and the relationships among subtopics within the same chapter. This practice alone might provide the ideational anchorage Ausubel considers desirable.

Another approach was the making of a structured overview out of the symbols equivalent to the words of vocabulary. If a scheme could be developed that conveyed mathematical meaning rather than logical meaning, as Earle's seemed to do, its impact might be correspondingly greater.

Summary

To help children comprehend explanations in the middle school mathematics textbook, the teacher can use exercises such as those described. It should be pointed out, however, that both the drills and the advanced organizer techniques described require direct teacher guidance if they are to be helpful. Giving the activities to students without the proper preparation from the teacher is not likely to be effective.

TEACHING COMPREHENSION OF PROBLEMS

As has been stated earlier, two kinds of problems are encountered in mathematics: the word problem and the concept-testing problem. In both kinds of problems, the teacher must be concerned with the language units of words, sentences, paragraphs, and chapter segments. Because most problems are presented in paragraphs, however, the majority of the following suggestions focus on that language unit.

Word Problems

One of the most complete statements about the reading of word problems was made by Smith (*12*) when she suggested that there were four basic questions to be asked when attacking word problems. These classic questions are as follows:

1. What is the whole situation?
2. What am I asked to find?
3. What am I given?
4. What process will I use?

Some writers have suggested the addition of the question, "What is an estimate of the answer?" It has been suggested that teachers should inculcate in their pupils the habit of asking themselves these questions every time they approach a word problem.

In any case, methods of inculcating the habit of asking these questions can vary a great deal. A teacher may first guide the students through many sessions in which the questions are answered orally and then make the assumption that they can pose the questions themselves.

On the other hand, it may be well to give extra practice by supplying a reading study guide in which the students must supply the written answers on blank spaces opposite each question. Such a procedure allows the teacher to pinpoint exactly the stage at which a pupil had difficulty in his attempts to solve the problem.

An intermediate step might be the supplying of a reading study guide with questions and multiple-choice answers. Such skill building practices would help bridge the gap between oral discussion in class and independent filling-in of blanks. A sample study guide follows:

Example: A homeowner insured his house for a value of $16,000. His premium for three years was $75. What rate of premium per year was being charged?

What am I to find?

(a) the premium for 3 years
(b) the premium for 1 year
(c) the yearly rate of premium payment

What am I given?

(a) house value
(b) 3 year premium
(c) rate of premium per year

What processes will I use?

(a) division, then division again
(b) division, then multiplication
(c) multiplication, then division

What is an estimate of the answer?

(a) below 1%

(b) between 10% and 20%

(c) between 3% and 5%

Another technique is one in which the student is presented with problems from which some essential information is missing. His task is simply to identify what is missing. Again, this can be made simpler initially by having multiple choice items supplied until the students become accustomed to the type of thinking needed.

Example: What is needed to do the problem?

Frank Harris is a mechanic's helper in an automobile shop. He is paid at the rate of $1.25 an hour. How much does he earn in a week?

(a) his wage per hour

(b) his hours of work

(c) what kind of work he does

A third technique is the "hidden numbers" exercise. This exercise focuses on a specific piece of information not actually included, but needed if the student is to solve the problem. For example, if he is asked to find the length of a room in yards and the only measurements quoted are in feet, he must know how many feet there are in a yard.

Example: What is the hidden number?

Mr. Smith wants to cover the floor of a room with wall to wall carpeting. The room is 10 feet by 14 feet and the carpet will cost him $10.95 a square yard. How much will the carpeting cost?

(a) the cost per square yard

(b) the number of square feet in one square yard

(c) the size of the carpet

In another activity called the "easy numbers" exercise, students are taught to turn "difficult" numbers into "easy" numbers as a way to make the relationship clear.

Example: What numbers would be easy to work with and give you a quick estimate of the answer?

A rectangular room is 30 feet long and 15 feet wide. What is its perimeter?

In the "draw a diagram" exercise, students are encouraged to produce a diagram from the facts given in the problem as a way of improving their grasp of a situation. In a problem about room measurement, for example, students would sketch the room roughly to get a mental picture.

Example: Draw a rough diagram before you try to obtain the answer.

Mr. Smith has a lot 60 feet wide by 100 feet deep. He wants to make a garden by stretching his fence across the lot about 13 feet from the end of the lot. What will be the area of the garden?

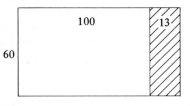

A sixth technique is called the "structured response" exercise and is especially useful with algebra problems. The teacher provides a framework into which the student fits his response until he can recall and use the framework when it is not before him.

Example: Fill in the blanks to work toward your answer.

One angle of a triangle is twice the smallest angle and the third angle is 16 degrees less than twice the middle-sized angle. Find the angles.

The smallest angle _____

The second angle _____ 2x _____

The third angle _____

Sum of angles (agebraic) _____ x + 2x + (2x-16) _____

Sum of angles of any triangle _____

Equation _____

(and so on)

Note: The teacher should supply some answers at first, gradually reducing cues.

Concept-Testing Problems

Some children find the single sentence problem among the most difficult, probably because it continues such a heavy density of vocabulary and instructions. The phrase and clause meaning and structured cloze exercises cited earlier could be adapted to such problems. An additional suggestion would be the "matching solutions to problems" exercise.

Here students are given a set of problems and an accompanying set of solutions with which to match them.

Example: Match the solutions to the problems.

1. Show that (3+4) +6 and   (a)   (3+4) +6
   3+(4+6) are names for   7+   6
   the same number   13

2. Find the product of   (b)   (8+7) +2
   8, 7, and 2   15   +2
                        17

3. Find the sum of 8, 7, and 2   (c) (3+4) +6 = 3+(4+6)

$$(3+4) \quad +6 = 3+(4+6)$$
$$7 \quad +6 \quad 3+10$$
$$13 \quad 13$$

4. Find the sum of 3, 4, and 6

(d) 8(7) 2
     56 2
  112

(e) 8 7 (2)

The paucity of examples given for the concept-testing problem should make it clear that opinion is still much divided about what one should do, beyond strengthening meaning vocabulary, to improve the student's ability to handle the concept problem. This is still very much an area for research.

CONCLUSION

The mathematics teacher, no less than other content teachers in the middle school, must be concerned with reading, since the degree to which the students grasp math concepts is highly related to their skill in interpreting the rhetoric of the textbook. To accomplish this aspect of the teaching task, the teacher must familiarize himself with the demands of the basic writing patterns found in the textbook, directly assist students in interpreting these patterns, and provide practice exercises such as those suggested here to insure that the skill is mastered.

References

1. Aiken, Lewis R. "Language Factors in Learning Mathematics," *Review of Educational Research,* 2 (Summer 1972), 359-385.

2. Ausubel, David P. *The Psychology of Meaningful Verbal Learning.* New York: Grune and Stratton, 1963, 15.

3. Barron, Richard F. "The Use of the Advance Organizer," in Harold L. Herber and Peter L. Sanders (Eds.), *Research in Reading in the Content Areas: First Year Report.* Syracuse: Syracuse University Reading and Language Arts Center, 1969.

4. Call, Russell J., and Neal A. Wiggin. "Reading and Mathematics," *Mathematics Teacher,* 59 (February 1966), 149-157. Reprinted in Robert Karlin (Ed.), *Teaching Reading in High School.* Indianapolis: Bobbs-Merrill, 1969.

5. Davis, Frederick B. "Psychometric Research On Comprehension in Reading," *Reading Research Quarterly,* 7 (Summer 1972), 628-695.

6. Durrell, Donald D. *Improving Reading Instruction.* New York: Harcourt Brace Jovanovich, 1956, 287-288.

7. Earle, Richard A. "Use of the Structured Overview in Mathematics Classes," in Harold L. Herber and Peter L. Sanders (Eds.), *Research in Reading in the Content Areas: First Year Report.* Syracuse: Syracuse University Reading and Language Arts Center, 1969.

8. Estes, Thomas E., Daniel C. Mills, and Richard F. Barron. "Three Methods of Introducing Students to a Reading Learning Task in the Content Subjects," in Harold L. Herber and Peter L. Sanders (Eds.), *Research in Reading in the Content Areas: First Year Report.* Syracuse: Syracuse University Reading and Language Arts Center, 1969.

9. Herber, Harold L. *Teaching Reading in the Content Areas.* Englewood Cliffs, New Jersey: Prentice-Hall, 1970.

10. Paige, J. M., and H. A. Simon. "Cognitive Processes in Solving Algebra Problems," in B. Kleinmutz (Ed.), *Problem Solving: Research, Method, and Theory.* New York: Wiley, 1966, 51-119.

11. Peters, Max, and William L. Schaaf. *Mathematics: A Modern Approach* (2nd ed.). New York: Van Nostrand, 1965, 1968, 252.

12. Smith, Nila Banton. "Patterns of Writing in Different Subject Areas," *Journal of Reading,* 7 (November 1964), 97-102.

CHAPTER SEVENTEEN

TECHNIQUES FOR IMPROVING
COMPREHENSION IN SCIENCE

Michael R. McElwee
Milwaukee, Wisconsin, Public Schools

The middle school science teacher is confronted with several special problems regarding reading in his content. As a specialist who has been educated to teach a specific area of the curriculum, he has not been trained to teach reading skills. Because of this, many middle school science teachers do not consider the teaching of reading to be part of their job description and assume that the pupil arrives in the class possessing the necessary skills to achieve academic success. This assumption is contradicted when the science teacher discovers that many of his students cannot read the assigned textbook or any of the supplementary commercial or teacher prepared materials. Giving assigned reading tasks soon appears to be a waste of time as many of the students do not comprehend the material and come to class inadequately prepared for the specific unit.

A second problem, unique to the science teacher, is that of having students participate in laboratory sessions which are an integral part of teaching in any area of science. The laboratory sessions allow the students flexibility in discovering concepts individually or in small groups. Because of this more individualized type of instruction, the teacher does not have adequate time to work with all students on a one-to-one or two-to-one basis. Consequently, students must be able to work independently most of the time during the laboratory sessions. To assist in this regard, laboratory manuals are often prepared to direct the student through a task and ask specific questions to insure that he will develop a complete understanding of the concept being presented. When the student is unable to read the laboratory manual, however, he becomes frustrated, disinterested, and feels that there is little sense in attempting to complete a task in which there is no achievable goal. The student's energy, which should have been directed to problem solving and discovering new concepts, is directed in other areas and the science teacher is faced with a classroom management problem, in addition to trying to teach.

A third problem facing the science teacher is finding time during the class session to teach adequately the reading comprehension skills which students need to understand the printed science materials. This is a difficult task for many science teachers as they must relinquish time from the teaching of science to include the teaching of reading skills. The decision should not be a difficult one to make, for the effective teacher of science realizes that little learning will take place unless students can comprehend printed science materials.

A fourth problem faced by the middle school science teacher is determining what reading comprehension skills should be taught and how they should be taught. As stated previously, science teachers are trained to teach science, not reading, and therefore do not necessarily have the knowledge or resources readily available to teach reading comprehension. This problem is compounded if the middle school does not have a reading consultant who can be called upon to provide assistance.

This chapter provides three areas of assistance for the middle school science teacher. First, the conditions which affect comprehension in science are specified. Second, the specific comprehension skills in science are discussed, including word meanings; organization and structure skills; main idea identification; literal, inferential, and critical reading; and other reading skills needed to comprehend science material. Finally, the third section is a hypothetical classroom illustration in which the principles of the first two sections are used.

CONDITIONS AFFECTING COMPREHENSION

The first task of the science teacher is creating classroom conditions which encourage comprehension. These conditions are similar to the prerequisites of decoding, experience, interest, and thinking skills discussed in Chapter 13. The strategy for controlling these variables is basically the same for science as for other content areas. The following hypothetical situation is provided in illustration.

The classroom being observed is a sixth grade science class and the unit currently being studied deals with shorelines formed by waves. The teacher has divided his students into four groups: one group is working at a laboratory table examining and comparing sand from different beaches; a second group is working on constructing a model of a shoreline which has been eroded by waves; a third group is doing independent reading, using materials related to the formation of shorelines; and the fourth group is working with the teacher in getting ready to read the textbook chapter about shorelines.

The teacher has insured that there will be a limited number of distractions during the class session by providing an activity for each student. To handle routine questions that may arise, the teacher has designated a leader for each of the three independently working groups.

Of the four groups, the one working with the teacher will spend about fifteen minutes on the specific reading skills required in reading the textbook chapter. If the day's lesson deals with the use of prefixes and how they change the meaning of root words, the prefixes to be taught are taken from words used in the science textbook such as *irregular* shoreline and shorelines of *submergence* and *emergence.*

Meanwhile, the group involved in independent reading is using materials written at a lower reading level, since these students have difficulty decoding the assigned textbook. The teacher has previously set the purpose for reading these materials by asking how many students have ever seen the shoreline of an ocean and if they know how the shoreline was formed. The students page through the chapter; look at the paragraph headings, pictures, and text; and formulate some questions regarding the formation of shorelines for which they might find answers. Once the students form their questions, they read independently to find the answers.

Of the remaining two groups, the one working at the laboratory table consists of a group of excellent readers who have chosen to pursue in depth an aspect of the study of shorelines which is of particular interest to them. To this end, the teacher has provided them with appropriate supplementary reading material and has helped them collect the samples of sand from the high school earth science teacher. The other group has already read the textbook chapter, using a study guide prepared by the teacher, and is now preparing the model which they will use in reporting their study to the class.

As described in Chapter 13, the objectives, activities, and evaluations are differentiated to account for student differences and to create conditions conducive to good comprehension. The decoding variable is controlled by giving each student material he can read; interest is created because students have been involved in the planning and setting of group purposes; experience is controlled by using pictures and models of shorelines with students who have not visited or lived near the sea; and comprehension is aided by teaching the specific word skills to those who need them.

TECHNIQUES FOR TEACHING COMPREHENSION IN MIDDLE SCHOOL SCIENCE

Duffy et al. (*1*) identify four major categories of operational skills employed in reading comprehension: 1) teaching word meanings; 2) teaching organization and structure skills; 3) teaching fact and inference skills; and 4) teaching evaluation and judgment skills. Since these thinking skills are appropriate to science instruction, the following sections describe both the skills and appropriate techniques for teaching these skills within a science class.

Teaching Word Meanings

The teaching of word meanings involves the teaching of concepts. A concept is the organization and integration of a student's perceptions of an object or idea and is particularly crucial in science. For instance, a student may have one perception of a mountain — that of a mountain formed by a volcano. He may then be exposed to a second perception of a fold mountain — and a third perception of a fault-block mountain. The student then integrates these three perceptions into a concept for the word *mountain*, which could mean a volcanic mountain, a fold mountain, or a fault-block mountain. Successful science teaching is related to the successful teaching of such science concepts or word meanings.

The first major task in the teaching of word meanings is recognizing the differences between content words and function words. Content words are those words, usually nouns, which signal tangible meaning in a sentence. Function words are those words which signal relationships among the content words in the sentence. For example, in the sentence "This dome was formed thousands of years ago," the content words are *dome, thousands*, and *years*; the function words are *this, was, of*, and *ago*.

The science teacher's major concern will be with content words since the technical vocabulary words of science usually fall into this category. The first step in teaching content word meanings is to provide students with experiences with the word. In teaching the content word *dome*, it is unlikely that the teacher will be able to take the students outside of the classroom to examine their neighborhood geological dome. When providing a direct experience for the content word is impossible, the teacher must provide students with second-hand or vicarious experiences dealing with the word to be taught. Vicarious experiences would include the use of films, filmstrips, filmloops, pictures, or even a simple illustration drawn on the chalkboard. Next, the teacher eliminates the use of visual aids in providing experience and presents the word within the context of a sentence to derive a meaning. Often times, as in the sentence "This dome was formed thousands of years ago," there is little in the way of context clues to help the student obtain a meaning. From the sample sentence, students may learn that some domes are very old, but it is unlikely that they will learn the meaning for the word *dome*. The teacher must then provide additional sentences of his own to assist students in deriving meaning by using context clues. Sentences such as "The men climbed to the top of the dome" would be more useful in determining the meaning of the word. Finally, the use of a dictionary definition may be introduced as a means of providing greater specificity in the word meaning.

As the teacher is providing such vicarious experiences for the teaching of the content word, he should state the distinct characteristics of the word. For example, while teaching the word *dome*, the teacher would direct attention to the ovalness or roundness of the rock layers and to the way they move away radially from a central high point. The similarities and differences of domes might be compared with kames or the characteristics of basins in which the rock layers are circular but move to a central low point. Throughout, the teacher is also continually using the name of the content word so that the students learn to attach the word label to the new concept.

The teacher should also expose students to any multiple meanings of new words. For instance, the meaning of the word *dome* in an earth science class is entirely different from the meaning encountered in reference to a cathedral's dome, the dome of the state capitol building, or to the slang use of dome in referring to a person's head.

Because of the heavy load of technical vocabulary typically found in middle school science, the teacher must not take casually his responsibility for teaching word meanings. Effective teaching of terminology, using the techniques described here, is often the difference between successful and unsuccessful comprehension of middle school science material.

Teaching Organization and Structure Skills

In the area of relationships, students should be taught how concepts within a paragraph go together and what words are used to tie the concepts together. The relationship words are usually function words which signal the organization of a paragraph as to events or objects in a series, chronological order, comparisons, and cause and effect.

The following is a paragraph containing words which signal chronological order:

> The water cycle consists of three phases. First, the sun's rays evaporate water from the surface of the ocean. Next, the winds carry the water from the surface of the ocean and over the land in the form of water vapor. Finally, some of the water vapor, which has condensed to form clouds, may fall as rain or snow and it may seep through the rocks and eventually return to the ocean.

The function words which signal chronological order are *first, next*, and *finally*. In teaching such relationship thinking, the teacher can reproduce the paragraph on an overhead transparency or write it on the chalkboard and direct the students' attention to the function words by underlining or circling the words and talking through the paragraph with the students to show them how these function words signal chronological order and sequence of events. This, of course, is a reading comprehension skill but without an understanding of the relationship signalled, the science learning would not take place.

Classification skills allow students to take major ideas or concepts within a reading situation and organize them according to their similarities. Using classification, the student is able to accept or reject concepts according to category, a thinking skill which is crucial in science. For example, if the students are categorizing lakes in earth science, they would put *crique lakes, kettle lakes*, and *rock basin lakes* in a category of lakes formed by glaciers. However, *crater lakes* would be placed in a separate category as lakes being formed by volcanos. In addition to being a useful science skill in itself, the skill of classification is also a prerequisite for obtaining the main idea from what is read.

In teaching how to locate the main idea, the teacher must first insure that students can classify major science concepts according to similarities and differences. The second step is to teach students how the common name for the major classifications becomes the main idea of the selection. When teaching students how to find the main idea, direct their attention first to reading the entire paragraph and then to looking for the common elements within the paragraph which can be classified into one category. Using the previous example of *crique lakes, kettle lakes*, and *rock basin lakes*, students would classify these as lakes formed by glaciers, thus identifying the main idea of the paragraph. The teacher should model this activity for students and show them how it works by giving them copies of paragraphs, classifying the concepts in the paragraphs, and demonstrating how the major classification becomes the main idea.

Teaching Fact Skills

Much of the reading which takes place in the sciences is done at the factual or literal level. That is, much science reading involves gathering information which is specifically presented in the textbook. When students are reading for literal comprehension, they are answering questions which ask who, what, where, when, why, or how. A literal question might be, "In which rocks is magnetite found?" or "What is a stalactite?" In answering these questions, the students return to the text and locate the specific fact, as stated by the author. In addition, students read literally to recall details, main ideas, cause and effect relationships, and sequence. The fundamental task here is to teach pupils how to locate the answers to such factual questions.

A modeling technique is probably most useful here. For each new student, duplicate a few short science paragraphs with comprehension questions. In the first paragraph, underline those statements which deal with the "where" of the story, pointing out those sections to your students and discussing with them how they know that these tell "where." The same techniques would be used for the second paragraph. This time, statements dealing with the "what" of the paragraph would be underlined and then discussed with the students. The third paragraph would be unmarked and students would be asked to identify the "where" and "what" of the paragraph on their own. This same technique could be used to model reading for detail, sequence, and cause and effect.

Teaching Evaluative Reading Skills

The fourth major skill to be taught is evaluative or critical reading. When using this skill, students read a selection and accept or reject statements based on their critical evaluation of the selection. The students must be taught to see the difference between fact and opinion, reality and fantasy, extreme statements of bias, qualifications of the author, emotion-laden words, stereotypes, and figures of speech. The students are making judgments which go beyond the printed page.

Students may not use evaluation or inferential comprehension skills as much as they use literal comprehension skills in reading their science textbook. However, they may encounter in newspapers, magazines, television, or radio science issues which require critical evaluation. Current issues, such as the expansion of expressways at the cost of eliminating green space in a city or the effects of a nuclear power plant on the environment, are dealt with by the mass media every day and they should be integrated into the science curriculum, since the middle school student must be taught to react to these issues in an evaluative manner.

A technique for teaching evaluation reading skills is to provide sample paragraphs containing words which reflect bias or opinion. The teacher circles the words or statements which signal opinion or bias on the part of the author and discusses them with the students. Next, the students are given paragraphs containing biased statements and are allowed to identify them on their own. Finally, a class discussion is held to determine if the statements selected were biased and why. A second technique would be to print, side by side, two paragraphs dealing with a current ecological topic. One paragraph should be written in a purely factual manner, while the other should be written in an opinionated and biased manner. The students read each paragraph and then discuss which article is the most factual and why.

Other Skills

In addition to the basic comprehension skills mentioned, the science teacher must also help students read tables, charts, and graphs to interpret the information presented. All too often, teachers expect students to have these skills developed before coming to class but frequently, middle school children have never been taught to interpret scientific material which is presented graphically. To increase student comprehension, the science teacher must take the responsibility for this task.

In addition, the science teacher should teach students how to use other aids in the text. For instance, he should direct the students' attention to words or phrases presented in italics, to the use of underlining, and to subheads or subtitles since these are all devices which the textbook author uses to signal what is of particular importance.

Following directions is another crucial skill in middle school science. Some students may not need any instruction in this area but others will. For these, begin with easy tasks consisting of only three or four directions and gradually expand the number of directions needed for each task until the students demonstrate competency in following directions.

Finally, students must be helped to use all their skills while reading their science textbooks. One way of helping them do this is to type a selection from the text on the left hand side of the paper while using the right side for teacher comments, indicating the reading skills which will aid the students' comprehension of the materials. For example, the main idea could be highlighted or the way context clues aid in discovering the meaning of a particular word, could be noted.

DESCRIPTION OF A MIDDLE SCHOOL SCIENCE CLASSROOM

Novak's *Facilities for Secondary School Science Teaching* (2), which is a report of a study conducted by the National Science Teachers Association, deals in part with planning appropriate instructional space in a science class. The areas of consideration are laboratory space, lecture-discussion space, individual and small-group study areas, integrated learning areas, and areas for special projects and special purposes. The following is a description of an ideal middle school science classroom in which reading skills are also taught:

> At the south end of the room, there would be student desks, sufficient chalkboard space, a screen for large group presentations, and a laboratory table for demonstrations. At the back of the large group presentation area and off to one side, would be a teacher's desk and a teacher's preparation area. The middle of the room would contain student laboratory tables with storage shelves along the walls and some bulletin boards, chalkboards, and a laboratory table for demonstration purposes. The area at the north end of the room would be divided into two sections: one section would provide space for small group meetings to discuss topics of special interest and to be used for the teaching of reading skills to small groups of students. This area would contain a few student desks and a chalkboard. The larger area at the north end of the room would contain study carrels for students doing independent studies or viewing individualized audiovisual presentations. Table space would be available for small group or individual class projects. In addition, this area would contain shelves for books and magazines, storage space for student projects and equipment, and additional bulletin board space. The different areas of the room could be left undivided to create an open atmosphere or they could be separated by using portable room dividers. These dividers would contain additional storage space.

With teacher ingenuity, such a classroom could be fashioned from existing space and materials in many modern middle school science rooms. The result would be the flexibility needed to conduct a diversified science program while also providing the reading help needed by the students. For instance, there is designated space for whole group instruction of concepts and for demonstration of laboratory experiments as is found in most standard science classes. In addition, however, space has been created to accommodate individual and small group instruction. These can be used for independent group work and special skill instruction, following the suggestions described in Chapter 13 and earlier in this chapter.

SUMMARY

The middle school science teacher is faced with many problems in meeting the reading needs of his students, not the least of which is that he has not been trained to teach reading. However, part of the uniqueness of the middle school is its commitment to meet such needs. Teachers who truly share this philosophy can organize the physical aspects of the science room and schedule the time to meet the goals of both science and improved reading within the science classroom.

References

1. Duffy, Gerald G. et al. *How To Teach Reading Systematically*. New York: Harper and Row, 1973, 193.
2. Novak, Joseph D. *Facilities For Secondary School Science Teaching*. Washington, D.C.: National Science Teachers Association, 1972.

CHAPTER EIGHTEEN

TECHNIQUES FOR DEVELOPING STUDY SKILLS

James E. Walker
University of Kentucky

The curriculum of the middle school requires that the student regularly go beyond the task of learning to read into the more complicated area of reading to learn, since he must now use reading as a means for learning a variety of subject matters. This area of reading is termed *study-reading.*

Study-reading is not something a middle school student comes equipped with naturally. To the contrary, it is composed of a variety of skills which must be taught within the framework of the content areas. This chapter describes principles and techniques applicable to study-reading, with an emphasis on those strategies which hold promise for making the middle school student a more efficient learner in all areas of the curriculum.

APPLICABLE PRINCIPLES

Definition of Study Skills

Webster's dictionary defines *study* as "a process of acquiring by one's own efforts knowledge of a subject." This definition assumes that a student has already learned how to read (8). This is supported by Smith (16), who defines study skills as "those skills used when we intend to *do something with* content while reading it or after finishing the reading." Unfortunately, such a definition can lead us to pay too much attention to methods of study and too little attention to the elements involved in a self-directed approach to how to study.

Emphasis on self-directed study is more utilitarian than concentration on methods alone. This emphasis is perhaps most appreciated when we consider the results of a factor analysis of study skills (11). The analysis showed that the components of study skills were: 1) morale and self-confidence, 2) scholarly drive and values, 3) study mechanics, and 4) planning to get the work done.

Three of these components have to do with aspects of self-direction while only one component relates to skills per se (5).

It is therefore necessary, when looking at study skills, to develop a definition which includes both the mechanical and the self-directional aspects of study. Factors related to self-direction are termed nonspecific study skills. What we know as mechanical factors are termed specific study skills (11).

Study Skills in the Middle School

By the time a student reaches the middle school, he may be able to read but he does not necessarily know how to study. To say that a pupil who knows how to read will also know how to make use of reference and illustrative materials is a good case of assumptive teaching. If a pupil lacks the necessary skills, his resistance is virtually guaranteed. Similarly, if a pupil lacks confidence in using the skills, we are again virtually guaranteed to meet his resistance. Note that both skills and confidence are included in the broader definition of study skills.

Study Skills in the Content Areas

A phenomenon that becomes evident in the middle school is the transition from narrative writing to the straight exposition materials commonly found in the content areas. Dulin (4) illustrates the difference by saying that reading a narrative selection is like the long, sloping left-hand side of a Gaussian Curve — the story builds and then drops off with the climax and denouement. On the other hand, expository writing is more like a series of small, then larger waves embodying paragraphs, subsections, sections, chapters, and units.

Differences in reading content related materials might be succinctly summarized as residing in 1) the technical vocabulary in each field; 2) the patterns of mental organization required to read printed materials of each field; and 3) the devices, symbols, and illustrations characteristic of each field. Each of these factors calls for specific teaching (12). In addition, students need to recognize the function of the different kinds of content materials they are required to read, particularly in view of the noticeable increase in the number of texts and supplementary materials commonly found in the middle school.

Because of the special demands of the content areas, study skills are learned best within the context in which they are to be used. This is equivalent to saying that such skills need to be functional and not taught in isolation. Herber (8) supports this view (as does Fillmer in Chapter 3 of this book) when he says that the reading program pervades all the content areas. And while it is true that all teachers are not teachers of reading, content teachers should think of study skills, as Catterson (3) states, "not as *something* to teach, but as a *way* to teach — a way of teaching which advances not only the students' knowledge of subject matter but his ability to learn other subject matter independently and at will." Catterson speaks not about a unit on study to be added to an already overloaded course outline, but something that should just be part of good teaching. Artley (*1*) continues the argument by saying, "The teaching of a particular subject is the teaching of the study of that subject; and that makes inescapable the fact that every teacher is a teacher of . . . study."

The Middle School Teacher's Role

Perhaps the middle school teacher's greatest contribution as a teacher of study lies in the motivational aspects of learning. To be motivated, one must succeed. Bloom (*2*) expresses his concern for the intellectual and personality consequences of a "lack of clear success in the learning tasks of the school" and suggests that if school learning is seen as frustrating and even impossible by a sizable proportion of students, then little can be done to kindle a genuine interest in further learning. Hence, one clear way to improve study skills is to provide the success experiences which are the basis of motivation.

In addition, students should receive direct instruction in improving skills rather than a trial and error approach. According to modern theories of learning, the pupil learns best when he 1) wants something, 2) perceives something, 3) does something, and 4) gets satisfaction from the learning experience (*18*). All these elements should be present in effective instruction in study. The point here is that extensive reading and rereading is not the way to improve study skills (*10*). Both teachers and students need to understand what assignments are required in a subject and what the assignments require of a student. In addition, questions such as the following need to be answered if mastery learning is to take place. What particular type of reading is asked for in the different content areas? When should notes be taken? How? In what kind of book? How should they be organized? Is there a special use of the library for a certain subject? What reference works would be especially useful? What are the standards for written work?

Study Skills Objectives

In planning study skills instruction, a middle school team should plan specific instructional objectives. Gronlund's *Stating Behavioral Objectives for Classroom Instruction* (*7*) is a handy and inexpensive resource. For example, Gronlund lists some of the following key words for study behaviors: arrange, chart, compile, diagram, itemize, locate, map, quote, search, sort, and underline. There are further listings for art, drama, music, language, mathematics, and laboratory science.

Study Skills Diagnosis

As in any area, diagnosis is a crucial aspect of instruction in study skills. A number of standardized instruments are available for diagnosing students' abilities in study skills. For Grades 3-9, the Iowa Test of Work-Study Skills is suitable. For Grades 6-9, the SRA Achievement Series: Work-Study Skills is also suitable. Other instruments are, for Grades 7-9, the Stanford Achievement Test: Study Skills; and for Grades 7-12, the Spitzer Study Skills Test.

If time for testing is at a minimum, the middle school teacher might consider using *Evaluating Reading and Study Skills in the Secondary Classroom* (*19*). Models are provided for short, informal diagnosis in fifteen content areas. There are also tests to determine students' backgrounds and when and how students learn best.

Summary

It can be seen that developing study skills among middle school students involves several principles: 1) study skills should include effective factors of self-direction as well as skills, 2) skills and attitudes must be taught, 3) study skills should be developed functionally within the framework of the content areas, 4) the teacher's focus should be on motivational aspects and on direct instruction, and 5) instruction should be based on specific diagnosis and should be designed to achieve specific objectives.

GENERAL CLASSROOM TECHNIQUES

There are many teaching techniques which could be incorporated into everyday classroom instruction for the improvement of study skills and habits. These techniques also include suggestions for reading and study beyond the confines of the classroom.

The SQ3R Method

The Survey, Question, Read, Recite, and Review method of study is probably well known, although there are many variations of this strategy. College and adult reading and study skills instructors often express disappointment when they realize that many students know about the SQ3R method but do not use it in their own study. The reason is that students fail to internalize the process. If the study process is not internalized, it does not become a habitual practice for the student; simply to explain the meaning of SQ3R is not adequate teaching.

One way to help students internalize SQ3R is by careful teaching of the *survey* or previewing step. Previewing is not the same thing as studying the content; it is an aid to help the reader know what to study. To avoid cluttering this step with complexities, teachers find it helpful to start with small segments of assignments until students are capable of working with much larger units of reading and study assignments, remembering that the objective is to provide the learner with a certain anticipation and expectancy which will contribute to improving rate, comprehension, and concentration.

Another way to help students internalize the SQ3R method is to concentrate more on the *Q*, the *Question*. This emphasis is equated with purpose-setting (*14*). A good reminder to students is to have an index card in their textbooks and at their regular places of study. On the card are terms which can be used both for setting purposes and for anticipating possible essay examination questions (6). While some terms apply more to one content area than to another, the following sample list is illustrative:

enumerate	define	trace
evaluate	compare	interpret
contrast	discuss	prove
explain	criticize	illustrate
describe	justify	summarize

For any given assignment, two or three such purpose-setting terms could help the student plan good questions. The pupil is directed to read for content and to answer the questions he has posed, which will require that he knows what he reads. Planning questions is good study.

Assignments

One of the most critical ways in which teachers can assist students to become better learners is to reconsider the way in which assignments are made. Teachers can readily see the lack of specific direction inherent in telling students to "Read Chapter Six for tomorrow and we'll discuss it" (17). That could mean one thing to the teacher and something quite different to the student; it is not fair to expect students to read the teacher's mind.

Another general study technique related to assignments is the similarity of outlining, notetaking, summarizing, and underlining. The appropriateness of each depends very often on the subject studied and the teacher's manner of conducting class sessions. In formal outlining and in summarizing, students can be given shorter selections as models until they are capable of dealing with longer selections and lecture sessions.

Finally, assignments can be improved by using the concept of purpose sentences (13). Three sentences which may help a student think effectively about any given class or assignment are:

1. The teacher spent most of the hour giving us information about . . . .
2. The teacher spent most of the hour giving an opinion on . . . .
3. The teacher spent most of the hour recreating the drama or style of . . . .

These examples should be modified to fit the context of the various content areas and the sentences should be modified to help students clarify what they read. Such sentences serve as guidelines for organizing thoughts gained during instruction and study-reading.

Examinations

A technique applicable to most content areas relates to written assignments and especially to examinations. Students often complain that there is not sufficient time to outline essay answers, or they do not know how. Students improve markedly when teachers insist that "idea sheets" be submitted for each essay question. When pupils can list two, five, or ten ideas for each question before attempting to write a full answer, they have a noticeable advantage in organizing answers. For each question, students take a colored pencil and mark each listed idea in terms of where it best relates to an answer and in what order it needs to be treated. Irrelevant facts and ideas are crossed out. The students then proceed to write their answers in full, working from a brief listing of ideas grouped in an organized manner. Outlining for examination questions is further simplified if students have received direct instruction regarding the organizational patterns of cause and effect, time and sequence, simple listing, and comparison and contrast.

To aid in the actual writing of an examination question which demands a lengthy answer, an understanding of full and half signals and transition phrases is encouraged. Full signals plainly say, "Here is the next point." Half signals are transition expressions such as "finally," "another," and "moreover." Answers from prior examinations can provide models which will assist students.

The analogy question is another aspect of test taking which can bewilder students. Analogy items can be an excellent informal means for developing vocabulary since the student is without the aid of contextual clues but, to be effective teachers must explain the analogy thinking pattern to students.

Reading Rate

Students can be taught to increase their reading rates without elaborate techniques. It should be emphasized that rates depend on what and why we are reading. Again, establishing purposes is essential.

There are several possible classifications of materials as far as adjusting rates is concerned. Study-type reading is thoughtful and reflective. In evaluating and drawing conclusions, the rate will of necessity be slow. For recreational reading, such as newspapers and most fiction, the rate is high. The process of skimming and scanning is appropriate for more accelerated reading such as when a student is searching research materials for a discussion of a particular topic (11). Students need to be taught that rates are not so much a matter of making the eyes move faster or slower but a matter of understanding the purpose of the reading (15).

If only to serve as a reminder to students, an informal way to improve rates is to have once-a-week timed readings. Occasional exercises in skimming for ideas and scanning to answer specific questions help students to improve their overall efficiency. Finding a name, a quote, the climax of a story, locating a chapter and subtopic for review are other examples of exercises which should be included as regular activities in content classes (9).

Using skills books with easy articles of equal length, students can be paced through the selections in about one minute, using the SQ and the SQ3R method.

With the book closed at the end of a minute, students can verbally or in writing indicate everything they know about the selection. With increasingly difficult materials, rate and comprehension can be increased while also reinforcing the SQ3R technique.

An elaboration of the above procedure is to have approximately ten articles which students skim in order to find the three particular articles which have the most bearing on a given topic. In the process, using SQ3R, students are asked to evaluate and determine why they would select these three articles for a research paper or unit project. This technique also helps students select and evaluate resource materials. Students have often heard of some of these techniques but teachers seldom insist on the use of them in the classroom.

A Potpourri of Suggestions

There are a number of functional materials which can be used to enliven instruction in study skills. For instance, TV guides, timetables, telephone directories (including the yellow pages), catalogs, menus, maps, and weather charts are all good functional materials for middle grade students.

Another suggestion is to encourage students to work more efficiently by writing down the expected completion time for an assignment or by graphing on a simple pie graph the different allotments of time for the day's activities. Some students also find it helpful to use a study crutch such as wearing a certain hat while studying at home or patting the stomach of a stone Buddha replica. Students should be encouraged to suggest similar ideas which serve as a reminder of why they are studying for a particular period of time. Many more suggestions for suitable activities are available in reading activity books.

CONCLUSION

Busy teachers could not possibly incorporate in their respective content areas all the suggestions offered in this chapter. It is hoped, however, that some of the techniques will be useful. The SQ3R method, the nature of assignments, the procedure for writing class examinations, and the regular improvement of reading rates are all areas which might be further explored by individuals or groups of teachers in the various content subjects in the middle school. If students are to learn for mastery, they must use efficient study habits and such habits must be taught functionally within the framework of the various curriculum areas in the middle school.

References

1. Artley, A. Sterl. "Effective Study — Its Nature and Nurture," in J. Allen Figurel (Ed.), *Forging Ahead in Reading*, 1967 Proceedings, Volume 12, Part 1. Newark, Delaware: International Reading Association, 1968, 10-19.
2. Bloom, Benjamin. "Learning for Mastery," unpublished manuscript.

3. Catterson, Jane H. "Successful Study Skills Programs," in Harold L. Herber (Ed.), *Developing Study Skills in Secondary Schools*. Newark, Delaware: International Reading Association, 1965, 156-169.

4. Dulin, Kenneth A. "Skill Training for All Secondary Teachers," *Journal of Reading*, 15 (November 1971), 109-114.

5. Entwhistle, D. R. "Evaluations of Study Skills Courses: A Review," *Journal of Educational Research*, 53 (1960), 243-251.

6. Gilbert, Doris W. *Study in Depth*. Englewood Cliffs, New Jersey: Prentice-Hall, 1966.

7. Gronlund, Normand E. *Stating Behavioral Objectives for Classroom Instruction*. New York: Macmillan, 1970.

8. Herber, Harold L. "Developing Study Skills in Secondary Schools," in Harold L. Herber (Ed.), *Developing Study Skills in Secondary Schools*. Newark, Delaware: International Reading Association, 1965, 1-12.

9. McCullough, Constance. "Reading in the Intermediate Grades," in Nelson B. Henry (Ed.), *Development in and through Reading*. National Society for the Study of Education, 1961, 288-304.

10. Moore, Walter J. "What Does Research in Reading Reveal About Reading in the Content Fields?" in Agnella M. Gunn (Ed.), *What We Know About High School Reading*. Urbana, Illinois: National Council of Teachers of English, 1969.

11. Otto, Wayne, and Richard A. McMenemy. *Corrective and Remedial Teaching: Principles and Practices*. Boston: Houghton Mifflin, 1966.

12. Russell, David, and Henry Fea. "Research on Teaching Reading," in Nathan Gage (Ed.), *Handbook of Research on Teaching*. Chicago: Rand McNally, 1963, 865-928.

13. Simms, Theodore F. *Improving College Study Skills*. Beverly Hills, California: Glencoe Press, 1970.

14. Smith, Arthur E. "The Effectiveness of Training Students to Generate Their Own Questions Prior to Reading," unpublished doctoral dissertation, Syracuse University, 1972.

15. Smith, James A. *Creative Teaching of Reading and Literature in the Elementary School*. Boston: Allyn and Bacon, 1967.

16. Smith, Nila B. *Be a Better Reader, Foundations A*, Teacher's Edition. Englewood Cliffs, New Jersey: Prentice-Hall, 1968.

17. Spache, Evelyn. *Reading Activities for Child Involvement*. Boston: Allyn and Bacon, 1972.

18. Strang, Ruth. *Guided Study and Homework*. Washington, D.C.: National Education Association, 1955.

19. Viox, Ruth G. *Evaluating Reading and Study Skills in the Secondary Classroom*. Newark, Delaware: International Reading Association, 1968.

CHAPTER NINETEEN

TECHNIQUES FOR DEVELOPING READING INTERESTS AND ATTITUDES

Thomas E. Culliton, Jr.
Boston University

One aim of the middle school is to establish habits which will enable its students to be independent, self-directing learners long after their formal educations have been completed. Therefore, a middle school reading program should not only insure mastery of the skills of reading but should also instill the lifelong habit of the use of reading.

While skills instruction is an integral component of a reading program, Robinson (18) points out that "Learning to read is a rather fruitless activity if it is not utilized beyond school assignments." Krathwohl, Bloom, and Masia (15) also emphasize the interrelatedness of cognitive and affective behaviors as well as the focus on promoting permanent use of acquired skills:

> In the cognitive domain we are concerned that the student shall be able to do a task when requested. In the affective domain, we are more concerned that he *does do* it when it is appropriate after he has learned that he can do it.

It cannot be assumed that the *can do* student *does do* it. The school must attend to the interest and attitude behaviors which hold promise for fulfilling our ultimate goal despite the difficulties in evaluating these (2).

INTEREST AND ATTITUDE IN READING

Getzels (9) defines interest as a

> ... characteristic disposition, organized through experience which impels an individual to seek out particular objects, activities ... for attention or acquisition.

Interest is a two-edged sword, always to be used in conjunction with cognitive skills. It may be used as the most promising means for practice in and improvement of cognitive skills of reading, or it may be the goal to be attained through the use of cognitive skills. Neither aspect can be overlooked, nor should either be emphasized at the expense of the other.

If interests are organized through experience, it is the results of these experiences which will determine the nature of attitude. It is to the extent that the seeking out of a goal is satisfied by reading that the student's attitude will move in a positive direction. The opposite is also true. Getzels (*10*) emphasizes the distinction, saying:

> An attitude is a disposition to react in a particular direction with regard to a given object or event. We do not ordinarily speak of being driven by an attitude; we are necessarily driven by our interests.

THE INTERESTS OF MIDDLE SCHOOL CHILDREN

Strang (*24*) points out that "... interests are both a cause and a result of adolescent behavior." What are the interests, then, that children bring to the middle school and that may be used as the starting point for a successful reading program?

Getzels (*9*) identifies the following interests as the ones which all children attempt to internalize: "... instrumental ... status ... transcendent ... aesthetic. . . . recreational . . . ." A review of the research, however, reveals that most of the research has been in the areas of aesthetic and recreational interests; i.e., in relation to growth in literary appreciation. While these contributions cannot be minimized, the development of a lifetime interest in reading requires that we include all areas with which the adult, as well as the child, will be concerned.

For instance, Gunn (*11*) suggests approaching the problem through self-image related values such as:

1. The need to be loved.
2. The need to love others.
3. The ego, the strong drive for sense of self . . . . Helping the ego to adjust to environmental demands and pressures.
4. The acquisition impulse.
5. The drive toward finding pleasure, joy, or satisfaction.

Similarly, Witty (*30*) advocates the planning of a reading program around ten developmental tasks of the child's life while Durrell (*4*) advocates the careful planning of a reading program around activities that will lead students to the discovery of the infinite number of ways in which reading may be used, saying:

> Reading is incidental to action, and perhaps the major use of reading is to expand the choices and increase the effectiveness of action.

Use of existing interests to increase depth and breadth of understanding and to discover new and more permanent interests is the most effective way of using the two-edged sword of interest. This is not meant to derogate the role of voluntary, self-selection programs. Research and results of teaching strategies geared to the development of literary appreciation attest to the worth of such programs. However, interests must be interpreted broadly enough to include the content of every discipline for expanding and improving reading.

DEVELOPING READING INTERESTS IN THE VARIOUS DISCIPLINES

Strickland's comments (26) regarding interests clearly indicate the content teacher's responsibility:

> Interests do not grow in a vacuum. They are stimulated by experience. It would be folly to try to build a curriculum entirely about children's expressed interests because each child's interests are limited to what he has had a chance to be interested in. There are many things he might become interested in if opportunity afforded. The teacher's task, then, is not only to feed the interests the child already possesses but to open up new avenues of interest and opportunity.

Barbe (1) concurs and elaborates.

> Developing permanent interests in reading must be the goal of every teacher regardless of the particular subject she may be teaching.

Herman (12) refers specifically to social studies, saying:

> Of all the curriculum areas, the social studies area offers a framework within which the fundamental use of the skills of language arts can be taught effectively.

Similarly, science offers areas of interest for every young adolescent. As Friskey (8) points out:

> Science cooks in our kitchen and roars in an African safari through our living rooms. It saves us from polio. It looks at the wonders of the ocean bottom and into the hot core of the earth. It makes food from seaweed, raises crops in the desert, and saves the cattle of Afghanistan from the rinderpest. It reads the whole fascinating story of mankind in rocks and artifacts.

In order to facilitate interest-arousing uses of reading in every content area, Durrell (4) reclassified the uses of reading according to the psychological tasks involved:

- imaginative reading
- history and travel reading
- "world about you" reading
- attitudes, ideals, and personal growth reading.

Each of these may be used in a variety of ways in every content area. There is no limit to the number or nature of activities which may be successfully accomplished through these uses. Suggested techniques for each of the four uses of reading are detailed in the following sections.

IMAGINATIVE READING

Imaginative reading involves the reading of fiction, poetry, and plays. It requires the ability to form mental imagery of the material being read. Students unable to visualize while reading do not tend to participate extensively in imaginative reading. The provision of planned experiences, as well as the sharing of these reading experiences through varied media, may aid this type of student.

Reading of Fiction

Fiction is usually read in individualized reading programs, voluntary reading periods, literature classes, and at-home recreational reading.

Various studies investigating the reading preferences of middle grade and young adolescent children have yielded surprisingly similar results throughout the years. Although specific topics have varied, general themes have remained constant. Reviews and studies conducted by Walby (27), MacKintosh (16), and Witty (31), report that realistic adventure, mystery, and biography predominate. Animal stories, home-centered tales, and career interests are also prominent. Sizemore's review (23) of the literature added humor to the list and also noted that students in grades seven and eight began to express definite interests in fictional stories dealing with personal problem solving by teenagers with whom they could identify. This trend was verified by Fine and Rackliffe (7), who found that while fiction still dominated the field, more interest was expressed in the teenage novel which provides the opportunity for vicarious problem solving. They concluded:

> The ten titles most often selected by the pupils come under the categories of teen-age stories, adventure, and humor. Four of the top ten titles were in the teen-age story category; thus indicating a strong interest of a majority of students in all grades (7-9), at all levels, and of both sexes in reading material which deals directly with people their own age who have problems similar to their own.

These studies not only determined the content preferences of young adolescents, but also noted definite age and sex patterns. Carlsen (3) attributes the distinction of interests by sex to acculturation but, regarding age, he unequivocally states:

> ... chronological age is more important than is mental age in determining what a child will enjoy reading. The average and the above-average thirteen year old will be interested in reading the same kind of books.

Klein's investigation (14) of the relationship between the sex and the occupation of a main character in fiction and the interest and comprehension of the reader led him to conclude:

> ... that concern for meeting girls' interests should be no less than concern for meeting boys' interests.

Norvell's investigation (*17*) of the numbers and kinds of periodicals in which intermediate grades were interested also emphasized sex differences. Using 147 classrooms in Connecticut, Illinois, Massachusetts, and Ohio, he found that of the top five preferences listed by boys and girls, only one was listed by both. Norvell also remarked that the decline in book reading was being accompanied by an increase in periodical reading.

As a result of these and similar studies, we may expect middle school students to possess interests in fiction ranging from animal stories to vicarious adolescent problem solving. While knowledge of group preferences and tendencies is important, it is, however, only a starting point for the acquisition of a variety of books at multiple levels. There must also be specific topic preferences of a particular school, particular class, and, in the case of the reluctant reader, a particular child (*13, 20, 28*). This is an important aspect of promoting interest in reading, especially in view of the research by Schulte (*21*), Walby (*27*), and Sizemore (*23*) which noted a decrease in the amount of recreational reading which seems to begin at about grade five.

While providing the right book for a particular child is crucial, other techniques are also recommended for expanding interests in the reading of fiction.

1. Provide a conducive environment which would include:
   a. a book-loving teacher,
   b. accessibility to a wide variety of high-interest books,
   c. accessibility to reading material on a student's independent reading level,
   d. time to read independently, and the
   e. opportunity to share reading experiences with others.

2. Provide opportunities which may stimulate a new interest:
   a. oral reading of intriguing selections by the teacher,
   b. multimedia presentation of a theme in literature accompanied by suggestions of related titles, and
   c. suggestions of specific titles related to results of individual interest inventories and conferences.

3. Provide opportunities for sharing activities to stimulate the interest of peers:
   a. construction of an original book jacket portraying the most interesting event in a story;
   b. construction of a mural showing one or several scenes leading to the climax of a story in which the climactic scene is omitted and the group attempts to anticipate an appropriate end;
   c. portrayals of interesting scenes to be used with an opaque projector

while the individual student narrates the appropriate part of the story corresponding to the scene;

d. construction of a map portraying the main setting(s) of a book;
e. composition by students of exchange letters between the main characters in books being read;
f. portrayal of an incident in the book in cartoon fashion, accompanied by an intriguing caption;
g. portrayal of one important incident in a story in comic strip style with careful attention given to the sequence of events;
h. construction of three-dimensional building(s) or particular place(s) in the book with the student narrating what happened in the specific place(s);
i. selection of a favorite character from a book and the writing of his biography (some facts may have to be added by the student and these should be consistent with the information from the book);
j. taping of a short part of the book which has a dynamic monologue or dialogue with the student changing his voice to imitate that of the character(s) as imagined by him with other students listening to the tape to determine how accurately they can ascertain certain information about the character.

These techniques for sharing and using peer influence are representative of ways in which individualized reading for pleasure — and incidentally developing fluency, power, rate, and vocabulary — may be reintegrated with other components of the language arts such as writing, speaking, and listening. Also, for those students less facile in verbal ability, the assistance of media is helpful.

Participation in Oral Literary Experiences

Oral literary experiences include oral reading of plays, poetry, choral readings, and dramatizations. While valuable for all students, they may be especially helpful to those students who have difficulty in the sustained reading of fiction since these techniques give the student auditory clues to the context of the imaginative experience.

1. *Oral Reading of Plays.* The importance of play reading as an essential part of a well-integrated reading program is recognized by all educators. Children participate eagerly regardless of level of ability. Durrell and Crossley (5) emphasize the following values of this type of reading:

   • provides an outlet for youthful imaginations
   • fosters reading of fiction by stimulating sensory images
   • contributes to the social growth of individuals
   • improves expression, enriches vocabulary, and improves reading comprehension
   • promotes speech fluency and broadens speaking vocabulary
   • provides for practice in two of the four major cues cited by linguists as essential to understanding in reading

- gives opportunity to regulate voice intonation and promotes understanding of meaningful structural units.

2. *Poetry and Choral Reading*. In introducing poetry or choral reading, two elements are essential: teacher interest in the genre and appropriateness of the selection in terms of student interest. Whitehead (*29*) lists the following interest areas from which to choose selections: adventure, animals, everyday occurrences, historical ballads, humor, narrative, and science.

Many teachers prefer to introduce selections by reading them orally to the students. This preference may be determined by teacher knowledge of the needs of students and will be influenced by the degree of interest and pleasure students have previously derived from experiences in listening. The following suggestions are made for those who have acquired such readiness for group participation in oral reading:

a. give each student his own mimeographed selection
b. ask each student to underline those words in poetry which would be stressed; i.e., those sections of a choral reading which should be differentiated
c. ask the class to listen to different oral interpretations of the same selection
d. have the group discuss and choose the most appropriate group interpretation.

3. *Dramatization*. The success of this technique depends upon the emotional climate in the classroom and the interest of the topic. The following suggestions are suitable for the middle school student and can be drawn from imaginative reading or content specialties:

a. dramatization of a famous historical incident
b. dramatization of a climactic scene from imaginative reading
c. improvisation of a telephone conversation or dialogue between two fictional or famous characters
d. staging of an appropriate imaginary happening in the life of a famous person
e. staging of an interview with a famous person
f. dramatization of the reception of the news of a famous event from the point of view of different types of people
g. dramatization of the results of a given illogical scientific situation
h. charades, using appropriate topics from learnings or independent reading.

Participation in Humorous Reading

The young adolescent's liking for zany, slapstick humor is often in evidence and should be used. Humor is expressed in many places and can often be related to content area topics being studied, such as: American folklore, tall tales, humorous anecdotes about historical characters, jokes from periodicals, and cartoons reflecting current events.

HISTORY AND TRAVEL READING

The chief psychological task involved in history and travel reading is how to develop concepts for that which is removed by time and distance from immediate and concrete experience.

Herman's review of research (*12*) cites several studies validating the concept approach to social studies. The following techniques have consequently been selected not only for their role in stimulating permanent interest, but also for their value in concept building:

1. *Provision of multimedia presentations*
   a. realia from past or different lands
   b. audiovisual presentations
   c. oral reading of plays related to the topic

2. *Investigation of objects reflecting knowledge of the concepts*
   a. radio and television programs
   b. stamp collections
   c. airline and steamship schedules
   d. periodical articles
   e. oral readings of strong but suitable selections from historical documents

3. *Provision of appropriate reading materials*
   a. multilevel texts
   b. easy trade books
   c. junior new publications
   d. textbooks rewritten by able students
   e. pupil specialties

4. *Use of existing interests*
   a. reading of biographies
   b. adventure as a source of concept enrichment

5. *Development of time concepts*
   a. time line
   b. writing of autobiographies
   c. writing of biographies

6. *Pupil specialties* (individual or group). Experimentation with and use of this technique is described in detail by Durrell and Savignano (*6*). Briefly, it is suggested that the teacher examine the course of study approximately six weeks in advance. A list of those topics which receive inadequate treatment in the text should be compiled and presented to the class. Using various research techniques taught during basic skills instruction, the students may select those topics they wish to investigate individually or as

part of a team. The technique is incomplete without a culminating (hopefully) multimedia presentation to the class. Specific topics presented to the students should reflect their needs in terms of both concept development and those interests amenable to expansion.

7. *Reading in relation to field trips and travel*
   a. In preparing for field trips, the class may form interest groups for the purpose of investigating and reporting to the rest of the class on the one preferred aspect of the topic. Begin by giving the class a choice from a carefully chosen list. Help them to eventually formulate their own lists from which to choose.
   b. After a field trip, the class may construct various types of exhibits; each introclass group concentrating on its preferred area.
   c. The entrance of new students, moving days, and summer holidays provide the opportunity of investigating all aspects of the travel experience; e.g., map construction, best means of reaching destinations, costs, and description of areas to ascertain new ways of living.
   d. The invitation of a person who has traveled to other countries to visit the classroom should be preceded by the preparation of exhibits prepared by children interested in the visitor's area of special knowledge.

8. *Integration with total language arts programs.* The following activities may stem from knowledge acquired in pursuit of a pupil's special interests. These may be initiated individually or in teams:
   a. creation of a ship log kept by a traveler, explorer, or discoverer
   b. production of a "You Are There" program
   c. composition of letters from sailors, explorers, and travelers to relatives or friends at home
   d. writing of stories of historical events from viewpoints suggested by given titles; e.g., The Gull that Flew Over the Santa Maria
   e. writing a guide to a new land for an immigrant
   f. creation of a tourist's guidebook
   g. formation of a set of rules for a new settlement or enterprise; e.g., Rules for Space Travel
   h. creation of a newspaper pertinent to an environment or period being studied
   i. composition of the diary of a historical character
   j. compilation of an illustrated dictionary of one class of objects peculiar to the unit
   k. preparation of a "Who's Who" of specific historical periods
   l. compilation of a series of bulletins from war correspondents
   m. narration of the history of a particular area accompanied with illustrations
   n. creation of folktales and yarns similar to those of the specific period

o. study and writing or recounting of the effects of a new mode of transportation upon the development of an area
p. investigation of area of public vs. private transportation in different regions
q. planning of a transportation system for the local community
r. stimulation of critical response to current problematic events analogous to historical topics
s. selection and description of a favorite event through adaptation of new words to an old tune
t. writing of editorials representing two sides of a controversial issue
u. writing of stories to explain names of specific countries, towns and cities, or objects of interest
v. narrating of the story of the growth of an important industry in an area.

The above listing of techniques emphasizes the fact that developing a reading program around the uses of reading in no way implies neglect of skills instruction. Rather, it demands more efficient instruction and provides the opportunity for self-directing, self-correcting, and highly efficient practice in these skills.

"WORLD ABOUT YOU" READING

This is perhaps the most promising area for the expansion of interests. It uses the child's immediate environment and expands his horizons, aspirations, and concepts in a practical way. It attends to instrumental, aesthetic, recreational, and vocational interests of the real world and is relevant to every content area in the academic world. This type of reading should be used in every possible way.

A wide range of reading materials will be required: catalogs, periodicals, newspapers, government publications, and advertising materials. The following techniques may be facilitated by means of pupil specialties, team projects, field trips, experiments, collections, construction activities, and audiovisual aids.

1. *Reading related to consumer education*
   a. Stimulate interest by means of a directed lesson. Have available a large variety of advertising materials pertinent to those objects of which young adolescents are the main consumers; clothes, records, sports equipment, and bicycles. Have pairs of students choose at least two advertisements regarding one object in which they are interested. Have students compare the value offered with the price required. Quality, guarantees, and desire of the consumer should be considered.
   b. Encourage students to present to their peers, evidence of wise choices made in actual purchases.
   c. Stimulate comparison shopping in purchasing materials required for hobbies, family purchases for the home, and birthday and Christmas presents.

2. *Reading related to hobbies and recreational interests*
    a. Class survey of television preferences; construct a chart depicting the results. Maintain a list of the "top five" programs.
    b. Using the above, construct a *TV Guide* for classroom use.
    c. Encourage demonstrations of proper ways to execute essential procedures in a favored sport.
    d. Diagram and explain possible offensive or defensive strategies in games such as football, hockey, track, and chess.
    e. Maintain interest centers of students' collections and hobbies. Items, processes, and techniques involved should be explained orally to the class and captioned for placement at the interest center.
    f. Display recipes and results.
    g. Exhibit items constructed, accompanied by directions for construction. Students may leave only directions without revealing the name of the final product as a booster device.
3. *Reading related to local community*
    a. Compare and contrast the past and present of various facets of community life. Report on changes which have occurred and foster creative thinking by predicting the community's future.
    b. Investigate important sites of the community.
    c. Trace and relate the stories of famous people born in the community.
4. *Reading related to career interests*
    a. Use typical interests in biography of the young adolescent. Relate this interest to the life work of famous people.
    b. Expand growing interest in careers by fostering interest in the roles of various community members.
5. *Reading related specifically to content areas*
    a. Investigate the utility and implementation in the modern world of basic scientific principles.
    b. Explore varied career roles suggested by units in science, social studies, or mathematics.
    c. Maintain weather charts utilizing local, national, and international (satellite) reports for data.

READING FOR ATTITUDES, IDEALS, AND PERSONAL GROWTH

Factual content material as well as literary material may be used to develop attitudes, ideals, and personal growth. The following techniques are suggested:

1. Encourage investigation of the motives behind the contributions of famous people and promote discussion which will lead students to realize the impact of these discoveries on their own daily lives.
2. Stimulate the writing of essays dealing with the importance of these contributions to the individual student.

3. Examine periodical essays and newspaper editorials dealing with controversial issues.
4. Develop a literary unit on the theme of "Successful Failures," dealing with the need for persistence in solving problems. This may be developed through fiction and biography.
5. Relate values of a main character to the reader's values.
   a. Present a word related to the theme of the story to the group, encourage association of other words to the given word through the small group discussion technique, compare the associations of readers with associations made by the character.
   b. Allow students to change endings of books to satisfy personal values.
6. Foster pupil-social growth through use of team learning techniques, team projects, student planning, and evaluation of specific techniques.
7. Provide for student mutual aid in classroom work.
8. Use procedures suggested by authorities in the development of literary appreciation.

CONCLUSION

The relationship between motivation and achievement is not clearly defined although, operationally, we assume it is positive. Some research is available, however. Schnayer (22) investigated the relationship between interest level and comprehension level and found that:

> ... interest as a factor of reading comprehension is significantly more important for the lower ability groups.

Robinson (19) contends that retarded readers can develop permanent interest in reading if they are given choices in and the opportunity for wide reading in books at their independent level. This will allow them the opportunity they need to practice the skills being taught in conjunction with wide reading and thus foster an improvement of attitude through successful accomplishment. Strang, Phelps, and Withrow (25) concur and state:

> For all these readers, the most generally approved recommendation is to provide easy, interesting reading.

Finally, relationship between reading ability and reading interests is clarified by Carlsen (3):

> ... those things young people want to read about are related to their chronological age regardless of the level of their reading ability. Therefore, an eighth grader who has twelfth grade reading ability does not usually have twelfth grade reading interests, nor does the one with a fourth grade reading ability have fourth grade reading interests ....

The techniques listed in this chapter can be used with a variety of materials and at varied levels of performance. If such a variety is accessible to the student, not only for directed skills instruction but for implementation of a program emphasizing the uses of reading, each child will proceed toward development of permanent and positive reading attitudes and interests.

References

1. Barbe, Walter. "Interests and the Teaching of Reading," *Education*, 83 (April 1963), 486.
2. Barrett, Thomas C. "Goals of the Reading Program: The Basis for Evaluation," *The Evaluation of Children's Reading Achievement*, Perspectives in Reading, No. 8. Newark, Delaware: International Reading Association, 1967.
3. Carlsen, G. Robert. *Books and the Teenage Reader*. New York: Harper and Row, 1971, 3, 22.
4. Durrell, Donald D. *Improving Reading Instruction*. New York: World Book, 1956, 310, 313.
5. Durrell, Donald, and Alice B. Crossley. *Favorite Plays for Classroom Reading*. Boston: Plays, 1965.
6. Durrell, Donald, and Leonard J. Savignano. "Classroom Enrichment through Pupil Specialties," *Journal of Education*, 138 (February 1956), 1-31.
7. Fine, Bert E., and Lillian T. Rackliffe. "Development and Trail of A Reading Interest Inventory for Grades Seven, Eight, and Nine," unpublished dissertation, Boston University, 1968.
8. Friskey, Margaret. "Science," in J. Allen Figurel (Ed.), *Reading for Effective Living*, Proceedings of the International Reading Association, 3, 1958. New York: Scholastic Magazines, 78.
9. Getzels, Jacob W. "The Nature of Reading Interests," *Developing Permanent Interest in Reading*, Annual Conference on Reading, 18. Chicago: University of Chicago, 1956, 7, 9.
10. Getzels, Jacob W. "The Problem of Interests: A Reconsideration," *Reading: Seventy-Five Years of Progress*, Annual Conference on Reading, 28. Chicago: University of Chicago, 1966, 98.
11. Gunn, M. Agnella. "Promoting a Love Affair with Books," in Mildred A. Dawson (Ed.), *Combining Research Results and Good Practice*, 1966 Proceedings, Volume 11, Part 2. Newark, Delaware: International Reading Association, 1967, 37.
12. Herman, Wayne L., Jr. "Reading and Other Language Arts in Social Studies Instruction: Persistent Problems," in Ralph Preston (Ed.), *A New Look at Reading in the Social Studies*, Perspectives in Reading, No. 12. Newark, Delaware: International Reading Association, 1969, 15.
13. Jan-Tausch, Evelyn. "Discovery and Measurement of Interests in Reading," in Dorothy De Boer (Ed.), *Reading Diagnosis and Evaluation*, 1968 Proceedings, Volume 13, Part 4. Newark, Delaware: International Reading Association, 1970.

14. Klein, Howard A. "Interest and Comprehension in Sex-Typed Materials," in Jane H. Catterson (Ed.), *Children and Literature*. Newark, Delaware: International Reading Association, 1970, 64.

15. Krathwohl, David R., Benjamin S. Bloom, and Bertram B. Masia. *Taxonomy of Educational Objectives – Handbook II: Affection Domain*. New York: David McKay, 1964, 60.

16. MacKintosh, Helen K. "Children's Interest in Literature and the Reading Program," *Reading Teacher*, 10 (February 1957), 138-143.

17. Norvell, George W. "The Challenge of Periodicals in Education," *Elementary English*, 43 (April 1966), 402-408.

18. Robinson, H. Alan. "Developing Lifetime Readers," *Journal of Reading*, 11 (January 1968), 261.

19. Robinson, Helen, "Can Retarded Readers Develop a Permanent Interest in Reading?" *Reading Teacher*, 12 (April 1959), 235-239.

20. Robinson, Helen M. "What Research Says to the Teacher of Reading," *Reading Teacher*, 8 (February 1955), 91, 173-177.

21. Schulte, Emerita S. "Independent Reading Interests of Children in Grades Four, Five and Six," in J. Allen Figurel (Ed.), *Reading and Realism*, 1968 Proceedings, Volume 13, Part 1. Newark, Delaware: International Reading Association, 1969.

22. Shnayer, Sidney W. "Relationship between Reading Interest and Reading Comprehension," in J. Allen Figurel (Ed.), *Reading and Realism*, 1968 Proceedings, Volume 13, Part 1. Newark, Delaware: International Reading Association, 1969, 700.

23. Sizemore, Robert A. "Reading Interests in Junior High School," *Education*, 83 (April 1963), 473-479.

24. Strang, Ruth. "Scope of Adolescent Interests," *Education*, 83 (April 1963), 463.

25. Strang, Ruth, Ethlyne Phelps, and Dorothy Withro. *Gateways to Readable Books* (4th ed.). New York: H. W. Wilson, 1966, 11.

26. Strickland, Ruth G. "Making the Most of Children's Interest in the Teaching of Reading," *Reading Teacher*, 10 (February 1957), 37.

27. Walby, Grace S. "A Survey of Current Reading Interests in Grades Four through Six," *Developing Permanent Interest in Reading*, Annual Conference on Reading, 18. Chicago: University of Chicago, 1956.

28. Washburn, Carol. "Reading Interests," *Elementary English*, 49 (April 1972), 538-541.

29. Whitehead, Robert. *Children's Literature: Strategies of Teaching*. Englewood Cliffs, New Jersey: Prentice-Hall, 1968, 110.

30. Witty, Paul. "Meeting Developmental Needs Through Reading," *Education*, 84 (April 1964), 451-458.

31. Witty, Paul. "Pupil Interests in the Elementary Grades," *Education*, 83 (April 1963).

PART FOUR

The Future

CHAPTER TWENTY

MIDDLE SCHOOL
READING PROGRAMS
IN THE FUTURE

Paul S. George
University of Florida

On September 17, 1787, Benjamin Franklin emerged from Independence Hall in Philadelphia after adding his signature to the document which was to become our nation's constitution. A woman rushed from the crowd that had gathered in the street, her eyes wide with excitement. Hurrying up to Franklin, she asked the old statesman, "Well, Dr. Franklin, what have we got?" Franklin paused for a moment and then replied, "A republic, Madam, if you can keep it."

Franklin's wisdom, revealed in this remark, served the young nation well and the applicability of his advice remains remarkably current. American educators today would be wise to pay close attention to Franklin's remarks. Certainly the education of American youth in the closing years of the twentieth century demands the same wise planning and cautious husbandry which Franklin recommended for our young republic.

This is particularly true in the middle schools where hopeful new programs are emerging. The question posed in the previous chapter and repeated here is, "Can we keep them?" The answer lies in the way in which several crucial factors are handled. The first deals with the nature of emerging adolescence as a developmental stage, as it exists now and how it might change in the future. The second is the nature of the middle school, including its past and future, as it affects reading programs for this age group. Third, a revised and expanded vision of the role of middle school reading teachers is necessary for successful programs to survive. Finally, teachers who can implement this expanded role must be prepared.

The preceding chapters of this book describe in detail the efforts of concerned educators to provide the guidelines upon which a quality program of reading and learning skills can be built. Whether we can keep such a program depends upon the vision of those who adapt and apply these factors in middle schools in the several decades ahead.

EMERGING ADOLESCENCE: TODAY AND TOMORROW

"Emerging adolescence" is a phrase used to bring together two discrete but adjoining phases in human development — preadolescence and early adolescence. Eichhorn (*1*) has suggested the term "transescence" as a synonym for emerging adolescence, emphasizing that the importance of the period lies in the fact that it is a time of change from childhood to young adulthood. In this chapter adolescence and transescence, are used interchangeably.

Providing quality reading programs for middle schools and their students depends largely upon the extent to which educators are familiar with and take into account the unique characteristics of preadolescence and early adolescence as developmental phases in the lives of American students. Not only must educators be familiar with those physical, intellectual, and socioemotional characteristics as they are today, but they must recognize the inevitability of the continuing change which will occur in the nature of emerging adolescence over the next quarter century.

In order for the middle school to avoid the ossification which overtook earlier efforts to educate the in-between-ager, educators must dispel the illusion that changes in the nature of the middle school youth have come to an end. Rather, the assumption that these changes have only begun seems to be a more plausible hypothesis. The emerging adolescent learner seems to be changing as rapidly as the society surrounding him. Change is the central fact of life for students in the ten to fourteen age group. Some have said that change may be one of the few things that any two transescents have in common at one time.

EMERGING ADOLESCENCE TODAY

One of the changes that takes place during these years is a transformation in the intellectual abilities possessed by the middle school youngster. Piaget and other developmental psychologists have revealed that transescence is a period during which mental operations undergo a transformation from concrete to formal operations. That is, students begin to be able to deal with more abstract, symbolic concepts. The ability to think in more accurate ways about the past and the future, to be able to visualize things in ways other than as they are, becomes more developed. In short, middle school age students are capable of dealing with more complex language and concepts than the typical elementary school age student.

The transformation in intellectual capacity develops concomitantly with the onset of puberty, the most dynamic and thoroughgoing of the changes through which middle school students must pass. Without hypothesizing about the biochemical interrelationships between the onset of puberty and other factors in this stage of development, most developmental psychologists agree that the impact of puberty upon the total life of transescents is tremendous.

During the preadolescent years, ages nine through eleven, the movement toward sexual maturity is evidenced primarily by a curiosity regarding all things sexual. Typically, this brings a withdrawal from contact with members of the opposite sex where new kinds of relationships or more mature interrelationships are required. In the years of early adolescence, however, this reticent curiosity takes an about-face, becoming an almost obsessive concern with sex. Havighurst has clearly outlined the sexually oriented developmental tasks which begin to occupy large portions of the mental and social time and effort during and beyond the early adolescent years (2).

Very closely related to the appearance of primary and secondary sexual characteristics, and another hallmark of the culture of pubescence, is the transescent's almost overwhelming need for peer acceptance and approval. Appearing early in the middle school years and growing stronger as adolescence becomes complete, the power of the peer group becomes a crucial factor in the educational process. Once condemned by parents, teachers, and other adults as a pernicious influence in the lives of students, peer group influence is now viewed by psychologists as a positive sign of the transition from childhood to adulthood. The peer group, say these scholars, plays an important role in securing the independence of the transescent from the total dominance of parental influence. As such, its presence is to be viewed as a desirable, healthy part of the life of the in-between-ager, and not to be too thoroughly condemned or discouraged.

The power of the peer group in the lives of middle school students brings a concomitant need for independence and autonomy which appears sporadically at first, but becomes more pressing toward the end of the middle school years. This demand for independence and autonomy, alternating as it frequently does with a need for the security and structure represented by adult authority figures, makes the transescent a seemingly enigmatic figure. This situation often results in a rather hostile resentment towards and resistance of adult authority which makes the transescent seem to the uninitiated teacher, to be a rather undesirable student with whom to work.

The appearance of new and sometimes startling erotic sensations bring serious value conflicts. When the clash occurs between what parents and society say is bad and what the transescent discovers to be pleasurable, values connected with sexual behavior are challenged, often resulting in a weakening of the total value structure of the struggling youth. Frequently, the transescent youth finds himself faced with the need to restructure his whole system of values. This need to rebuild a personal system of values seems destined to be one of the central concerns of the transescent.

During the years of transescence, for the second and perhaps last time in the average human life (barring individual differences and major traumatic experiences) the self-concept becomes fluid and flexible. The impact of tremendous physical, mental, and social change demands an intensive effort to achieve a successful reintegration of the self. Middle schoolers are often uncertain of their personal worth, their value in other's eyes, their abilities, and potentials. They need frequent opportunities to perceive themselves in essentially positive ways and need success experiences upon which to construct a positive concept of personal worth.

Physically, the emerging adolescent is faced with mastering a new body in muscular and skeletal terms. Frequently, these changes in size, appearance, and function, propelled by a seemingly inexhaustible source of energy, become rather complex sources of anxiety and self-consciousness. They seem to account for a great deal of the status determination in interpersonal relationship hierarchies among transescents. In this way, the interconnectedness of physical and social change in the lives of middle school students is easily demonstrated.

This interconnectedness is demonstrated again in the transescent's need to bring about a major transformation in interpersonal relationships with parents, teachers, and peers. Achieving young adulthood physically, brings with it the demand by society that the youth act socially in more adult ways. This means that the young person must abandon the style of interaction which characterized childhood and adopt a wholly different, more mature, pattern of interpersonal behavior. The patterns of interaction which characterize adulthood must be adopted, and cooperation from understanding parents and teachers is essential.

The task of sex role identification is, in a way, a part of this new pattern of relationships. Each transescent must, during this period, put the finishing touches on his or her conception of the proper adult sexual role. This developmental task becomes more and more difficult in contemporary American society, as a societal consensus on proper masculine and feminine role behavior becomes increasingly unlikely. Transescents seem to be on their own, the responsibility for guiding them in learning sex roles partially abdicated by society.

One result of these demands upon transescents is that frequently some volatile emotions will accompany the process. The transescent years are described in psychology texts and popular literature as the most confusing and demanding, in emotional terms, of all the years in human life. The mood of the typical middle school student changes abruptly, swinging from one emotional level to another, from peak to trough with little obvious external provocation. Even more draining, perhaps, is the fact that the causes for such pitching and tossing emotionally, are frequently just as mysterious to the student experiencing them as they are to those nearby.

Finally, the typical transescent today appears to blossom in terms of personal interests in much the same way as he does in physical and mental development. Most middle school youth seem to have a continuing supply of rapidly multiplying, but superficial, personal interests. The world appears to be a smorgasbord. The transescent tastes, nibbles, and samples a wide variety of hobbies, ideas, subjects, and types of people, and moves on. Emerging adolescence is an important period for determining the direction in which tastes, interests, and talents lie. The middle school and its reading programs must be prepared to facilitate this quest for identity.

Emerging Adolescence Tomorrow

What will the preadolescents and early adolescents of the early twenty-first century be like? This is a question which should assume as much importance in our deliberations as a clear conceptualization of the present characteristics of this group of learners. If we plan for the present only, our efforts are doomed to fall short of the mark.

Some will say that we cannot predict the future; that we cannot know what the nature of emerging adolescence will be fifty years from now. And they will be correct. However, the inability to know the future is the basic reason to plan for it. Planning for today must be supplemented by contingency planning for tomorrow, even if that planning seems based on hunches, hopes, and guesswork.

Guessing about the future characteristics of the most volatile age group in our society is a risky but necessary business. Possibly the least hazardous hypothesis is that certain present influences for change in western society will accelerate. This acceleration can be expected to produce a similar acceleration or intensification of the related changes occurring in the nature of emerging adolescence. If this occurs, what will the client of middle school reading programs be like in the years to come?

Extrapolating from the data being gathered on the nature of transescence, we might logically expect to find middle school students who possess a greater ability to deal with symbolic ideas and abstract ideas than today's students. If the impact of changing schools, media, and nutrition continues, students may possess an intellectual sophistication far greater than that of students in the schools today.

We may find the onset of puberty and the appearance of erotic sensations occurring at an even earlier date than today. Evidence that the development of adult sexual potential is continuing to occur at earlier ages is being discussed by authorities in growth and development in many western nations. There is some research to show that pubescence begins, on the average, almost five years earlier than it did a century ago. If Booth Tarkington were to rewrite his book, *Seventeen*, he now would have to call it *Twelve*.

The continuing changes occurring in the socialization of American youth and the changing patterns of family life may signal an increasing importance for the role of the peer group in the life of middle school youth. Although it is difficult to imagine, further changes in the family structure and social mobility may make the emerging adolescent's need for peer acceptance and approval even more powerful in the future than it is at mid-century. Peer pressure may have an even greater impact on who reads and who does not.

Related to the need for stronger peer group ties, the need to assert autonomy and independence will probably be more pronounced. The resentment of and resistance to adult authority which is concomitant with the drive for independence will need to be dealt with then, as now. To be effective, adults must be perceived as facilitators of, rather than barriers to, autonomy and independence.

Regarding the development of values and the enriching of the self-concept, the future promises anything but the proverbial rose garden. If the present movement toward ever greater pluralism in values continues at the current rate, the task of building a system of values will have assumed almost bewildering proportions by the beginning of the next century. Youth will be desperately in need of the skills of value clarification. In the same way, the emerging adolescent in American schools in the 1970s will need to continue to develop, test, and change his perceptions of self. The future may bring even greater flexibility and fluidity to the developing self-concept of the transescent.

It is not easy to accept and learn a socially approved adult masculine or feminine sex role. Achieving a satisfactory sex role identification shows every prospect of becoming more difficult in the years to come, as the distinction between the behaviors appropriate for the sexes becomes increasingly indistinct.

Summary

The attempt to synthesize the various possibilities and achieve a sort of sneak preview of the transescent learner of the twenty-first century yields an interesting picture. The emerging adolescent of the future will probably possess many of the traits which now identify him. The curiosity, the needs, the ebullient emotions, the extreme idealism will all be there. Along with those characteristics, quite possibly there will be a number of traits which add up to learners who will be on their own in many ways. They will have to carve out their own concepts of self, create their own value systems, and describe their own sex-role identification. The middle school learners of the twenty-first century will probably be brighter and more knowledgeable, will mature earlier and live in a world where very little is defined or delimited. Designing an educational experience which will provide the learning tools appropriate for the citizen of the twenty-first century is the crucial task of today, not tomorrow. If we wait until the end of this century to prepare the educational plan for the next we will assure failure.

THE NATURE OF THE MIDDLE SCHOOL

A strong case can be built to support the statement that educational programs for transescents, including reading, either have been minimally effective or nonexistent. A glance at the history of American education for in-between-agers seems to suggest that, with few exceptions, the years between primary school and high school have been thoroughly and consistently ignored. Future plans must insure that such an educational wasteland is not perpetuated.

Implications from the Past

In the late nineteenth century, there was a great deal of criticism of the 8-4 plan of school grade organization. The criticism, however, was not focused on the unique nature of emerging adolescents. Rather, it came initially from faculty and administrators who were concerned about the expansion of elementary and high school. They wished to avoid the resultant increase in the average age of students entering college, preferring to reduce the time students spent in the public school program and to facilitate entrance to college at an earlier age (*3*).

The Report of the Committee of Ten on Secondary School Studies, presented in 1893, illustrated one of the directions that the middle years of schooling would take in the decades to come. The report, one of the most influential in the history of American education, had one major effect: the extension downward of the curriculum and instructional program of the high school into the upper years of the elementary school, with the expected attendant effects on the teaching of reading and other skills. It was only after this report emerged that public school educators began to take the first small steps toward the development of educational programs for emerging adolescents. Beginning in 1895 with the Committee on College Entrance Requirements, the public schools began the still incomplete process of securing independence from the domination of higher education.

The years between 1895 and 1918 saw a procession of committees and reports, all of which were to have some effect on the teaching of reading. The results of these deliberations had two major effects. The first was a shift away from a total emphasis on the preparation of the college bound student to a program accommodating a more varied student population. The second was acceptance of an elementary program reduced from eight years to six, with a six year secondary program divided into two three-year segments. The proposed organizational structures shifted from an 8-4 to a 6-6 to the 6-3-3 plan. With the 6-3-3 organization, the separate school building for in-between-agers became a reality, and an authentically unique program became a possibility.

The new junior high school played an important role in the development of education for emerging adolescents. It signalled the recognition by educators at all levels of the uniqueness of this phase of growing up. It also symbolized the determination of public school educators to provide an appropriate educational program for the students in junior high schools, a program which dealt with what they believed to be the needs of early adolescence rather than a tightly prescribed college preparatory experience.

As was pointed out in Chapter 2, however, the junior high school was destined to fall somewhat short of its goals. Perhaps it failed to achieve its objective because many American high schools, to which successful junior high school students graduated, found it difficult to offer realistic, attractive alternatives to college preparatory programs. Maybe it fell short of its goals because the junior high school, in many cases, was staffed by teachers who had been prepared for and consequently preferred to teach at another level. Possibly the junior high school fell short because those same teachers received no special training to prepare them to implement a program different from the high school.

Often teachers seeking high school positions were placed in junior high schools, with promises of high school assignments when and if an opening occurred. No one told them that the junior high school had a special mission and teachers, therefore, acted as if it had none. It is easy to understand how, under such circumstances, the junior high school became just that, a pale shadow of the school to which its teachers looked for guidance and upon which their career aspirations were focused.

The curriculum tended to become either a watered down version of the high school curriculum or it reflected the teacher's desires to prepare the students for the too narrow objective of success in the high school. Public school seventh and eighth grades had previously been staffed by teachers who were oriented more toward the elementary program, with its emphasis on the basic skills. These two grades now passed into the hands of teachers who had a decidedly secondary orientation. This change in staffing patterns seems to have brought a profound change in attitude toward reading.

The old saw about the differences between elementary and secondary teachers, while often exaggerated, probably earned its status because there was enough truth in the claims to make them stick. Certainly one of the most frequently cited differences is the reported expectation on the part of the secondary teachers that pupils master all basic skills of reading prior to entrance to secondary school. Secondary teachers, so the hypothesis goes, deny any responsibility for teaching reading.

Insofar as reading programs are concerned, the evolution of the junior high school has been, in this writer's opinion, even less successful than other academic programs at that level. The overall effect on work in reading and other basic skills seems to have been the termination of reading instruction in those grades. Had the junior high school not emerged when it did, however, the result would probably have been the same or worse since the 6-6 organization would have postponed indefinitely any transition to the middle school concept. The junior high school, then, was a positive step forward in terms of recognizing the uniqueness of the emerging adolescent student. Regarding the acquisition of the skills of reading, however, progress was less positive.

As a result, by the time the typical early adolescent got to high school, assuming he could read, any of a number of negative reading experiences may have occurred. He may have been required, for example, to read books which were too difficult or were of little interest. The transescent may have been required to overanalyze books (e.g., long book reports) rather than to enjoy them. Quite possibly, he lacked the time or place to become lost in a book either at home or school. He may have been compared unfavorably, from time to time, with other students of higher reading ability, with the expected damage to ego and desire for reading (1).

Often the in-between-age reader lacked examples, among both peers and adults at home and school, who considered reading important or who were concerned that the student continue to develop his skills. Access to suitable reading materials may have been difficult, or he may never have learned how to locate such materials. At any rate, the typical sixth grader could expect little in terms of reading improvement in the next three years of school.

The Future Role of the Middle School

In the past ten years, the number of middle schools in the United States has doubled, redoubled, and redoubled again until the number is close to 5,000. There are now about as many middle schools as there are junior high schools. As a result, the future of reading in American society depends, at least in part, upon the successful implementation of the middle school concept. This requires that schools for transescents change their philosophies and their programs as well as their names. If this happens, the educational goals now being established for this age student may be realized. Aspects of the middle school program which will influence the future success of middle school reading programs require some examination here.

For instance, we can expect that, for the foreseeable future, individualized instruction will be a central mode for middle school educational efforts. Comprehensive instructional designs for individualizing, such as the Kettering Foundations Individually Guided Education (IGE), may spread throughout the nation's middle schools. The use of the learning stations' approach to classroom organization will become more and more the norm, and unipacs or learning activity kits will provide further opportunity for effective individualization. The thrust of accountability in education will bring about a continuum of objectives for each subject area, including reading, replacing the large units of the curriculum currently found. Individual student diagnosis and prescription will often be supplemented by Computer Managed Instruction (CMI), and record keeping will no longer be a task handled by teachers. Individualizing will have many facets.

Educators should also anticipate an extended emphasis on increasing student independence and responsibility. Hopefully, middle school faculties have learned that passive learners do not make active citizens. The need for self-initiating, self-directed learners at higher levels of schooling demands the development of these propensities at the middle school or earlier. As a result, authentic programs of independent study will operate for students of every ability level. Increased opportunity for student decision making will be common.

A special brand of team teaching — the interdisciplinary approach — also promises to make a strong bid for popularity in the coming years. This implies that teams of teachers representing a variety of disciplines will, in some way, plan and teach together. On some teams, each teacher will teach every subject. On others, teachers will contribute aspects of their own areas to an interdisciplinary unit theme, such as Ecology, The American Dream, or Latin America. In spite of the difficulty of such an approach, it will quite possibly become a central concern of most middle schools.

New physical plants for the middle schools of the remainder of this century will be flexible open-space facilities. There are now many open-space facilities, but frequently these buildings are as rigid and inflexible as the self-contained classrooms they replaced. The physical plant's flexibility coming in the next few years will change the nature of the task of the middle school teacher, permitting a much greater diversity of instructional activity than either totally open or self-contained schools have allowed.

Along with the increase in individualized instruction will come more flexible groupings of students. Instances where students of a variety of ages will be temporarily convened for the presentation and mastery of a specific group of objectives will be common. The practice of grouping students strictly by chronological age has much less appeal when dealing with middle schoolers who often have little in common except change. Some middle school educators have begun to advocate student grouping on the basis of physical size and maturity.

Additionally, variety in the size of instructional groupings will be even more common. The one-on-one instructional setting, peer teaching, and extensive use of small, temporary learning groups will occur frequently. Much of this will be an attempt by teachers to provide a greater variety of learning alternatives. From these alternatives, individual students will choose various elements, designing large portions of their educational program themselves.

Exploration will also become a central theme of the middle school of the future. The rapid increase in cognitive skills and self-awareness, which are known to be signals of emerging adolescence, requires a school which facilitates the exploration of interests, areas of knowledge, bodily changes, and a host of other areas. Exploratory programs will be available in all areas of the traditional curriculum, as well as in the expressive arts and special interest programs ranging far beyond the usual fare.

Perhaps more significantly, insofar as reading programs are concerned, the skills of continued learning must receive a great deal of attention in the middle schools during the next several decades. The traditional communication skills, such as writing and reading, will continue to be served while skills such as listening and viewing, which up to this time have received little attention, will be emphasized in a greater variety of programs. The skills of thinking (hypothesizing, questioning, inferring, contrasting and comparing, generalizing, predicting, analyzing) will receive special treatment and study skills, such as library usage, laboratory work, and organizing and presenting information, will be a common focus. These skills, so vital to future success in education, have been left primarily to chance until now. Since ours is now an information-rich society and not an information-poor one, learning how to learn becomes far more important than the mastery of an arbitrarily selected list of curriculum objectives. While few teachers in today's middle schools are prepared for this necessary shift in emphasis, it is a primary concern for the future.

Finally, one of the most important future roles of the middle school is that it serve as an avenue for innovation and change at other levels. It is hoped that change in the middle school will mean an upward diffusion of change to the high school level. There is some evidence that diffusion is beginning to occur in small ways. It may even make sense to predict that before the end of this century, general education — that portion common to all — will terminate shortly after the end of the middle school years. The student would then be presented with a number of educational alternatives. One alternative might be early college admission, another might be vocational education, while a third might be national service of some kind. Each would imply an early end to compulsory attendance in the high school as it is now designed.

Summary

Past educational programs for the transescent have not been particularly outstanding. In pondering both the present and the future of the emerging middle school, it is crucial that this mistake not be repeated. The future middle school's educational program in general and the reading program in particular must capitalize on the unique concepts inherent in middle school theory in order to achieve its educational goals.

THE FUTURE OF THE MIDDLE SCHOOL READING PROGRAM

What does all of this signify for the future of middle school reading programs? To use Franklin's phrase, what must we do "to keep" the middle school reading programs which are about to be given life? With an idea of what the future may hold for the middle school and its occupants, what strategies should planners of reading programs pursue? How can we plan for tomorrow rather than today? The answers to such questions are important to the establishment of a middle school reading program that will last beyond the present decade.

The one major recommendation to be made here is that the horizons of reading programs and the role descriptions of middle school reading teachers must be expanded to include a far greater conception of the task. The decades-old stereotype of the special reading teacher in the upper grades and junior high schools must be destroyed or that stereotype will destroy the future of the very middle school reading programs it was meant to serve. The role of the reading teacher as a lone wolf, existing in isolation or floating from school to school, must be eliminated. The classroom teacher's mental picture of the reading teacher as that lucky girl who has only five kids in her classes must be replaced. The student's rejection of instruction in remedial reading, or worse, his rejection of himself when forced to participate, must be erased. Only by responding to these imperatives, will the middle schools of the future have effective instructional programs in learning skills.

An expanded conception of the task means that we must do away with solitary reading teachers. Reading teachers must be replaced by teachers who are specialists in teaching all the skills necessary for continued learning in today's middle schools; not just one of those skills, even though it may be the most important one. Instead of special reading teachers, the middle schools must be staffed by teachers of the skills of continued learning.

What would be the role expectations of such a teacher? How would the learning skills teacher be different from the traditional special reading teacher? Where would this teacher fit into the scheme of things in a middle school?

First, the learning skills teacher would remain a specialist. Reading programs in the junior high school failed when they depended upon all teachers being teachers of reading. Similarly, the skills of continued learning have been and will continue to be ignored as long as all teachers are asked to assume responsibility for instruction in these areas. The learning skills teacher must be a specialist of a different sort. He must throw off the clinician's cloak, emerge from the refuge of the remedial reading laboratory, and join the mainstream of life in the middle school.

The learning skills teacher in tomorrow's middle school must be a full-fledged member of the teaching team. He, along with a small group of his team members, must assume the responsibility for a major portion of the instructional program of a group of youth, ages ten to fourteen. Within this domain, he will insure that each student receives instruction in the appropriate learning skills — those skills needed to become a self-initiating, independent learner.

The interdisciplinary academic program will be complete only when the reading teacher of the past becomes the learning skills teacher of the modern middle school teaching team. When the social studies, science, and language arts teachers work together to teach an interdisciplinary unit on "Ecology in America," for example, the learning skills teacher must be there to plan the most effective strategies for assuring the acquisition of the appropriate learning skills. The learning skills teacher must be a fifth wheel of a different sort.

The learning skills teacher will play a vital role in the life of the teaching team. He must be able to demonstrate the crucial importance of the skills of continued learning to the other members of the teaching team. He must help the team choose academic themes which also permit a focus on special aspects of important continued learning skills. He must encourage the team to develop learning objectives which also facilitate the mastery of these learning skills in a properly sequential manner. He must aid the team in designing learning activities which demand the use of the appropriate skills. Finally, he must provide the expertise which will allow the team to evaluate the acquisition of the learning skills by the students.

This new role for the reading teacher carries a number of important implications for middle schools. It means, that the learning skills will really be taught as a part of the academic content, and that these skills will be recognized as worthwhile academic content themselves. It means that acquisition of these skills will not be left to chance. It means that the teaching of reading will not be viewed as an escape from the classroom, if indeed it ever was. More importantly, perhaps, it means that the teaching of continued learning skills, in addition to reading, will be legitimized. Viewing, listening, speaking clearly, questioning and predicting, as well as reading, will be recognized as crucial learning tools. The skills of critical and analytical thinking and of library, laboratory, and media usage will move closer to center stage. Today's middle school reading teachers must be the learning skills teachers of tomorrow. No one else is able or willing to do the job.

As middle schools move toward the goal of the interdisciplinary team approach to instruction described above, some interim efforts will be necessary. For some time to come, there will be fewer learning skills specialists than the schools will require. During that interim, the specialist must continue to assume the roles specified in Chapter 5 of this book, including those of developer, counselor, and facilitator of the second-chance experience. It is in the provision of the latter that contemporary middle school reading programs can move closer to the learning skills approach. If the stigma of nonreading can be avoided or circumvented, and other learning skills substituted, many nonreading students can and will respond to the opportunity to learn to read in the middle school years.

This movement demands reading teachers, or learning skills specialists, who see themselves as involved in the personal development of individual middle school students. The reading program of the middle school must be staffed by teacher-counselors who believe that growth in the feelings of self-worth, adequacy, and confidence are often more conducive to the learning process than the direct teaching of reading. The teacher-counselor involved in middle school reading programs must see the relationship between the self-concept, general learning skills, and ability to read, and work for the improvement of all. When this happens, the philosophy of the middle school and the goals of its future reading programs will be in harmony.

PREPARING TEACHERS FOR MIDDLE SCHOOL READING PROGRAMS

Successful middle school programs which emphasize the skills of continued learning depend upon a steady supply of properly trained teachers, both academic and skills specialists. The early efforts to improve programs for emerging adolescence, notably the junior high school, have failed to fully achieve their goals largely because of the lack of teachers who perceived clearly the purposes of the programs. Similarly, the middle school cannot last long without properly trained teachers.

Even if all teachers are not expected to be reading teachers, the general climate of the school must be favorable to a continuing focus on those skills. The existence of this favorable climate depends upon the understanding and commitment of all the teachers in the school, not just those whose primary responsibility is the teaching of learning skills. We must, therefore, design training programs for all middle school teachers to include the development of competencies in the area of the skills of continued learning.

This means that in the future all programs in middle school teacher education should include the completion of a course in the teaching of reading as a minimum requirement. The middle school teacher education programs at the University of Florida require the completion of at least one course in the teaching of reading, in both graduate and undergraduate phases. Hopefully, these will become courses or series of courses which develop the commitment and provide the necessary techniques for producing independent learners.

While a single course may be adequate for most middle school teachers, the learning skills specialist must know almost everything there is to know about reading and the other learning skills since the typical middle school class will contain students who range from K-12 in skills and reading abilities. The effective middle school learning skills teacher must be comfortable in remedial, developmental, and recreational skills areas and must be able to articulate the skills program from K-12.

In addition, middle school learning skills specialists must receive intensive training in the psychology of learning and the nature of preadolescence and early adolescence. Teachers must understand the intellectual, physical, and socio-emotional characteristics of middle school students in order to facilitate personal growth. They should be familiar enough with the learning theories of behavioristic and perceptual psychology to apply the principles in the classroom. Recognizing the importance of the self-concept in learning to read and being able to do something about it, knowing how to break the skills of learning into smaller pieces, and providing rewards at the appropriate time, are crucial skills too frequently ignored. But the day is over when the preparation of reading specialists can occur in isolation, without a continuing input from learning theory or the psychology, physiology, and sociology of transescence. The learning skills specialist must function as a member of an interdisciplinary team. He will need a thorough familiarity with the academic fare of the middle school curriculum, especially if the skills are to be taught in the regular classroom rather than in isolation. Ideally, the learning skills specialist on the teaching team will have some formal study in each of the four major subject areas of social studies, language arts, science, and math. If this is combined with formal study in the skills area for each academic teacher, the future of the skills program will be secure.

Finally, the learning skills teacher must acquire management competencies which allow him to individualize skill instruction for large numbers of students and which facilitate successful team teaching. The task of successfully designing curriculum and instructional systems for developing learning skills within the context of the academic program demands organization and teamwork of the highest order.

If we wish to prepare learning skills specialists for tomorrow, we must begin today by designing and implementing teacher training programs which look far beyond the present. The future of the middle school demands teachers with a unique preparation which develops a thorough understanding of the skills necessary for successful learning. It is up to the teacher education institutions to equip the specialist to develop these skills with middle school students.

SUMMARY

Reading programs for the middle school must leap into the future, even if it is largely a leap of faith. We cannot wait until tomorrow to prepare programs for the students of tomorrow; this is why earlier programs fell short of their goals.

This leap into the future should emphasize the skills of continued learning. The learning specialist, in addition to being an expert reading teacher, must also possess an in-depth knowledge of the transescent youngster with whom he works, an understanding of the emerging middle school concept, and the ability to work as a team member in interdisciplinary learning situations. This person must be, in effect, the transitional link between the elementary and secondary schools. While this may be a most difficult job, the authentic middle school cannot survive without it.

References

1. Eichhorn, Donald H. *The Middle School*. New York: Center for Applied Research in Education, 1966.

2. Havighurst, Robert J. *Developmental Tasks and Education* (3rd ed.). New York: David McKay, 1972.

3. Howard, Alvin W., and George C. Stoumbis. *The Junior High and Middle School: Issues and Practices*. Scranton, Pennsylvania: Intext Educational Publishers, 1970.

4. Kohen-Raz, Reuven. *The Child From Nine to Thirteen*. Chicago: Aldine-Atherton Press, 1972.